to,

Grandad

Happy Reading

All our LOVE

Alan, Yasmin & Chevon

x x x

x x

x

The Last of the Regiments

THEIR RISE AND FALL

Also available from Brassey's

BAYNES
The Forgotten Victor: General Sir Richard O'Connor

BAYNES
Soldiers of Scotland

CLAYTON
France, Soldiers and Africa

DIETZ
Garrison : Ten British Military Towns

JOLLY
Military Man, Family Man

MATTHEWS & BROWN
The Challenge of Military Leadership

MATTHEWS & BROWN
The Parameters of Military Ethics

PERKINS
A Fortunate Soldier

WILLIAMS
Judy O'Grady and the Colonel's Lady

The Last of the Regiments

THEIR RISE AND FALL

Peter Dietz

BRASSEY'S (UK)

(a member of the Maxwell Pergamon Publishing Corporation plc)

LONDON · OXFORD · WASHINGTON · NEW YORK · BEIJING
FRANKFURT · SÃO PAULO · SYDNEY · TOKYO · TORONTO

UK (Editorial)	Brassey's (UK) Ltd., 24 Gray's Inn Road, London WC1X 8HR, England
(Orders, all except North America)	Brassey's (UK) Ltd., Headington Hill Hall, Oxford OX3 0BW, England
USA (Editorial)	Brassey's (US) Inc., 8000 Westpark Drive, Fourth Floor, McLean, Virginia 22102, USA
(Orders, North America)	Brassey's (US) Inc., Front and Brown Streets, Riverside, New Jersey 08075, USA Tel (toll free): 800 257 5755
PEOPLE'S REPUBLIC OF CHINA	Pergamon Press, Room 4037, Qianmen Hotel, Beijing, People's Republic of China
FEDERAL REPUBLIC OF GERMANY	Pergamon Press GmbH, Hammerweg 6, D–6242 Kronberg, Federal Republic of Germany
BRAZIL	Pergamon Editora Ltda, Rua Eça de Queiros, 346, CEP 04011, Paraiso, São Paulo, Brazil
AUSTRALIA	Brassey's Australia Pty Ltd., PO Box 544, Potts Point, N.S.W. 2011, Australia
JAPAN	Pergamon Press, 5th Floor, Matsuoka Central Building, 1-7-1 Nishishinjuku, Shinjuku-ku, Tokyo 160, Japan
CANADA	Pergamon Press Canada Ltd., Suite No. 271, 253 College Street, Toronto, Ontario, Canada M5T 1R5

First edition 1990

Library of Congress Cataloging in Publication Data
Dietz, Peter.
The last of the regiments: their rise and fall/Peter Dietz.—
1st ed.   p. cm.
Includes bibliographical references
1. Great Britain. Army—History. 2. Great Britain. Army—Organization—History. 3. Great Britain. Army—Military life—History. I. Title.
UA649.D53   1990   355.3'0941—dc20   89-17318

British Library Cataloguing in Publication Data
Dietz, Peter
The last of the regiments: their rise and fall.
1. Great Britain. Army. Regiments, history
I. Title
355.3'1'0941

ISBN 0-08-034761-4

Printed in Great Britain by BPCC Wheatons Ltd, Exeter

For Vivien and Suzanne

With Love

Contents

Preface

ALTHOUGH this book started out as an analysis of the regimental system it has become something of a personal history of the British Army. I was at first concerned to show where some of the main features of army and regimental life originated and where they are now heading. This led me into an historical, chronological format. However, I have singled out, in addition to my main narrative, what seems to me to be the important aspects of military life for closer study. Cutting across the historical presentation, I examine the concept of honour, the oath of loyalty, morale, cohesion and disintegration and the practical differences between the Regiments on one hand and the Corps on the other. I have followed these themes where they would lead me and this has meant that events and persons sometimes crop up in more than one chapter and furthermore, out of strict chronological order. I can only hope that what I have to say about the various themes makes the zig-zagging worth while.

My admiration for and debt to Sir John Fortescue will be obvious to any reader of this book and I hope my quotations from his thirteen-volume study will encourage anyone who has not had the pleasure of reading his work, to dip into it at least. The scale of his work does present a challenge, but despite its being dated by some more recent military histories continuous pleasure can be guaranteed by his style and learning. It was a particular joy also to read Mason's book *A Matter of Honour* and I defy anyone to read of the British connection with the Indian sub-continent, especially the military connection, without being moved. It is interesting to compare Mason with Fortescue on eighteenth- and nineteenth-century India and I am indebted to both authors as much for their inspiration as for their admirable histories.

My more recent sources will be well known to most readers and I would only like to add thanks to Ruth Jolly for her recent account of the military family and its problems in *Military Man–Family Man*. She brings together for the first time some of the social difficulties which have surely always been present in the Services but which it has usually been possible to ignore. The increasingly frequent appearance of these problems on the front pages of the newspapers and elsewhere means that any restructuring of the Army or of service life in the near future will have to take them seriously, and perhaps only for the first time.

St Ives   *PJD*
Cornwall
January 1989

Acknowledgements

I WOULD like to thank the Chief Librarians, archivists and staff of the following Institutions for their unfailing courtesy, kindness and attention to my sometimes trivial demands: The Ministry of Defence Central Library, Whitehall: The Library of The Royal United Services Institute for Defence Studies: The Prince Consort's Library, Aldershot: The Gibraltar Garrison Library: the Cornwall County Library Service, especially its Branches in Penwith: The Penzance Library, Morrab Gardens, Penzance. I would also like to thank The British Library and The Public Record Office for help over a long period of years. Lorna Swift, Command Consultant Librarian at Headquarters United Kingdom Land Forces, has given much practical help with the provision of source material.

The following publishers have kindly given permission to quote from the material shown for which they hold the copyright: The Macmillan Publishing Company for material from *European Society In Upheaval* by Peter N. Stearns. Copyright © 1967 by Peter N. Stearns: *The Making Of A Gentleman* and *The Squire And His Relations*, both by E Wingfield Stratford and *Morale* by John Baynes. Hodder & Stoughton for *Autobiography* by Richard Burdon Haldane published in 1929: Collins for permission to quote from *Asquith* by Roy Jenkins: Macmillan Accounts and Administration Ltd. for permission to quote from *A Matter Of Honour* by Philip Mason. Jonathan Cape Ltd., for *Face Of Battle* by John Keegan, copyright John Keegan 1976: Penguin Books Ltd., for *The Penguin Atlas Of Medieval History* by Colin McEvedy, 1972: George Weidenfeld & Nicolson Ltd., for *The German Officer Corps In Society And State, 1650–1945* by Karl Demeter: Constable Publishers for permission to quote from *The Old Lie* by Peter Parker: Oxford University Press for material from *Roman Britain* by Peter Salway, 1981 and *The British Army* by W S Hamer, 1970: Harrap for *The Story of Army Education* by Colonel A C T White VC: Martin Secker & Warburg for *The Rise And Fall Of The Third Reich* by William Shirer.

The Controller of Her Majesty's Stationery Office has given permission for quotations from The Statement On The Defence Estimates 1986, 7 and 8, from The Report by The Comptroller and Auditor General (236) on Ministry of Defence: Costs and Financial Control of British Forces in Germany: he has also allowed me to use The Army List Part 1, 1987, as source material in Appendix I.

I would like to thank Brassey's (UK) Publishers for permission to quote from *Military Man–Family Man* by Ruth Jolly and *Hitler's Gladiator* by Charles Messenger. Finally, I would like to thank my wife Vivien for her researches, frequent re-readings and constant encouragement.

Introduction

All conservative institutions look back to a golden age which in some mysterious way, is supposed to contain a blueprint for the future. The British Army is no exception, but how can this blueprint fit a society which, we are told, is changing not only rapidly but at an exponential rate?[1]

Even if this rate of change is only perceived rather than experienced, its effects can surely be felt by us and our institutions in countless ways. The Army, and the whole apparatus of our Armed Forces is now subject to technological and social change in a way which it has never before experienced. The replacement of bronze by iron in the manufacture of edged weapons, the gradual supremacy of the armoured horseman and the introduction of the feudal land tenure system which supported him, the long drawn out and slowly achieved domination of the battlefield by handguns and artillery, all introduced fundamental change. But the impact of these changes was gradual and spread over many centuries. By contrast, mechanisation, armoured vehicles and the aeroplane have probably made their maximum impact in a very few decades. Nuclear weapons may have an even shorter life. These innovations, together with parallel changes in society in political, economic and industrial organisation have had their inevitable effect on military organisation and also, if more slowly, on the military ethos. Armies are conservative institutions, organised and preconditioned to resist change, or at least to adapt to change very slowly indeed. This attitude to change reflects the unique relationship between the Armed Forces and the State which has called them into being and which mutually they serve to legitimise.

Not only are armies slow to adapt to change but they are slower usually than the civilian population as a whole. So that, quite apart from having to struggle hard to keep abreast of 'the state of the art' in weapons technology, surveillance techniques and communications methods and equipment, the soldier is expected to be constantly aware

1

of changing patterns of authority, education, morality and public beliefs and expectations. Without this regular updating, demanded more and more frequently by governments and the concerned public, the Armed Forces are threatened with isolation from their parent society and are in danger of ending up as the defenders of an anachronistic, outdated and obsolescent way of life. What is worse, they may become the household troops of an oligarchy devoted only to its own supremacy and survival.

These conditions can be far more bewildering for the soldier today than they were in the nineteenth century, when the rate of social progress also caused serious tensions between sections of the Forces and some parts of society. It should not be surprising that there is some loss of direction and uncertain notes are heard to come from the trumpet. As well as the possibility of alienation from some sections of society at large, there is also a danger of divergent forces at work within the Armed Services themselves. It has been noted, and this will be expanded upon in a later chapter, that those sections of the Armed Forces which are more intimately concerned with technology; electrical and electronic engineers and operators; communications and transport operatives and even tank, helicopter and plane crews, because of the very nature of their work, are better able and more willing to keep pace with the speed of events outside the barracks than the members of some other arms and services. That these other, less technical, troops may be seen in a crisis as more immediately useful can only enhance the danger of misunderstandings.

What makes this potential lack of sympathy and possible divergence of aims and interests more serious is that traditionally, and for very good reasons, which we shall explore, the military ethos, style, tone and very model of the good soldier has been set and maintained from the beginning by the fighting troops of the Army. It could not be otherwise. Leaving aside the 'super élites' within the fighting troops it is the 'teeth arms' and not the supporting 'tail', despite its growing demands on manpower and financial resources, which still have the prestige, and for its leaders, the first call upon positions of power and influence. Even though there is considerable acknowledgement of the contribution made by the technicians, mechanics and operators, there is an uneasy gulf between the warrior and the technical expert. It is already just possible to envisage a war fought entirely between the scientists and technicians on opposing sides and the possibility becomes more credible day by day. Nevertheless, the constant irritant of seemingly disproportionate rewards and career horizons stemming from the 'tooth and tail' stereotype can only enhance the dangers of unfamiliarity, rivalry and alienation, focused as they are today by the impact of unprecedentedly rapid social change.[2] 'Tooth and Tail' profiles of General Officers in the British Army are set out in Appendix I. Some social, educational and family characteristics of British Major Generals in the 1986 Army List are shown in Appendix II.

Alienation within the Forces must lead, however it is caused, to a lack of common purpose which is likely to be enhanced by a politico-military philosophy of nuclear deterrence. The over-riding assumption of an army, if not a nation, which shelters under a nuclear umbrella must be that serious war is impossible.[3] However hard the army trains and however realistic it tries to make its exercises, the belief must be widespread that a grand theatrical performance is taking place which has no meaning or purpose off the stage. In its way, this performance is not unlike the great European, post-harvest manoeuvres which took place annually before the First World War. It was impossible for pre-1914 society to connect with or anticipate the horror, carnage and sheer immobility of the war which was to follow. Had the connection been made by the actors and their audience before the event, it is surely inconceivable that the tragic aftermath could have followed.

Unlike the rest of Europe, Britain rarely engaged in large scale manoeuvres. This was mainly because Britain had no great conscripted army on the continental pattern to exercise and, more important, the bulk of what there was of it was stationed overseas in the Empire. Senior British officers, staff officers, instructors and students all had to content themselves with an exploration on bicycles of the great European battlefields where so many of their forbears had won glory. Tactical exercises without troops were the normal thing, even when training areas did become available, usually on appropriated common land. It was in the Empire, and especially in India, that the regiment and the military system based upon it, flourished and developed into a self-perpetuating institution eminently suited to fighting the hundreds of 'small wars' which brought honour and glory and frequently death to the nineteenth century British soldier.[4]

A lack of purpose or confusion over aims leads immediately to certain practical problems within the Armed Forces. One obvious problem is how to go about recruiting enough young men as officers and soldiers at a price which does not radically warp the employment structure into jeopardising the national economy. Apart from the size of the age groups from which the Forces must be recruited, there appears to be an upper limit to the number of young men who will come forward to enlist voluntarily in the absence of a clearly defined external threat. The limit appears to be independent of economic considerations except within fairly narrow margins.[5] Pay, unless it is increased quite disproportionately, and even then only in the short run, and even unemployment, unless it is massive, and again only in the short run, would seem only to have the effect of improving the prolongation rate and reducing premature retirement rather than of attracting more recruits. This is certainly not unimportant but the evidence is that recruiting is much more susceptible to negative factors than to positive ones. Falling prestige through lack of purpose and clearly defined and stated aims and the rapid decline of so many seemingly glamorous, adventure-promising overseas stations are important negative factors which now act against recruiting.

A posting to the British Army of the Rhine, which today represents the centre of gravity of the British Army, is no longer regarded as an acceptable substitute for service in the Far East or some other exotic overseas station. Even when it was considered to be financially advantageous to serve in Germany, many, if not most, soldiers and some officers, especially if they were married, would have preferred to remain in the United Kingdom. Now that the money rewards have been reduced, however logically and however little they served in the past as a direct inducement, the perceived loss of cash is seen as a real disincentive to recruitment and even more to the retention of men coming to the end of their engagements in Germany.

Coupled with the widespread unpopularity of Germany as a present day posting, but equally important in its own right in its effect on recruiting and retention rates, is the military family problem. It is a commonplace that the age of marriage for young people in Britain has fallen sharply in recent years and the Army has not been exempt from this phenomenom. The 1986 statement on the Defence Estimates shows that almost 75 per cent of all officers in the three Services taken together are married, whilst well over 50 per cent of non-commissioned servicemen are also married. In the age groups over nineteen years of age, again for the three Services taken together, the percentage for marrieds rises to nearly 75 per cent and is still rising.

In the last five years, the number of young servicemen who are married has risen by over 9,000 whilst the total number of servicemen, of whom the Army will have the lion's share, has increased by only about 2,000. This change from what was formerly almost an unmarried army to an almost fully married one, has meant a growing concern on the part of the serviceman, and even more of his wife, with the question of quarters, children's education, welfare and amenities. Not only does a young wife expect to be provided with accommodation but she expects it to be of a standard equal to that available in civil life. She expects to be able to live in a civil community and in a house which she and her husband are buying rather than renting if she so wishes. Political propaganda and to some extent service advice encourages this attitude.[6] But expectations over housing are only one of the many influences for dissatisfaction in contemporary Service

life. A report in *The Sunday Times* of 12 July 1987 refers to an investigation by Air Vice Marshal Robson into early retirement and general
dissatisfaction with life in the Royal Air Force. The report mentions
family unrest, and specifically cites the desire to own a home as a
cause. The investigation was concerned with the Royal Air Force but
the general feeling in all three Services is the same. *The Times* published an article recently on service wives and careers which supports
the widespread impression of unease amongst service families. An
article by Michael Evans, the paper's Defence Correspondent,
appeared on the 7 July 1987, just before the report of the Royal Air
Force investigation. In it, Evans says that the Ministry of Defence is
considering reorganisation of the Army's tours of duty to give longer
periods in one posting and to help wives build a career. The late Chief
of the General Staff is reported as saying that the regimental system
remained 'the bedrock of the Army', and there was no question of
giving it up. General Sir Nigel Bagnall went on to say that any proposal
that would damage that traditional way of life in the Army would be
unacceptable. However, he said, traditions had to be adjusted.[7] The
instrumental view of occupations is now widespread in Britain. An
uncongenial job is accepted merely as a means towards providing a
pleasant home and family life, where long periods of leisure allow
for the cultivation of hobbies, sports and pastimes which, in their
enjoyment with family and friends, provide the main purpose in life.
The Services have not escaped this philosophy and, while it may not
be an ignoble vision for someone in a dead-end occupation or working
without hope of betterment on an automated production line, it does
not fit well with the generally accepted picture of service life. The
five day week syndrome which is manifested in a reluctance to serve
abroad, in a nine-till-five working day and in the attitude that time
after 'working hours' and especially at week ends is entirely private,
whilst it does not completely dominate service life, is now an important
factor. Many wives prefer to stay in their own homes, possibly well
away from army installations but near their or their husband's family.
In the past it was only a relatively few officers who commuted regularly between their duty stations in Germany and their homes in the
United Kingdom, now the practice is much more widespread. Not
only does operational efficiency suffer directly in these circumstances
but this situation leads to a restless, discontented army whose way of
life and whose tacit contract with the soldier has rested upon an
entirely different ethos, similar perhaps to the one General Bagnall
had in mind and which he called 'the bedrock of the Army'. This
ethos, surviving from an earlier and only half-remembered time,
viewed from a sufficient distance, may really have the appearance of
a golden age.

The surviving image of the great days of the Army is concocted from a heady mixture of myth and legends, with much of the harsh reality drained out. The legends tell of Wellington's army in the Peninsula and at Waterloo, of a charge at Balaclava and a 'Thin Red Line'; of hard fought battles in India and on the 'Frontier' and in many another barely remembered place. The stories and legends can be recorded and commemorated for only a little longer in the sad museums of the Corps and Regiments still surviving in the remnants of Victorian military architecture in our old county towns. When they have gone, it will be easier to accept myths which picture a 'tail-less' army, certainly with its quota of crime and rascality but without social problems unless venereal disease be included and this was only regarded as the inevitable price of a robust, male orientated society.[8] The perennial problems of recruiting and desertion and isolation from normal life, are forgotten or glossed over. But it is from the myths and legends that the military ideal is constructed. The modern concept of a 'lean' army is of an army without a tail, without families and their supporting services, engaged, as far as possible, for short service without pension and isolated from what some see as the subversive influences of political and social education. That this is a perverted view of some modern military ideas may be accepted but that it stems from a popular but mistaken vision of the historical past is also not to be doubted.

Of course it is cliché to say that we see and interpret the past in a way which best fits our view of the contemporary world. It would be fatuous to say that the received view of military history is more than partial, or that it provides in its more accessible forms a guide to present action. John Keegan, writing in his book, *The Face of Battle*, illustrates the dilemma precisely in the chapter titled 'The History of Military History' when he says that an historian is bound to become either an obscurantist or a publicist. He points approvingly at Creasy and his *Fifteen Decisive Battles of the World* and suggests, of course with tongue in cheek, that an eye catching title and a jolly good read may be the most important and certainly the most profitable thing to aim at. But none of this is to decry soldiers or to disbelieve or to pour scorn on their countless genuinely heroic actions in the past. What we would do however and what this book sets out to do is to discover, in so far as it remains possible at this remove, what motivates the soldier to sacrifice himself in so many thankless situations. At the same time we shall try to examine the role of military organisations and especially the archetypal British regiment, kindred organisations in other countries, and its predecessors and descendants. It may then be possible to assess more accurately whether a 'passing of the regiments', such as we may now be witnessing, will mean the end of the British

Army or merely its transition to a new form of Armed Forces, in other words to another 'New Model'.

The word 'model' is somewhat out of favour with orthodox military writers and thinkers. No doubt this is because of its sociological connotation and the use to which it has been put in the devising of theories about war and revolution which are alleged by their authors to have predictive value. Yet, Cromwell's New Model Army, formed and trained by him during the English Civil War, has always enjoyed the admiration of soldiers. It has been held up as worthy of emulation by military planners who could see that to be an efficient and trustworthy fighting instrument, an army must have more than good equipment and good training. Even when led by brave and intelligent officers, good soldiers need something more. Cromwell's regiments believed in the rightness of their cause and in God's support against an enemy who had turned away from the Puritan ideals of simplicity and piety. Their common beliefs bound them in a brotherhood which has provided a pattern sought after by all great military commanders since then.[9] These underlying beliefs may not be the whole story where success in battle is concerned and they are not in themselves a sufficient guarantee of victory. But given the material pre-requisites for success, they can remove most of the uncertainty in their contribution to the soldier's morale and his determination to engage in combat with the enemy.[10] Where the physical conditions do not point to victory, it seems that strongly held beliefs, shared with comrades in close proximity, will slow the onset of disintegration and often delay to the bitter end the moment of defeat. A 'New Model', if it is to be a worthy successor to the illustrious armies of the past, must be imbued with the 'fighter spirit' however it is to be induced. It is this spirit which we shall be looking for in this study of organisation and ethos.

1

The Origins of the British Army

It is difficult to find a satisfactory starting place except the beginning. Some military historians date the foundation of the modern British Army from the Saint Valentine's Day parade in 1661 when the recently restored Charles II took Monk's Regiment of Foot from the army of the old Commonwealth into his own service, eventually to become the Coldstream Guards. Other writers would set the date a little before this, in 1645, when Cromwell's New Model Army, already including Monk's regiment, was established by the Long Parliament. Fortescue, in his classic history of the British Army[1] begins his study, after a brief reference to the organisation of the English army under Harald, with a description of the Battle of Hastings. But to find the true origins of the beliefs and customs which inform the behaviour and the way of thinking of the modern Army it is necessary to look a thousand years before the arrival of the Normans.

When Sir Sibbald David Scott presented his study of the Army in 1866[2] he made the point that there was no history of Britain before the Romans. If there was no history, there could be no military history and so he decided that the Roman invasion was the place to start his work. The writings of Caesar and Tacitus are unique as a record of early warfare in these islands and make the Roman Army in Britain a useful and natural point of departure for our investigation. During the thousand years between the Roman invasion of Britain and the rather more accomplished fact of the Norman Conquest, at least three military systems left strong traces in our military fabric which are still discernible today. To call all three of these sometimes loose and ad hoc battle arrangements systems may be to formalise the impossible. However, the Romans, the Saxons and the Normans have each contributed to the development of the British Army and have left recognisable elements which have survived the centuries. These survivals can still influence the shape and will of our armed forces, and even when they are reduced to myths and legends exert an enormous power.

Discipline from the Romans

In their first warlike contact with the Roman Legions, the loose combinations of tribal warriors in the South of England came face to face with close ranked, highly disciplined soldiers who were able to overcome superior numbers and sometimes superior valour and commitment. It is likely that, for many of the British tribesmen opposed to the Roman legions, the idea of Rome, for many years after the successful invasion of 43 AD, could only exist as a picture of close ranks of identically armed and armoured men, moving in unison, faceless and almost inhuman. It would not have been necessary to dehumanise the enemy for our ancestors as now seems necessary for many modern armies before they are loosed in battle.[3] Creatures from another planet could seem much closer to our ancestors than to us and this is probably how the Romans were at first regarded. As the native British became more familiar with Roman military organisation, and quickly learned that legionaries could also be killed, it was the uniformity of their high quality weapons and the standardised production and supply of them that would most have impressed the barbarian mind. In the first and second centuries AD, good weapons and armour, adequate rations and all the necessaries of war were still being produced regularly and systematically for the Roman armies deployed across Europe, North Africa and Asia Minor. Effective weapons and armour were an essential part of every warrior's equipment but in the Roman Army, weapons were not given individual names and did not partake of magical powers and, however finely wrought, did not enter into primitive mythology. Enemy weapons and armour would have been seized as part of the honours and trophies of war but, regardless of their value in decorative or in exchange terms, they were never taken to replace the standard equipment. A utilitarian view of the soldier's equipment could be accepted, if only briefly, by those Britons who enrolled as auxiliaries in the Roman forces. The acceptance would have been made easier since until the end of the second century AD, and possibly later, Roman weapons were the best in the then known world. One of the reasons given for the catastrophic decline of Roman power is that by the end of the fourth century, the German soldier had a better sword, made of better steel, than the Roman legionary. Eventually, the Legions found that their methods and equipment were hopelessly obsolete, especially in their failure to grasp the new cavalry tactics so ably exploited by the

Goths.[4] In the meantime, the Legion, with its close order tactics, its disciplined, drilled reaction to attack and its almost rational observance of the essential parts of the state religion, (including, in later years, Christianity), left a memory of a fighting machine which in its professionalism and stoicism could be held up as worthy of emulation by British armies in India, the Peninsula and elsewhere many centuries later.

The Romans had come to Britain as invaders and colonists but as the *pax Romana* gradually spread through most of Britain, the native inhabitants came to see the Legions as their protection from the 'barbarian' tribes in the far North and West. By the fifth century, frantic appeals were being made to the remnants of Roman power in Gaul and on the Lower Rhine to protect an abandoned and defenceless province. Towards the end of the Roman occupation of Britain, the Eastern frontiers of the Empire were being more and more threatened and subjected to pressure waves from the nomadic barbarians moving westward out of Central Asia. Already, by the later half of the third century AD, the pressures were being felt in Britain. Salway points out[5] that complete stone walls became common around British towns by 270 AD and that by then also, the construction of the series of fortifications on the South East coast known as the 'Saxon Shore', was well under way. The purpose of the 'Saxon Shore' forts appears to have been partly as a defence against pirates from the North East and partly to safeguard communication across the narrowest part of the Channel but their erection does indicate a threat from outside the Island. As the legions were withdrawn to bolster the defences on the Rhine and the Danube, their place was increasingly taken over by the 'Auxillia' which were originally little more than a collection of barbarian levies, raised for the duration of a campaign and officered in part by Romans. Even before the withdrawal of the legions, the Auxillia were relied upon more and more for peace keeping and punitive raids throughout the Empire, whilst the Legions settled into garrison life with its continuous demands for fortress construction and road building. Agricola, at the battle of 'Mons Graupius' in AD 84 was already able to achieve victory over the Caledonian tribes using only his auxiliary forces. The Auxillia, even in Britain, were by no means all native. At 'Mons Graupius' Agricola used not only British but Batavian and Tungrian infantry from the lower Rhine as well as a considerable force of auxiliary cavalry. By AD 175 a new light force called 'Numeri', recruited from the frontier tribes, arrived in Britain in the person of 5,500 Sarmatian cavalry to reinforce the depleted garrison.

By the middle of the second century AD, native Britons would have been in contact with the Romans for more than a hundred years and, certainly in the southern half of Britain, it would have become an association of mutual advantage if not actual affection. Even by AD 60, at the time of the Boudiccan revolt, London was a flourishing mercantile centre.[6] The benefits of Roman civilisation, in the shape of goods imported from Gaul, the Rhine valley and as far away as the Mediterranean basin, would have been widely apparent by the turn of the century. Britons would have allied themselves with the Romans either as members of the 'Client' Kingdoms or more directly as auxiliary soldiers. Encouraged by a deliberate policy, the leading Britons consciously adopted the outward trappings of the Roman way of life. Tacitus, Agricola's son-in-law and biographer, in a passage quoted by Salway[7] says: 'Little by little there was a slide towards the allurements of degeneracy: assembly rooms, bathing establishments and smart dinner parties'. By quite early in the second century AD, much of Britain would have regarded the 'Roman' army with its legions, auxillia and additional irregular troops as 'our' army. But, like all standing armies everywhere, it would have suffered the opprobrium of having to act as a police force, dealing with crime, civil disturbance and minor revolt. The Romans had a well deserved reputation for brutal efficiency in their handling of disorder and unrest. However, under the circumstances then prevailing in Britain, this policy probably made more friends than enemies.

The reality of the Anglo-Roman association is reinforced by two other circumstances. From the early days of the Empire, when vast new areas for recruitment had been opened up in the conquered territories and among the surrendering tribes, it had become the practice to promise automatic Roman citizenship after an honourable career in the auxiliary forces. Similarly, the sons of auxiliary soldiers were eligible to enlist in the legions after the satisfactory completion of service by their fathers. This had been a jealously guarded honour restricted previously to Romans by birth. Perhaps even more important, the four legions which came to Britain in AD 43, II Augusta, IX Hispana, XIV Gemina and XX Valeria all became long term residents. New commanders were posted in from time to time and the ranks were reinforced as required. For example, in AD 60, 2,000 legionaries from Germany were brought over to bring the Ninth up to strength after it had been badly cut up in Boudicca's uprising. But the corpus of the legions remained in Britain and became associated over long periods of time with particular locations. The Ninth moved North to York and returned there after 'Mons Graupius' to stay, or at least to be based there, until it disappears in a mysterious, if not sinister manner, after last being recorded at York in AD 107–8. A tile with the official stamp of the legion dated 126 AD has been discovered at Nijmegen but theories suggest that the legion 'disappeared' during the Jewish wars of 130 AD or even as late as the Parthian wars of 161 AD. It was not unusual for a legion, badly beaten or in disgrace after a poor performance in battle, to be cashiered and removed from the military records.[8] Although the association of the Ninth with York is probably the best known of these contacts over a long period of time, the II, XIV and XX legions would all have developed strong local connections. This would have been especially so after the Emperor Severus, early in the third century, lifted the ban on soldiers having lawful wives. Sons of the inter-marriages would eventually serve in the 'local' legion and there would be the normal intercourse of trade and social contact. The colonies of veterans founded at York, Colchester and elsewhere would only have strengthened the process of integration. When the Ninth eventually marched out of York for the last time it was no doubt only one of many emotional and dramatic military events which bound the troops 'in garrison' to the civil community and brought them to be regarded as 'our army'.

To sum up this section, it may be said that the Romans, through their army bequeathed a common heritage to most of Europe. Whilst the heritage, at least in military terms, is rarely acknowledged, it does mark the beginning of the acceptance of discipline as the highest military virtue so that exemplary punishment could be understood and accepted as a means of enforcing it. The moral importance of loyalty and the oath of allegiance also stem from the Roman system and although they sometimes operated in a limited and arbitrary way, they introduced, perhaps for the first time, the idea of service and obligation and the acknowledgement of a higher duty. The Roman virtues were never quite as straightforward as they seemed, especially under the cynical rulers of the Empire but the vision of the Legion as a small, highly disciplined, well trained and dedicated body of soldiers, sternly and stoically performing their allotted tasks, if necessary to the death, is one which has commended itself to the British and has had an important role in the making of the self-image of the British Army.

Saxon Spirit and the Darker Virtues

Although the Roman virtues were never quite lost sight of in the Dark Ages or the confused period which led on into a new civilisation, other forces were at work which have also left their own peculiar mark on the military, no less than on the religious and literary history of the period. After the final withdrawal of the legions in AD 410, a flimsy imitation of Roman civilisation was left behind which only gradually disappeared into the mists of the Dark Ages. The period following the withdrawal was so obscure as at times to be almost unknowable but it has left us with a mass of myths and legends which still work away providing inspiration and a dimension of magicality not covered by orthodox religions. Arthur, 'The once and future King' had a real-life counter-part, but it is the Arthur of myth, legend and poetry who still provides the inspiration for many models of leadership. The young knight in armour, on a white horse, still has a most potent role to play as the ideal of the young officer everywhere. This phenomenon may be known cynically as the 'White Horse Syndrome'[9] but it encompasses the idea of the quest, adventure, the righting of wrongs, the officer as the embodiment of chivalry and above all, the notion of honour as the most important principle of the officer's life. Romantic, many of these concepts may be but none of them is ignoble. The fact that they are more likely to have emerged from the pragmatic and utilitarian feudal arrangement of society at the end of the Dark Ages is easily lost sight of in the bright light which surrounds the Knights of the Round Table.

We shall return to the legacy of the feudal system. Meanwhile, it is to be noted, almost all officer corps are bound by, and seem to require, systems which incorporate higher religious or spiritual beliefs. Whether genuinely held or not, these beliefs may act as an essential link between the leader and his men. A function of all leaders is to act as an ideal figure and, whilst shortfallings can be forgiven in oneself, higher standards are demanded of our leaders.

The one undisputed legacy from the later Dark Ages, attributed to the Anglo-Saxons and more particularly to Alfred and his son, was the obligation of all free land-owners to serve at the King's summons.[10] Whilst this type of obligation was widespread through Northern Europe by the eighth century, Alfred enforced and localised the arrangements and, by introducing a kind of shift system, made possible the almost continuous existence of a military force in being. The fyrd, the English name for the European '*Landwehr*', remained the legal and organisational basis of English armies until Tudor times. By then the continuous troubles in Ireland and the growing fear of Spanish ambitions prompted Cecil, Elizabeth's Secretary of State, to initiate an enquiry into the country's readiness and ability to defend itself. Even in pre-Norman times, the fyrd was modified by Canute, who, after his successful invasion of England, whilst returning most of his army to Denmark, retained 3,000 of his bodyguard as household troops. At a later date, the half-trained levies of the fyrd were stiffened by mercenaries hired from abroad, especially when a campaign in France or the Low Countries was contemplated.

Paradoxically, whilst an obligation to military service was becoming an accepted part of British life, another element, opposed at least in part to servitude and compulsory duty, was still evident in the warrior attitude of the native inhabitants. The warriors in the waves of invading tribes from beyond the old Roman walls and across the now unguarded North Sea,[11] fought as individuals. Their motivation was a personal one which, whilst it may have included loyalty to a King or a war leader, saw a warrior's life as the only acceptable one, in which each man should pursue his own personal destiny in battle. The rewards of this violent life-style were seen in terms of plunder, heroic prestige and an attachment to the pleasures of wassail made familiar to us from the great sagas. Great feasts, heavy drinking bouts and a rough enjoyment of story telling and minstrelsy would appear from the evidence of surviving poetry to be the only relaxation from the exercises of war. The invaders enjoyed a reputation for ferocity which was no doubt well earned but the reputation also owed something to the pious horror of the recently converted Christian onlookers observing successful barbarian invasions and raids taking place under the banner of Thor, the heathen God of Battle. In their writings, both Scott and Fortescue tend to deplore the influence of the Northern invaders and their whole philosophy and imply that the arrival of the Normans was an unmitigated blessing, rescuing the benighted British from the embarrassing excesses of Saxons and Vikings alike. A touch of Norman discipline was what was really needed. Scott, becoming lost in Victorian admiration for the newcomers says, 'A sluggish, sensual and degenerate race was refined and elevated by the advent of the chivalrous Normans.'[12]

Norman Chivalry and the Feudal Military State

Whatever we may think of the Normans, and indeed of their chivalry, their conquest of England was more effective and longer lasting than that of the Romans. Interestingly, in a Parliamentary by-election in March 1987, one candidate was able to accuse another of being a member of the feudal Norman aristocracy with some hope of his point being taken by the voters.[13] The description 'Norman', it seems, can still, after almost a thousand years, be used pejoratively. The Normans of the conquest were of course 'Northmen' in origin, like some of the earlier invaders of Britain. They had settled and colonised Normandy when it was ceded to the Danes by the French King in 911 AD. Colin McEvedy says that 'The resulting blend of Viking and Frank in the Duchy of Normandy produced a race of hybrid vigour, men who in their ambition and valour established a firmer authority over their subjects than had hitherto existed in the West'.[14]

By 1,000 AD, the Normans considered themselves, and were also considered by most of Europe to be amongst the finest soldiers in the world. As R H C Davis points out,[15] not only were the Normans good soldiers with a military organisation which was very advanced for its day, but they were also excellent propagandists who were able to manufacture a most plausible and exciting set of myths and legends about themselves. By the time of the conquest, the fame of the Norman Army was so widespread that it had become a magnet for booty and adventure-seeking Knights from the whole of Northern Europe. William's army at Hastings included sizeable contingents of Bretons, Flemish and French, making up perhaps a fifth of his army. Most of these non-Norman members of the invading army were given lands, along with their true Norman comrades, confiscated from the English. The King, who claimed the whole of England as his personal property, whether lay or ecclesiastical, installed his followers as his tenants. This represented a considerable tightening of the feudal system at a time when it had already begun to decline in England. The increased centralisation of power in the King's hands strengthened his military potential and was no doubt not approved of wholeheartedly by his Barons. However, they had little option since it was necessary to remain united and loyal in the face of a possible revolt and reconquest of the island by the English. The two armies at Hastings are both thought to have numbered between seven and eight thousand men. Such a small occupying force would have needed to react swiftly and in co-ordination against any possible threat. The constant danger and the disparity in overall numbers is also said to account for the enormous spate of castle-building that marks the decades immediately after the conquest. When the Domesday Book was made in 1086, only about six out of the 180 greater landlords and tenants-in-chief were still English and the feudal system was probably at its strongest—and needed to be, if the Normans were to hold what they had seized.

In the longer run, the growth of central power in the King's hands introduced a countervailing force, checking the arbitrary authority of the local land holders and chief tenants. The King's personal interest in commerce and trade hastened the full re-introduction of a money-based economy. The obligation to serve was only generally acceptable in defence of the homeland and so a considerable amount of negotiation and fund raising would be necessary before the King could mount an expedition abroad. Money payments in place of personal obligations in service and kind were necessary to support the King's political ambitions. Even so, it was the feudal, hierarchical structure of society which provided the military organisation of Norman Britain. The duty of the Norman nobility to bring their armed knights and retainers to join the King's host when summoned was never in doubt although there was confusion in the dynastic conflicts which eventually brought the Angevins to the throne in 1154. It was this accepted duty to organise and command in battle their own locally provided troops that gave to military command, especially at the lower levels, its essentially rural nature. It is a commonplace that, until recently, the most fertile and most approved-of ground for the recruitment of young officers has been the shires. The rural aristocracy first regarded military service as an obligation and only later as the one steady source of employment for younger sons which, whilst allowing them to continue to indulge in congenial country pursuits, also provided a prestigious if poorly paid career.

Just as the arrival of the 'Northmen' in France produced a new injection of vigour and gave rise to the hybrid Norman sub-race, so also did the conquest of England by the Normans and their allies bring them into a new and lusty combination with the largely Saxon and Danish native population. The restless and warlike qualities of the English armies, constantly displayed in their wars at home and in France over the next four centuries, might well be traced to this enforced admixture. In the end perhaps, Scott's effusive-seeming welcome to the Normans and his harsh strictures on the English of 1066 may have some justification, but hardly on the basis of chivalry opposed to native degeneracy.

The End of Chivalry and a New Honour for a New Army

Between the decline of the feudal system and the rise of a standing army in the late seventeenth century, the military forces in England were a confused and often 'ad hoc' mixture of peasants and yeomen who served through an obligation which pre-dated the Normans, together with household troops provided by the King and the higher nobility and mercenary troops from Britain and abroad, paid for by the King alone. Fortescue, writing of the later part of this period, when the long bow and the tactics that went with it were a thing of the past, says:

> The acknowledged leaders in hundred and parish and shire gave place to experts trained in foreign schools, men who swaggered about in plumed hats and velvet doublets and extravagant hose, swearing strange oaths of mingled blasphemy taught by Spanish Catholics and Lutheran Landsknecht, and prating of *besonois* and *alferez*, of camp-masters and rote-masters, of furriers and *hurenweibels*, of false brays, mines and counter mines, in one long insolent crow of military superiority.[16]

Fortescue had caught exactly the aggrieved tone of the archetypal 'old soldier', passed over and passed by, but he goes on to make the point that by the sixteenth century, war had become a profession and could no longer be tacked on as a mere appendage to the everyday life of the citizen.

Fortescue's marvellously intemperate language does however disguise the fact that at least some traces of that pre-professional army remained. A sense of obligation and loyalty, the feeling that armies were, or should be, made up of groups of neighbours and sometimes friends. That they partook of and believed in country virtues, including a rural sense of the right ordering of society, was an element preserved and carried forward into the future and into the heyday of the County Regiments.

The Tudor Queens, Mary and Elizabeth both, were in their turn forced to tackle the moribund state of their military forces. Mary was compelled to hire foreign mercenaries since she could not rely on her native troops, especially after her marriage to Philip of Spain. Italian harquebusiers and Swabian Landsknechte were regularly in her employ but, as Fortescue points out, she was the first to appoint Lords Lieutenant who were made responsible for the Shire forces. She also raised the pay of English soldiers going to join the Spanish at Saint Quentin from 6 pence to 8 pence per day. The increase of a third being necessary, presumably, to overcome any religious scruples. However, the new rate of 8 pence became general and remained in force for the next two hundred years. Even though more modern weapons were introduced through her reforms, the long bow was still accepted as a substitute for the arquebus at muster parades. Fortescue, ever ready to suspect treachery from abroad, hints that the clause in the Bill which accepted the equivalence of the long bow was inserted in the interests of Spain, the foremost and best equipped military power in Europe.

Elizabeth, unlike Mary, had a large popular following, despite her parsimony and double dealing. So she could dispense with foreign mercenaries. However, in spite of the demonstrable ineffectiveness of her militia, she could not be persuaded to form a standing army even under the immediate threat of the Spanish Armada. But long before the threat from Spain had become a reality, trouble in Scotland, where French troops were supporting the Catholic party, caused great concern in England. The small English force at Leith was in danger of being defeated and this could have been followed by a rising of the English Catholics who were numerous in the North. Corruption and inefficiency sapped the strength of the Queen's forces in Scotland where, of the 8,000 men on the rolls only 5,000 were with the colours whilst the other 3,000, whose pay went directly into the Captain's pockets, did not exist. After the death of Mary of Guise in 1560, mother of Mary Queen of Scots and Regent until her death, the French troops were withdrawn from Scotland. The tension was eased in the North of England and Elizabeth was recognised in Scotland as Queen of England. The way was thus opened for the eventual union

of Scotland and England although it was to take a further 150 years
to become reality.

The continuing troubles in Ireland, the disgraceful state of the
Queens's army in Scotland and the growing threat from Spain called
for a more drastic overhaul of defence measures than the Queen was
prepared to pay for, but Cecil, her Secretary, required all magistrates
to report on the condition of the population and the efficacy of
arrangements for defence of the realm. Reports coming in soon
showed that the fyrd was no longer capable of providing an adequate
defence force, largely it was said, because the gentlemen no longer
set an example 'The people were no longer trained to arms and the
country was passing through a social as well as a religious revolution'.[17]
The revolution reported to Cecil was undoubtedly a reality but it
had many causes, some of which were far from obvious. The rise of
Protestantism had encouraged the growth of a capitalist economy and
a rapidly growing merchant middle class. Towns, with their markets
and Charters, began to emerge as important sources of wealth in taxes
and other contributions to the royal exchequer. Not only did the
burgeoning towns foster a prosperous middle class but they also saw
the beginning of an urban proletariat which provided some less
savoury recruits for the Army and Navy.

The traditional country aristocracy turned away from a military
service where the new weapons were costly and distasteful and where
the new tactics were likely to be taught by one of the foreign-trained
coxcombs described by Fortescue. Even more disastrous to the image
of the Army as a worthwhile career was the new found popularity of
seafaring, and the widespread feeling amongst adventurous young
men that this was now to be their destiny. This turning away of country
gentlemen from their traditional role of leadership left the way open
for the rising middle class to fill the vacuum at least in part.

As Fortescue says:

> The people had awaked to the fact that their heritage was the sea; and the life of the
> corsair, free, stirring, lucrative and dangerous, appealed powerfully to a race at once
> adventurous and grasping, energetic and casual, bold and born gamblers.[18]

What he does not say is that seafaring has always been the traditional
way for an island people to escape from a narrow, repressive environment made increasingly so at this time by the fast growing influence
of Puritanism. Puritanism and the new rational book-keeping were
the bases of the new society. A new concept of honour, a personal,
autonomous honour as opposed to feudal honour of position, status
and birth, was becoming apparent. The new kind of honour was composed of 'moral quality', solid, permanent and more amenable to con-

tract and a commercial code than the more romantic pre-capitalistic honour code.[19] The new code was to become an overwhelming force in the next century. The new society accepted the early Stuart dynasty uneasily for a while. Then, exhausted and exasperated by royal, high-minded obscurantism, rose, formed the first 'New Model' army, and eventually executed their King. For a short time it seemed as if the Restoration of Charles II might put the clock back to Tudor times or before, but the new commercialism was by now too well entrenched and the new code was here to stay. The Army was left in a somewhat ambiguous position with regard to the Crown and Parliament which could only be resolved, in the future as in the past, on a personal basis.

2

The Tempering of the Regiments

By the end of the sixteenth century, some of the divergencies which were to distinguish the English and later the British Army and its officer corps from its continental counterparts were becoming obvious. Cecil's correspondents had already reported in Elizabeth's time how the natural leaders in the country, even amongst the rural aristocracy, had begun to turn from the old feudal beliefs to a new philosophy based on protestant capitalism. The new leaders no longer searched for the Holy Grail by way of a crusade but by way of a commercial venture to the Indies, where there would certainly be risk and adventure enough but also the prospect of a handsome profit on returning safe home. The English Army, and certainly individual English soldiers serving abroad, were, on the other hand, likely to find themselves in armies opposing the domination by Catholic Powers and Princes of a civil population who had found that their newly achieved civic and religious freedoms were worth fighting and dying for.

Before the outbreak of the English Civil War, both British and Scots soldiers had enlisted in privately raised and privately owned regiments as mercenaries, recruited to fight in Germany and the Low Countries. Sometimes this service abroad was sanctioned by the Crown and sometimes it was a refuge for fugitives, but usually the movement of soldiers from Britain was motivated by the hope of regular pay and occasional loot. However, when the men, and eventually whole regiments, returned, they brought new ideas of a military as well as of a religious and philosophical nature with them. The latest military notions were learned in the camps of the great military commanders of Europe. The Huguenots were joined in their battles and sieges against their French Catholic oppressors; the Dutch were joined in their revolt against the Spanish; many Englishmen joined the Danish service and many sought employment under Gustavus

Adolphus in the Thirty Years War. Under Adolphus particularly, the English and Scots were educated in what we would now call 'the state of the art' of the warfare of their day.

Almost all the leaders from both sides of the English Civil War learned their trade in the Dutch wars of 1625 to 1637. Fortescue tells us that Philip Skippon and John Cromwell, a kinsman of Oliver, were both wounded in Holland early in the Dutch wars. By 1637, Prince Rupert and Prince Maurice, sons of the Winter King, were, both working in the trenches before Breda with a recovered Skippon, Lord Warwick and George Goring. Meanwhile another Cromwell kinsman had arrived with Thomas Halifax, Jacob Astley, Thomas Culpepper, Balfour and Sandilands, and fresh volunteers continued to pour in. Herbert of Cherbury, Sir Faithful Fortescue, Sir Charles Slingsby and Captain George Monk, first Colonel of the Coldstream Guards, fought side by side and learned their business together before taking prominent parts, on opposite sides in the coming Civil War.[1]

Fortescue also mentions another occurrence at the Siege of Breda which anticipates many scenes in the English Civil War, where the New Model Army took its religious observances more seriously:

> There they were, Brave English Gentlemen, all wearing the scarfe of orange or blue, fighting side by side with the pupils of Francis Vere, learning their work for the days ahead when they would be divided into Cavaliers and Roundheads and flying at each others throats. It was a merry life enough, though with plenty of grim earnest. Before each relief marched off for the night to the trenches it drew off in 'parado' to the quarters of the colonel in command, heard prayers, sang a psalm and so went to its work; but though there was a preacher to every regiment and a sermon in the colonel's tent, there was no compulsion to attend, and there were few listeners except a handful of well-disposed persons.[2]

At the end of the sixteenth century, serfdom and peasantry were firmly established in France and the German States. Between the nobility and the lower orders, unlike in Britain, there was almost no middle condition. On the Continent, the Church and to some extent the Army had provided a means of upward mobility. In Northern Europe, outside Britain, the aristocracy could only be noble. In England, on the other hand, the squirearchy, landed gentry and even the yeoman class interposed between a small group of nobles and the lower classes. The growth of the middle class in Britain was closely associated with the growth of trade and commerce and the whole process was very much speeded up by the early arrival of the Industrial Revolution. But already by the seventeenth century, the comparative ease with which it was possible to rise in society and all the professions, including the Army, ensured the success of the Glorious Revolution of 1688 and made possible the next two hundred years of comparatively peaceful progress towards full democracy.[3]

This seemingly steady and inevitable progress was not without its setbacks and reverses and it occasioned acute tension from time to time, not least amongst the officers of the Army. Whilst protestant commercalism had become the accepted creed of the rising middle classes and indeed affected a proportion of the old aristocracy, it had not yet and would not for a long time affect the way of life of the country gentleman who, whilst he might invest some of his ready money in overseas enterprises, still lived in the country and still sub-scribed to the old code of honour and behaviour.

The changes in society in the early seventeenth century, epitomised by the 'new honour', were not so evident in the Army despite what Hans Spier says about the particular applicability of the new system to England at this time, 'where a thrusting, thriving middle class was making itself felt'.[4] Although the sea was undoubtedly a strong counter-attraction to adventurous young men, military service still presented a traditional way of life compatible with country interests and pursuits acceptable to the country gentleman still imbued with virtues that harked back to an earlier age. The ethos of the Knight and of feudalism was long dead for most practical purposes but, whilst out of fashion, it was present under the surface, unrecognised but still nurtured by the country necessities of paternalism and the need to provide leadership and rural organisation.

The clash between the two systems of honour and beliefs was to be seen in the sad spectacle of divided families, with brother fighting brother in the Civil War. In the Army, many officers, some of them senior, fought reluctantly but loyally for the King because of their oath and their allegiance to a royal commander who still claimed to rule with absolute, divinely inspired authority. It is likely that many of the great British soldiers had gone abroad to fight in the days before the Civil War in order to avoid some of the problems, arguments and pressures arising in the new society, As we have seen, they returned to take post on one side or the other. For some of those soldiers, as with some of their civilian counterparts, it must have been touch and go on which side they finally appeared. Typical of this split of loyalties, although he was a Scot, was the Earl of Montrose who was one of the principal instigators of the second Covenant. After raising most of Eastern Scotland for the Covenant, he found that his conscience would not allow him to fight directly against the King. Even as the Royalist fortunes in the Civil War declined, he raised a second army, this time to fight a brilliant campaign for the King in Scotland. But he was too late and, after the King surrendered, Montrose was forced to escape to Norway. Unfortunately, he returned to make a last desperate effort to save the royalist cause but his small army was easily defeated. Captured and tried by his Scottish enemies, he was executed at Edinburgh with barbaric ritual.

The New Regiments

After the restoration of the Stuarts in the person of Charles II, as King of England and Scotland, Scotland still maintained its own military establishment. One of the first acts of the new monarch was to replace the English garrisons which had been stationed in Scotland by Oliver Cromwell. Although the English garrisons had brought peace for almost the first time to most of Scotland, their withdrawal and replacement with native Scottish soldiers was highly popular. Futhermore, it brought onto the stage of history some of the oldest and most prestigious regiments of the British Army. The Scots Guards can trace their foundation back to 1662. The Royal Scots (The Royal Regiment), the senior line regiment of the British Army, was formed in 1633 under a warrant of Charles I for service under the French King and was placed on the British establishment at the Restoration. It did not finally return home until 1678. Independent troops of dragoons had been raised and disbanded in Scotland as threats to order arose and abated but in 1681 Lieutenant General Sir Thomas Dalyell of the Binns finally formed some independent troops of cavalry into The Royal Regiment of Scots Dragoons, later known as The Royal Scots Greys and now as The Royal Scots Dragoon Guards (Carabiniers and Greys). Many English regiments also date from this period. Charles' acceptance of Monk's Regiment of Foot, at one time in Cromwell's New Model Army, gave us the forerunner of the Coldstream Guards. Another consequence of the Restoration which was to be a great portent for the Army was the garrisoning of Tangier. The settlement at the Western end of the Mediterranean, at the entrance to the Straights of Gibraltar, had come to Britain, or rather to Charles, as part of the dowry of his Queen, Catherine of Braganza. The Tangier Horse was raised for service in the garrison and later became The Royal Dragoons, now The Blues and Royals. It remained there until the settlement was abandoned in 1680 on grounds of expense. The forerunners of both the Grenadier Guards and the Coldstream, The Royal Scots and the regiments which later became The Queen's Royal Regiment and the King's Own Royal Regiment, served there during the British occupation.

This time, which is widely regarded as the founding period of the British Army, marks the beginning of permanent British garrisons outside Europe. Like the Tangier settlement but with a longer and happier history, they have contributed enormously to the making of the image and the self-perceptions of the Army up to the present day. The regiments of the Restoration Army, since they were still the property of their respective Colonels, were still known by their names despite the frequent changes and subsequent confusion that this caused. It was not until 1751 that the seniority and ranking of regiments in the 'line of battle' was formalised into the official numbering of the regiments, although the numbering was shown on Colours from 1743. Territorial or county subtitles were not authorised until 1782 and even then only for some regiments. Indeed, it was not until the post-Cardwell amalgamations of 1881, when regiments were linked in pairs, that the familiar county designations came into being. What is taken by many people to be the very essence of the British regimental system, is thus seen to be of comparatively recent origin. In some proud regiments, the new territorial designations were accepted only grudgingly. Even now, a few regiments cling, quite unofficially but tenaciously, to the old numerical titles under which they gained their early battle honours.[5] All the battle honours of the many amalgamated regiments are today inherited by the newly enlarged regiments into which they have been, in many cases reluctantly, combined. The battle honours of The Queen's Regiment, which include the honours of ten of the old line regiments which have been put together over a period of time to form the present-day regiment, total more than two hundred battles from Tangier in 1662 to Korea in 1950. In themselves, the honours alone, with their dates, provide a brief but enlightening history of the British Army.[6]

Cromwell, as Protector, had managed to impose a standing army on England and Scotland. He retained that army under his own hand, leaving the maintenance of order in the country to the tender mercy of a force of militia cavalry under the orders of his specially appointed Major Generals. The hatred with which military rule was regarded during the Protectorate, especially in the country districts, fed the opposition to a standing army in the immediately following period of the Restoration and which, regardless of the popular and widely acclaimed victories of Marlborough and Wellington, survived until well into the nineteenth century. Fortescue writing in 1899 says:

> The memory of their dictatorship burned itself deep into the heart of the nation, and even now, after two centuries and a half, the vengeance of the nation upon the soldier remains insatiate and insatiable.[7]

Honour and the Clash of Loyalties

After the death of Charles II and the accession of James II, the Army was again thrown into confusion by the conflict between a

Catholic King and a Protestant parliament. It is not likely that there was much sympathy amongst army officers for the last of the Stuart Kings but loyalty and honour kept them to their duty. The situation led to a number of incidents which, whilst they were handled on the whole with common sense and humanity on both sides, were embarrassing to the Army and highlighted the gulf in thinking between the militia and the standing forces. A typical situation arose at York. By 1687 the garrison had been built up to ten companies. The city was already in a state of some resentment at the billeting within the walls of such a large force and at its continuous surveillance of the activities of the townspeople, most of whom favoured the replacement of James by his brother-in-law, William of Orange. The situation continued to worsen until August of the next year when King James moved the York garrison to Hull in anticipation of a landing there by William. A month later, one company was sent back to York to guard and keep order in the city. The garrison commander, Sir John Reresby, called up the militia to reinforce his command in the city but this turned out to be a grave mistake. A little later, an assembly of Yorkshire business men, meeting in the Guildhall, declared for William and the militia went over in a body to their support. They surprised and surrounded Sir John's company of regulars and disarmed them, one imagines with some connivance on the part of the troops themselves, whilst Sir John was arrested and held until the 'Glorious Revolution' was an accomplished fact.[8] The connivance of the troops, if not of the officers, seems likely since, during the commotion, the city gates were immediately secured by Lord Danby for William's party, without resistance. The next year, the military boot was firmly on the other foot when 6,000 Danish soldiers under the Duke of Wirtenberg were billeted in York on their way to fight for William in Ireland. It is doubtful if the citizens of York were any more welcoming to their Danish co-religionists than to the English soldiers of the previous year.

Fortescue speaks scathingly of the state of the British Army at this time. Rarely paid, frequently without rations or clothing, swindled by contractors and composed for the large part of raw recruits who were inadequately armed and trained, it is not surprising that the war in Ireland had to be sustained by Dutch and Danish troops. But there is no doubt that the appalling state of the Army reflected the cynical and confused state of the officers who had been prepared to fight for James but were prevented from doing so by popular sentiment, and who were expected to change their loyalties overnight. In another context Fortescue says, 'it is curious to note the extreme slowness with which the civilians learned that soldiers were after all men of flesh and blood, not puppets to be hugged or broken according to the caprice of the hour'.[9] Loyalty and discipline are the bases on which all armies must be built but problems of conscience do arise even in the most highly disciplined corps. The wars of religion, especially in the sixteenth century, had been fought between forces who, in the main, believed in the rightness of their cause. The Huguenot armies were composed of Protestants supported by their co-religionists from outside France. Similarly, the army of the Dutch States, in their revolt against Spanish rule, was solidly Protestant, aided by some of the German principalities and by English troops whenever Elizabeth thought this would be to her advantage. Mercenaries fought on both sides and were usually of the same religion as their employers, if they had one at all. In any case, they contrived not to be too outraged by the religious practices or intolerant excesses of their paymasters. Protestantism and dissent during the early Enlightenment in England, and well before similar events in France, led to a rejection of 'the divine right of Kings', putting the officer's oath and his personal loyalty at hazard. However, the oath of loyalty maintained and still maintains its importance in regulating the relationship between the soldier, especially the officer, and his employer. This has led to curious and occasionally deliberate misunderstandings, sometimes with tragic consequences. Most army officers in Britain, at least until recently, have believed that they stand in a special relationship with the monarch and that this relationship confers privileges of an extra-constitutional nature which we shall examine shortly.

It is necessary now to introduce events from the nineteenth century and later but we shall return to important issues in the previous two centuries which we may appear to be leaping over. However, the whole question of the officer's oath of loyalty, whether it be explicit, as in the German case, or implicit, as it often is elsewhere, together with the concept of honour which sustains it, is so important and so universal that it occurs through the whole of military history and we shall need to look at it again. Meanwhile it should be noted that after the 'Glorious Revolution' the loyalties of the British officer corps were never strained in quite the same way again. Both Marlborough and Wellington were associated with political factions and both owed more than a little to political favour but they were never required to act unconstitutionally or in violation of an oath. Nor indeed were they asked to oppose a personal loyalty to Sovereign or party against the constitution or legitimately elected parliament. Only in recent times does the problem seem to have reappeared with the Nuremberg Judgements which raise the question of personal conscience against the narrow concept of a duty subservient to all superior orders. In Germany, where the problem seemed so much more urgent when the army was being reconstructed after the Second World War, it gave rise to a whole new philosophy of leadership called *Innere Führung*.

Now however, personal conscience is a little out of fashion and soldiers are left, as they always have been, to make up their own minds and to take their chance with the consequences. That the problem is always with us is illustrated by events in Viet Nam and, on a less tragic level, by the spectacle of ex-members of our security services who use the plea of conscience to break an oath of secrecy, and with some degree of public support.

The Army and the Royal Connection

It is easily seen that many of the most famous regiments of the British Army are distinguished in their titles by including the name of the King or the Queen and that some of these titles date from the Restoration. Other regiments bear the names of other members of the Royal Family: but from the nineteenth century, the connection with royalty was not only revered but seen by some officers as a source of advancement and even profit. During the preparations for Queen Victoria's visit to Ireland in 1847, there was much competition to command the royal guards of honour and military escorts because it was still believed that the Queen could promote the lucky commander on the spot. This had apparently happened on her Scottish tour of 1846, although it was likely that this was an aberration and there is evidence that the authorities at 'The Horse Guards' were not going to let it happen again.[10] As late as 1904 however, when Major Lord Edward Gleichen was appointed to Berlin as a military attaché, he was summoned to Balmoral to receive his instructions from King Edward VIII. At the conclusion of his interview, he was given a brevet for promotion to Lieutenant Colonel. King Edward no doubt thought that he was entitled to award the promotion but Gleichen appears to have had no such illusion. In his memoirs, Gleichen explains that he had to persuade General Kelly-Kenny, the Adjutant General, who was also staying at Balmoral, to confirm the brevet promotion.[11]

There has been a suggestion that Haig, at that time General Officer Commanding at Aldershot, used the Royal relationship to save Brigadier Hubert Gough from his 'indiscretion' in the so-called Curragh Mutiny of 1914. But Haig had been a personal friend of both Edward VII and George V. His wife was a Lady-in-Waiting and his sister was often at Court, so his relationship was hardly typical of that of most officers to their sovereign even if, in the unlikely event, he had used it to Gough's advantage. On this point the evidence is almost non-existent but there is clear evidence that the King objected strongly when Sir Arthur Paget, at that time Commander-in-Chief, Ireland attempted to use the King's name directly, and without his knowledge, in persuading the recalcitrant officers in Ireland to carry on with their duties.[12] The flimsiness of the few cases supporting a special relationship with the Sovereign and royalty in general does suggest that, for some long time, the Army's, and expecially the officer's continuing relationship with the Crown has been based on rather different premises. From the middle of the nineteenth century royalty, in the person of Queen Victoria, captured the popular imagination. Before Victoria, the patronage of the House of Hannover could only have been regarded as a liability and never an asset, except on the occasion of a great military victory or the personal involvement in a victorious war of royal personalities, like the Duke of Cumberland.

George II had commanded the allied forces at the victorious battle of Dettingen in 1743, the last occasion on which a British King commanded his troops on the field of battle. Both George and his son Cumberland had the alarming experience of being carried away by their bolting horses during the battle. One can be sure that the British soldiers were amused by the incidents and remembered this, rather than royalty's other somewhat inept, although unquestionably brave, actions on the field of battle. Cumberland was, in fact, carried into the French infantry by his runaway horse and only extricated himself by fighting fiercely and, even then, only at the cost of a bullet wound in the foot. This kind of royal appearance could only excite sycophantic praise and Fortescue gives a stanza of what he calls 'doggerel effusion' from a broadsheet now in the British Museum which could rival the great McGonagal himself:

> Our noble generals played their parts,
> Our soldiers fought like thunder,
> Prince William too, that noble heart,
> In fight performed wonders.
> Though through the leg with bullet shot
> The Prince his wound regarded not,
> But still maintained his post and fought
> For glorious George of England.[13]

Although Cumberland gained for himself the unenviable title of 'Butcher' for his brutal conduct towards the defeated Highlanders after Culloden, it is probable that his actions were highly approved of by the general public in England and in the larger towns in Scotland. Exaggerated stories of the barbaric behaviour of the clansmen from the still barely known North of Scotland terrified the civilian population, who dreaded occupation by the wild hordes. The soldiers, no doubt, merely did their business and made no moral judgements. What the soldier approves of in the conduct of his superiors is often at variance with the common or reported view and also at times with the self-view of his own leaders. Esme Wingfield-Stratford, in the chapter titled 'Eccentrics and Barbarians' in his book *The Making of a*

Gentleman, says of the English squire, 'What pleased him as much as any victory was the fact that, while Massena's great army was starving outside the Lines of Torres Vedras, Viscount Wellington was enjoying excellent sport with a pack of English hounds behind them'.[14]

Despite the occasional evidence of media distortion or sycophancy, the personal popularity of the Sovereign from Victoria onwards, and of the royal family, amounting at times almost to adulation, has meant that they have been able to bring respect, prestige and glamour to all the organisations and people with whom they are closely associated. Lord Cardigan, in 1840, was perhaps the first of many to realise the importance of the royal connection where impressing the public was concerned. As commanding officer of the 11th Light Dragoons, he had become notorious as a bully, martinet and duellist. Stationed near London, he provided endless copy for the National newspapers and their cartoonists. He was a dreadful example, ready to hand, for the growing number of critics of the military and reformers in the House of Commons. Cardigan urgently needed a 'good press'. Providentially, he was selected with his regiment by Wellington to escort Prince Albert from Dover to London for his marriage to Queen Victoria. Cardigan made excellent use of his opportunity. Prince Albert agreed to become Colonel-in-Chief of Cardigan's regiment and its title was changed from the rather ordinary 11th Light Dragoons to the much more fashionable and prestigious 11th (Prince Albert's Own) Hussars. From being one of the most hated men in London, he became a hero overnight. His good fortune with the Royal Family must also have impressed his military superiors. When the Crimean War broke out in 1854, he was given command of the Light Brigade, but he and his regiment were idolised well before they gained immortality in their charge at Balaclava.[15]

Happily, the monarchy continues to be a most popular part of the British constitution and the continually growing influence of the media, especially of television, has enhanced the prestige and esteem enjoyed by the Royal Family. It is now this unique popularity which makes the close connection with royalty through royal Colonels-in-Chief and royal Commandants-in-Chief so sought after and prized by all the regiments and corps of the Army. There is now even a fear that over exposure of royalty by the media and the move towards a more 'popular', show-business kind of royal persona, of which there have been certain signs in recent years, could be counter-productive and might involve the Services in a re-examination of all their traditional connections.

Royalty and Loyalty and the German Army

By comparison, the German experience has been less happy. In his study of the German Officer Corps,[16] Karl Demeter shows how, whilst the absolutist concept of the State gave way to the constitutional during the nineteenth century, this development was not accepted in the majority of German states by their officer corps. In many of the states, officers refused to swear an oath of loyalty to the new constitutions introduced in 1848 and insisted on retaining their special position vis-a-vis the royal Head of State. In Prussia, although Frederick IV promised that the Army would take an oath to uphold the new constitution, in the event the officers would have none of it. This immeasurably strengthened the King's hand in dealing with the reformers so that he was able to revoke the quite liberal constitution of 1848 and impose a much less generous one in 1850. The German Army, united under the leadership of Prussia after the successful war against France in 1870, kept itself aloof from the democratic parliamentary process and relied on its special relationship with the Kaiser to maintain its privileged position. This special relationship of personal loyalty was ruthlessly used by Hitler after the demise of the Weimar Republic in 1933. To quote Demeter: 'It is hardly a matter for wonder if the corps of officers obeyed without resistance (although with occasional misgivings) when Blomberg, on 2 August 1934 – the very day after Hindenburg's death – boldly made the whole Wehrmacht swear allegiance to the new President and Supreme Commander, Adolf Hitler'. Some high-ranking officers were inclined to resign but had second thoughts. By 1944, when many of the generals had become sickened by the horrors of the Third Reich and, it must be added, appalled by the prospect of defeat, loyalty to the Fuehrer had become so ingrained that many officers stood idly by during the attempted coup in July. Others helped to suppress the revolt and, in some cases, persuaded the unsuccessful leaders to commit suicide rather than compromise the honour of the Army. The protagonists themselves probably thought more of the safety of their families and friends and the inevitability of torture and reprisals against involved and innocents alike in the event of being captured alive.[17]

The Legacy of the 'New Model'

To return to the seventeenth century; by its end the real legacy of the 'New Model' was becoming apparent. British troops under experienced officers had learned to march long distances, to stand steady with their comrades, to receive the musket and artillery fire of their opponents at close range without breaking or losing their cohesion and to reply in disciplined, devastating volleys to such effect that over the next two hundred years they were literally unbeatable. It was not only the high morale manifested in their marching and their steadiness under fire but the superior handling of their weapons which made their actions on the battlefield so often decisive.[18] With the renewed success of British arms on the Continent of Europe came the new myths and legends, but now rarely telling of heroic individual actions. The new stories were concerned with the exploits of British regiments, infantry and cavalry, against a foreign foe and always in superior numbers. The stories reached their apotheosis in describing the gaining and the holding of the Empire in India. Almost always the legends were based on fact but as in all great stories, they were often improved upon in the telling. The steadiness of the British ranks at Fontenoy in 1745 gave rise to the marvellous and typically 'Guards' story of how the French Guards, on being invited to fire first, refused, allegedly saying, *'Non messieurs, nous ne tirons jamais les premiers'*.

Fortescue, who could himself rarely refuse the chance to make a good legend describes that part of the action in classic terms:

> At last the crest of the ridge was gained and the ranks of the French battalions came suddenly into view little more than a hundred yards distant, their coats alone visible behind the breastwork. Next to the Forest of Barry, and exposed to the extreme right of the British, a line of red showed the presence of the Swiss Guards; next to them stood a line of blue, the four battalions of the French Guards, and next to the Guards a line of white, the regiments of Courtin, Aubeterre, and of the King, the choicest battalions of the French Army. Closer and closer came the British, still with arms shouldered, always silent, always with the same slow, measured tread, till they had advanced within fifty yards of the French. Then at length Lord Charles Hay of the First Guards stepped forward with a flask in hand and doffing his hat drank politely to his enemies. 'I hope, gentlemen,' he shouted, 'that you are going to wait for us today and not swim the Scheldt as you swam the Main at Dettingen. Men of the King's company', he continued, turning round to his own people, 'these are the French Guards, and I hope you are going to beat them today'; and the English Guards answered with a cheer. The French officers hurried to the front, for the appearance of the British was a surprise to them, and called for a cheer in reply, but only a half hearted murmur came from the French ranks, which quickly died away and gave place to a few sharp words of command; for the British were now within thirty yards. 'For what we are about to receive may the Lord make us truly thankful', murmured an English Guardsman as he looked down the barrels of the French muskets, but before his comrades around him had done laughing the French Guards had fired; and the turn of the British had come at last.
>
> For despite that deadly march through the crossfire of the French batteries to the muzzles of the French muskets, the scarlet ranks still glared unbroken through the smoke; and now the British muskets, so long shouldered, were levelled, and with crash upon crash the volleys rang out from end to end of the line, first the First Guards, then the Scots, then the Coldstreams, and so through brigade after brigade, two battalions loading while the third fired, a ceaseless, rolling, infernal fire. Down dropped the whole of the French front rank, blue coats, red coats and white, before the storm. Nineteen officers and six hundred men of the French and Swiss Guards fell at the first discharge; regiment Coutin was crushed out of existence; regiment Aubeterre, striving hard to stem the tide, was swept aside with a single imperious volley which laid half of its men on the ground. The British infantry were perfectly in hand; their officers could

be seen coolly tapping the muskets of the men with their canes so that every discharge might be low and deadly.[19]

A similar scene occurred at the battle of Minden in 1759, when six British battalions, supported by three Hanoverian battalions, advanced, independently of the remainder of the allied forces, into the heart of the French army and literally, calmly and methodically shot to pieces what should have been two overwhelming cavalry charges and, for good measure, a large force of French infantry. This famous feat is still commemorated every year in the six battalions descended from their forerunners at Minden. The early battles of the First World War were probably the last occasion where British musketry featured so importantly on a battlefield. At the battle of Mons and before the machine gun had come to dominate the battlefield, as it very soon did, the rate of fire and accuracy of the British infantry was so effective it is said, that the advancing German infantry were convinced that they were being held up by machine guns.[20]

The Legacy of the 'New Model' Across the World

The steadiness, discipline and expert musketry of the British infantry was the arbiter of battles in which they were involved on the continent of Europe. By 1704, a handful of British and Dutch marines under Prince George of Hesse-Darmstadt, had already brought a new and unexpected possession to England by 'The Surprise of Gibraltar', which, though captured for King Charles III, the British candidate for the Spanish throne, was kept for Queen Anne. At the time, the capture of Gibraltar was completely overshadowed by Marlborough's brilliant victory at Blenheim. Many Englishmen saw Gibraltar as another Tangier which would soak up men and treasure. However, the Treaty of Utrecht in 1713 finally confirmed Britain's possession of The Rock and it was not long before new interests and new policies proved that an easily defended base in the Western Mediterranean could more than pay its way. The treaty not only gave Britain an important naval base but transferred the 'Asiento', the monopoly of the slave trade in Spanish America from France to Britain. This was so important that, according to Trevelyan,[21] the finances of Britain in 1711 were planned on the assumption that the 'Asiento' would be wrested from France under the coming treaty. Another important concession was wrung from Spain following the Peace of Utrecht. The British were now allowed to send a ship every year to trade in the West Indies. Mahan[22] reports the story that the ship, after being anchored in West Indian waters, was kept continually supplied by other British trading ships, so that fresh cargo came in over one side of the ship as fast as the old was sent ashore over the other. Whatever the truth of the story, the agreement effectively broke the Spanish monopoly of trade in the Caribbean.

By the time of Queen Anne's death, in the year after the Treaty of Utrecht, British commercial interests were represented all round the globe mainly in companies set up to obtain a monopoly of trade in a particular area with the support of the government and the protection of the British Navy. Such companies carried on their business in Africa, Hudson's Bay, The Levant (that is to say, Turkey) and the Eastern Mediterranean and, most important of all, in India as the Honourable East India Company. Unlike the British colonies in North America, which could raise and, when necessary, pay for a militia on the British model, the Company settlements and trading posts were very much at the mercy of local rulers. This was acceptable as long as they were only likely to be threatened by untrained and ill-armed local armies equipped only with extremely primitive fire arms. But as trade rivalry with the Dutch and French grew, another dimension entered into the situation. The European soldiers trained and officered native forces and entered into the service of native rulers so that in India especially, where a largely warlike people provided good and willing military material, warfare soon resembled that of Europe. At first, this warfare consisted of maintaining British trading interests in small-scale conflicts between rival trading posts but this soon led to intrigue with native rulers in search of allies against their European rivals and eventually, as the superiority of European organisation and discipline became apparent, the situation was reversed. European help was sought by local Princelings against neighbouring chiefs or threatening overlords, and sometimes to assist in the straight-forward usurpation of power. By 1760, the combination of high morale, good discipline and effective training which had made the British infantry all but invincible in Europe, made the East India Company's armies equally feared on the Indian sub-continent. Regiments of Indian troops trained and supported by a small British element set the pattern for a force which eventually drove out any European remnants that posed a threat to British interests and finally expanded sufficiently to dominate the whole sub-continent.

The relationship of the British Army and the British soldier to India and the Indian Army is needless to say a complex and ambiguous one. The relationship, whether it is or was a real one, or whether it was as some suggest only the outpourings of romantic and sometimes overheated imaginations, is now almost impossible to clarify. What is certain is that to visit the Indian or Pakistan army on their home ground, or to be lucky enough to be really familiar with the memories and mysteries of our older regiments, or what is still preserved of them, is to be aware that imagination or not, the relationship was utterly self-fulfilling for the people involved. So strong was the vision that it coloured British military thinking, uniforms, equipment, architecture, food and social life almost up to the Second World War.

Whilst the British Army has been involved in all parts of the overseas world continuously since the eighteenth century, India has been by far the most important commitment outside Europe for more than three hundred years. We shall return to India in a later chapter. We have seen that Tangier was an early and unsuccessful attempt to set up a base at the Western end of the Mediterranean. But this was followed early in the eighteenth century by the successful occupation of Gibraltar and, less happily, of Port Mahon on the island of Minorca. Long before Tangier came to his son by way of a dowry, Charles I had shown an interest in Spain and its southern coastline, but luckily he was too preoccupied to pursue his ambition there. Even before the Restoration, Oliver Cromwell had also shown an imaginative interest in a project to capture The Rock of Gibraltar to further a forward maritime policy in the Mediterranean. According to Fortescue, this confirmed Cromwell's standing, along with Marlborough and Wellington, as one of Britian's foremost military thinkers. However, there is an apocryphal story, still told in the bars of Gibraltar, which does not really support this estimation. It is said that Cromwell actually dispatched a ship complete with Irish labourers whose task was to dig a wide trench across the sandy isthmus joining the Rock to Spain thus turning it into an island. Alas, the ingenious scheme was never tried out. Cromwell never attempted the Rock, and it is said the ship with the unfortunate Irish navvies was captured by the Spanish.

Nevertheless, having determined to make an enemy of Spain, Cromwell revived long standing ambitions against her in the Caribbean and on the Main. He conceived a plan to seize Hispaniola using as a base Barbados, which had been in British hands since 1628. Despite immense although seemingly not very efficient preparations in the English dockyards, which by their scale frightened the whole of Europe, the descent on the port of St. Domingo was a resounding failure, especially on the part of the military leadership. Determined to save something from the debacle, the expedition moved on to Jamaica and captured it easily in May 1655.

In the half-century following the capture of Gibraltar, Britain continued to expand into the Indian sub-continent and after the Peace of Paris in 1763, following the Seven Years War, British gains were enormous. In North America Britain gained the whole of the mainland from Canada south to Florida and from the Atlantic seaboard to the Great Lakes, the Ohio Valley and the Lower Mississippi. New gains in the West Indies came to join Barbados and Jamaica. In all the island possessions, from the oldest to the most recent, under a new if fragile peace, the inhabitants returned to a lucrative occupation which again perforce engaged the Army. The Colonies were prohibited from manufacturing any goods which could compete with the wares made in Britain; trade with the Colonies was prohibited in any but British built ships and certain articles of trade could only be imported into the Colonies by way of England. Evasion of these regulations was a profitable pastime, engaged-in all along the immense Atlantic seaboard of North America and in the West Indies and even in the British home islands. In Britain, the main peace-time task of the troops was to protect and reinforce the Preventive Service. Fortescue says, perhaps with tongue in cheek, that when The Isle of Man was annexed to the Crown in 1762, it was described by Burke as a citadel of smuggling, and it was found necessary to overawe the island by stationing a squadron of dragoons there.[23]

As was usual at the conclusion of a peace treaty, Parliament could not wait to reduce the military establishment to its normal abysmal peace-time level. After the Peace of Paris, this was effected by disbanding, or planning the disbandment of, all infantry line regiments junior to the Seventieth Foot and all cavalry regiments junior to the Eighteenth Light Dragoons. The reduced military establishment then made up a total of just over forty-five thousand men. Of these Gibraltar and Minorca took more than four thousand men, whilst the rest of the Colonies were allowed ten thousand men including the King's regiments in India. A part of the total was the irreducible twelve thousand men on the Irish establishment, leaving seventeen thousand five hundred men in Great Britain of whom three thousand were invalids. The remainder of the forty-five thousand was made up of artillerymen. Fortescue lists the overseas garrisons of that time as: Minorca, Gibraltar, Bermuda, the Bahamas, St. Vincent, Dominica, Tobago, Grenada and the Grenadines, Jamaica, New York, Halifax, Quebec, Mobile and Pensacola, as well as a chain of posts extending some three thousand miles from the St. Lawrence in the North to the Lower Mississippi in the South. He adds, in emphasising the overstretching of the reduced British Army, 'The whole of the West Indies were subject always to the danger of an insurrection either of Negro slaves or of savage natives; while the entire western frontier of North America lay exposed to attack by Indians.[24] But there were Militia regiments in some of the overseas territories such as North America, and the East India Company did have its own armies in India. The burden on the British troops was enormous but the Army could rely, as could Britain itself, upon a dominant, powerful and aggressive navy. The mobility that this naval supremacy ensured, and the reasonable expectation of supplies and reinforcements made up for the lack of numbers. In the absence of large-scale hostilities against a European enemy, the Army towards the end of the eighteenth century was back in what it probably regarded as its normal situation of deprivation.

A Hundred Years of the 'New Model'

A hundred years after the founding of the 'New Model' and its later incorporation into the first British standing army, it may be appropriate to sum up what had been achieved over that century and indeed what still survived from the earlier military organisations in Britain which we have briefly surveyed. The new 'small' army of 1770 was made up of Guards regiments; the Grenadiers (1st Guards until 1815), the Coldstream, and the Scots Guards (known as the 3rd Guards from 1713); seventy regiments of foot soldiers, numbered in strict seniority from the 1st Foot (The Royal Scots), to the 70th Foot (2nd Battalion The East Surrey Regiment); two regiments of Household Cavalry and twenty-five other regiments of cavalry. The artillery had increased from three to a remarkable thirty-one companies between 1741 and 1761, but it was not only in numerical strength that the artillery had been improved. The British batteries present at the battle of Minden won the admiration of the most critical artillerists in Europe.

The 'New Model' had laid down that an infantry regiment of the line or a regiment of dragoons, who were originally 'horsed infantry', should be composed of ten companies. After the disbandments of 1763, twelve of the remaining infantry regiments had two battalions with twenty-four companies between them. The cavalry, again based on the 'New Model', had six troops of horse for each regiment. However, the strength of an infantry company could be as high as one hundred and twenty men but it could and frequently did fall as low as fifty men in peacetime. The retention of low strength regiments allowed for a rapid expansion in times of crisis.[25]

What was most to be noticed in the infantry in the hundred years up to the Peace of Paris was the growth of discipline, and steadiness under fire, accompanied by the ability to reply at short range with devastatingly accurate and rapid volleys. The British performance at close range was aided by the heavy bullet which they customarily used. Only sixteen bullets to the pound for the British muskets against twenty-four in the French Army. But it was the combination of steadiness, efficiency and high morale which gave them the victory at Minden. To quote Fortescue again, 'At Dettingen the fire though deadly was unsteady; at Fontenoy it was nearly perfect; at Minden, where the British stood motionless until the French cavalry was within ten paces, it was quite admirable; at Quebec it was simply superlative'. He goes on to say that it was commonly supposed that this improvement was due to the adoption of Prussian methods but he found no grounds for the assumption. The British had nothing to learn from the Prussians either in the cavalry or the infantry. Marlborough taught them the superiority of shock action and platoon fire long before Frederick the Great was born.[26]

It would not be too fanciful to see another legacy, this time from Cromwell's Army, evident amongst the British soldiers fighting on the Continent and in India and in the Americas. Whilst there was not too much to be seen perhaps of the Puritan conscience or the Roundhead seriousness of purpose, there were signs of a new national awareness which encompassed the whole of the British Isles and which gave to British possessions overseas a new worth and meaning for the soldiers who acquired them and defended them. Fortescue says that the 'New Model' was responsible for the concept and ultimate unity of the 'British Isles' and it was this which first, as in so many later examples of unification, fanned the flames of patriotism and sustained the regiments in so many desperate encounters round the world.

Fortescue points also to a new breed of officer which emerged towards the end of the century. In the late sixteenth century and for much of the seventeenth there were influences at work which were at odds with the traditional country values and feudal sense of obligation which had once dominated the beliefs and ideas of the majority of army officers. Mercantilism, puritanism and the unlicensed freedom of the Restoration were equally inimical to an efficient officer corps. Despite this the period did produce some excellent officers and some very good regiments but it was not until after the 'Glorious Revolution' that fanaticism and bigotry, and perhaps one should add corruption and debauchery, became unacceptable to society at large. By the end of the seventeenth century, a certain balance had been restored. There was still corruption and jobbery but there had been a reassertion of the old virtues. Loyalty, honour, an appropriate paternalism and the notion of gentlemanly conduct, although perverted and debased at times as they certainly were, became what was expected once again of the officer. A new body of senior officers could be discerned emerging from their fellows, combining a real interest in the technicalities of their profession with the desire and ability to innovate. At the same time, they demonstrated humanitarian feelings, a genuine compassion towards their men and an understanding that their physical and spiritual wellbeing was an essential part of their battle worthiness. Amherst and Wolfe prepared the way for the Light Infantrymen and riflemen who were to come later, by training bodies of marksmen who, in philosophy as well as in tactics, could operate on something like equal terms with the individualistic Indians and backwoodsmen in the forests of North America. Howe, Washington, Forbes and Bouquet had initiated reforms in tactics and dress and were pointing their young officers towards the future. Only a few years later, John Moore had his baptism of fire from the insurgent Americans at Boston and began to learn the lessons which he applied so brilliantly in training the Light Division at Shorncliffe in the first years of the nineteenth century.

The use of regular soldiers from regular units in the training of riflemen and light infantrymen as skirmishers, rather than the use of auxiliaries or locally raised units, broke an important mould that went back to the Romans. We have already said that it was Marlborough rather than Frederick the Great who raised the British Army to its later condition of pre-eminence at the end of the eighteenth century. But Frederick did leave a system which could not be entirely ignored. The steadiness, the rigid formations coupled with battlefield mobility and the harsh discipline of his regiments impressed all who witnessed his troops on the battlefield or at exercise. Colonel David Dundas, who saw the Prussian Army at manoeuvres in 1785, was afraid that the less formal, looser and less uniformly regulated style of the British Army might suffer badly at the hands of an army trained under Frederick's rules. With the approval of the Headquarters in London, he produced a large volume of instructions based upon the Prussian system, ranging from the basic training of recruits to the manoeuvering of large formed bodies of troops. Whilst, even at the time, it was considered by many soldiers to be over detailed and too high in its standards, it did introduce a uniformity between regiments and between the various notions of their respective Colonels which had been seriously absent until then. The whole of battlefield movement was compressed into eighteen manoeuvres. 'General,' said Sir John Moore on meeting Dundas in 1804, 'that book of yours has done a great deal of good, and would be of great value if it were not for those eighteen manoeuvres'. Dundas, who could never suffer fools replied 'Why—ay, blockheads don't understand'. Which was certainly true and no doubt there were many blockheads in the Army, but John Moore was not one of them. His distillation and combination of the best elements of Prussian teaching and the experiences coming out of America, formed the basis of his training methods with the Light Division.[27]

If, in the eighteenth and nineteenth centuries, it was the remnants of a kind of enlightened feudalism, with all its faults, that produced an officer corps worthy of the troops it commanded, the soldiers themselves might have looked to an earlier model. The dour steadiness and graveyard humour that thanked God, 'for what we are about to receive', from the enemy muskets at point blank range, and the realisation that survival in battle depended upon unity and discipline, would not have seemed strange to the Roman legionaries nor perhaps to the Normans. Perhaps also it is not unfair, and may do no more than round out the picture, to agree that there was and still is in the British soldiers make-up a strain of Saxon wassail, which, however inconvenient and sometimes dangerously relaxing it may be, allows a very necessary relief from the stress of battle.[28]

3

The Golden Age of the Regiments

When war with France was resumed in 1793, following the execution of Louis XVI, it was to continue, with two short breaks, until 1815. The war increased in scale over this period so that almost no country and certainly no continent was not involved in the conflict. For Britain the two great battle areas were in Europe and the West Indies. India we will leave for the moment, noting only at this stage that the wars in the sub-continent had already begun to take on the character of training for the Generals and men who would later appear on the European stage. India and Europe, especially the Europe of the Iberian Peninsula, were to be the great anvils on which the British regimental system was to be forged into a definitive shape and tempered so that it would last for more than a further hundred years. In the West Indies, before Assaye and long before Wellington's first victories in Portugal, there was already a formidable British presence, made up partly of home-based troops and partly of locally raised regiments. This force was largely misdirected and the cost of maintaining it, in terms of men and treasure, became prohibitive. After the victory at Trafalgar, French overseas ambitions could be neutralised by the British Navy alone and an end was made to the squandering of scarce British troops on what were essentially secondary objectives. With aftersight it is difficult to see the West Indies campaigns as more than a side show concerned with the safeguarding of private profit.

By 1799 there were twelve black West Indian regiments, raised and paid for by the British. It was soon found necessary to enfranchise all the black soldiers in order to avoid the summary and arbitrary punishments inflicted by a planter magistracy, who feared and loathed any measure which might undermine the slave property status of the negro inhabitants of the islands. Properly trained and led, the negro regiments were loyal and fought no less bravely than the 'Company' troops in India. In St. Domingo the negro slaves in revolt under the leadership of Toussaint L'Ouverture showed that they could more than hold their own against French troops and the portion of the island now known as Haiti has remained a ramshackle but independent state to this day. The regiments raised by the British in the islands and on the mainland of South America were disbanded and raised again as the international or internal situation seemed to demand. This, in itself, is some evidence of the loyalty and value of local troops. When the islands achieved independent status, well after the Second World War, the black regiments, again very much in evidence, were taken over to be the nucleus of the forces of the new island states.

Yet, by the beginning of the nineteenth century it was already clear that the West Indies was not going to be another great springboard, like the early possessions in India, for almost limitless British expansion. Commercial and military enterprise was clearly seen to present more limited opportunities there than in other parts of the world, and Empire building ambitions were in the main directed elsewhere. The cost of maintaining British troops in the West Indies was immense. It was necessary to calculate a replacement of fifty per cent every year for every British regiment to make up for the deaths from yellow fever alone. Fortescue calculated that the cost of fighting the war against the French and Spanish in the Caribbean and on the South American mainland during the later part of the eighteenth century was greater in men than for the whole of Wellington's Peninsular Campaign.

In most years, however, the casualty rate from disease was not much higher in the West Indies than in the East Indies, and the Caribbean islands were much nearer for replacements than many of the Far Eastern garrisons. It was also easier to support the troops in the Caribbean islands where the strategy was predominantly maritime, than on the vast Indian sub-continent where, after the early campaigns, the Navy could rarely intervene in the fighting. At one stage in the struggle there was a vision, fostered by planter and emigré fortune hunters, of the whole of the South American land mass being liberated from Spain and Holland, making it ripe for British usurpation or at least for British commercial exploitation. But this idea was not followed up, because of the British need to find allies against revolutionary, and later Napoleonic, France. After the French invasion of Spain and Portugal and the opening of the Peninsular War, it was more than ever necessary to maintain both countries in their South American possessions. The Portuguese Royal House found a refuge in Brazil whilst the protection of the Royal Navy for the colonies of both countries ensured the co-operation of the people of Spain and Portugal in the internecine war in the Iberian Peninsular. So, in the end, there was no great South American hinterland ready to become a second India. There were two further factors which made India a more attractive prize than the scattered islands of the Caribbean and the mainland of Central and South America. The growing strength and the independent policy of the newly founded United States of America warned against an open ended commitment in what was already seen as a future sphere of their interest and influence. The war of 1812 against the United States, whilst it was an overwhelming victory for Britain, did demonstrate that a new force had risen, not necessarily, as Canning had suggested, to redress the balance of the Old World, but to claim a voice in the disposal of any of the spoils of war in the New.

It must also be said that Britain was in something of a false position in her war against the possessions of the continental powers in the Americas. Britain already possessed several islands which, like Jamaica, had been in British hands since 1655. All these islands were worked by slave labour under the plantation system. Furthermore, as we have seen, Britain had obtained the much prized 'Asiento', the exclusive right to carry on the slave trade in the Americas, as part of the Treaty of Utrecht in 1713. None of this was to be given up lightly. But already, towards the end of the eighteenth century, consciences were stirring in England as well as in 'enlightened' and revolutionary France. To further the aims of the revolution in France, the Directory had promised freedom to all slaves who rose against their royalist masters in the French colonies. In most of the French and Spanish islands an active revolt was in progress. Royalist emigrés and plantation owners encouraged the British to invade French possessions, claiming that they would be strongly supported by the white planters who, with a little assistance from the British forces, would quickly restore the *status quo*. Once engaged, the British quickly found that they had been duped by the plantation owners who, in the main were found to be corrupt, vicious and self-seeking. The planters and their friends had persuaded the government in London to pull their chestnuts from the fire for them whilst they intrigued against the naval and military commanders sent to succour them. The avarice and cruelty of the planters was not lost on the British officers, many of whom were surprisingly liberal in their sentiments. The planters were vehemently opposed to the raising of Negro regiments, knowing that this must eventually lead to the emancipation of the blacks. But they could offer nothing to stand against the promise of freedom already made in Paris except terror and harsh repression. The fifty per cent mortality rate of the British troops made the raising of black troops essential but this was only brought about in the face of bitter opposition from the planters in the British, as well as in the French and Spanish, islands. The British officers and their men could see that they were being sacrificed to fill the pockets of the plantation owners, who had the ear of the influential ministers at home.[1]

Fighting against the French revolutionary armies in Europe would have seemed little different from fighting the armies of Royalist France in the immediately preceding decades. The excesses of the Terror had effectively destroyed any sympathy there may have been for the revolutionaries, in the Army as much as with the civilian population at home. Any early influence the revolutionaries and their doctrines may have had was quickly swept away for the majority of people in Britain if not in Ireland, by the accounts of outrage, massacre and summary execution. In particular, the execution of Louis XVI and his Queen, even though inspired by the English regicides of the seventeenth century, destroyed any lingering doubts about the justice of the revolutionary cause. Anti-revolutionary propaganda was assiduously spread by the many aristocratic refugees who arrived in England anxious to raise funds and troops for the pro-Royalist armies which they hoped would restore the French monarchy and regain for them their confiscated estates.

The Regiments in an Age of Revolutions

The execution of the French King caused a crisis in the French Army not unlike the events of the Civil War and the Glorious Revolution in Britain. But the outcome for the French officer corps was much more serious than for the officers in Britain in the previous century. Immediately after the 'Flight to Varennes' in 1790, when the French Royal Family tried to escape to join their sympathisers in Austria, where an army was being raised to support them, a new oath of loyalty was tendered to all ranks of the French Army. The King's name was deliberately omitted from the new oath, and whilst many army officers were well educated and of superior intellect, enabling them to sympathise with at least some of the aims of the revolution, generations of hereditary service made them regard the King with a sentimental devotion amounting almost to superstition. They could not accept that the function of the King as fountainhead of all honour should be abolished. Thousands of officers resigned rather than take the new oath and, by September 1791, two thirds of the French officer corps had been driven from the service into exile in foreign lands, where they often joined the forces of their host country. The feudal bond between the Monarch and the nobility to which all French officers belonged was still extremely strong and was paradoxically strengthened by the centralising policies of the French Kings from Louis XIV onwards. But in Britain real feudalism had ceased to exist some hundreds of years earlier, and the majority of country gentlemen, from whose families most of the British officers came, were not members of the nobility. Thus, despite much heart searching, grumbling and occasional recalcitrance, the British officers could accept three changes of titular head whilst their French counterparts could not accept one.

Disenchantment with the revolution, which was growing stronger day by day in Britain, was not echoed in Ireland. A disaffected peasantry persecuted and permanently disadvantaged on account of their religion, ruled by an often absent Anglo-Irish aristocracy and suppressed by what must have seemed like an Anglo-Scottish army of occupation, could scarcely escape the attention of the French Directory looking for allies who could be used in diversions against Britain. Encouraged by the sporadic violence and some small but spontaneous risings, put down with typical inefficiency and brutality by the Irish Militia, the French planned several small-scale landings. It was hoped in Paris that these would be supported by a large-scale rising of the peasantry. The first and only landing to be even partially successful took place on the coast of Mayo in August 1798. A thousand French soldiers fought some small engagements, defeating on one occasion a largely irregular British force of seventeen-hundred men. But Humbert's French force failed to attract any reliable support and in the end the eight hundred French survivors were forced to surrender. However, it was not detestation of Jacobin excesses or the French attempts on Ireland nor, least of all, the machinations of the French emigrés, which finally made the British people the implacable enemies of France but the rise to supreme power of Napoleon Bonaparte, the 'Bogeyman of Europe'.

Although the civil population in Britain was not violently agitated by events in Europe, there were isolated manifestations of unrest and there was certainly a great deal of apprehension amongst the upper classes about the spread of radical ideas. The Army was not entirely immune to Jacobinism and its low and irregular pay, appalling living conditions and generally depressed status could have provided fertile ground for subversion. The artillerymen at Woolwich and even the Guards were involved in mildly disaffected behaviour but the soldiers did not refuse to carry out their duties and the actions of a few trouble makers were quickly disavowed by most of their comrades. These murmurings were quickly suppressed by a mixture of judicious concessions and seeming firmness. At the same time, in 1797, there were two much more serious outbreaks of unrest in the Navy which unquestionably amounted to mutiny. The Channel Fleet, lying at Spithead, refused to put to sea when ordered to do so, thus endangering the blockade of the French squadron sheltering at Brest. The men demanded fair wages, sufficient food, better care for the sick and protection from embezzlement. The demands were not unreasonable and had aroused some sympathy. Moreover, during the whole of the incident, the men insisted that should the French fleet put to sea and leave Brest, they would return to their duty and sail in pursuit at once. After negotiations, all the demands of the sailors were conceded and the Channel Fleet sailed for Brest to reimpose the blockade only a month after the outbreak of unrest. The mutiny at the Nore, which followed that at Spithead, was a much more muddled affair. Agitators had been at work in the North Sea Fleet and there was much confusion over the aims and demands of the men. But by June 1797, the authorities, confident of the support of the civil population and of their ability to keep the military under control, took a much firmer line. As resistance to their demands hardened, the mutineers quarrelled amongst themselves and finally capitulated. Their leader Richard Parker was hanged from the yard-arm of the *Sandwich*. But the two risings did bring about a significant improvement in conditions in the Fleet. Fortescue also points out that in May, between the two naval mutinies, the government suddenly granted the substantial increases of pay to the Army which had been entreated for many years.[2]

If Napoleon was able to unite France and restore the spirit and organisation of the French Nation and its army, he could also, ironically, be said to have some responsibility for a new unity and determination in Britain. The clear threat to British commerce in the enforcement of Napoleon's Berlin Decrees of 1806 which sought to exclude all British goods and shipping from the Continent, rebounded on its perpetrator. Even the threat of a French invasion from Boulogne, until it was finally laid to rest at Trafalgar, did not stir such passions nor so readily loosen British purse strings as the so-called Continental System. But Napoleon soon found that since Trafalgar he had no instrument to enforce his system around the coasts of Europe. Under the protection of the Royal Navy, Gibraltar and the Portuguese ports were used by the 'system breakers', and ships from Europe and the New World made them entrepots in the profitable business of thwarting the embargo on British trade. The invasion and partition of Portugal by France and Spain closed some of the loopholes for a short time but the British replied by carrying off the Portuguese King into exile in Brazil and at the same time, for good measure, seizing the Portuguese fleet. But the crucial event which precipitated the Peninsular War was the French usurpation of the Spanish throne and the spontaneous rising of the Spanish people against the occupying French armies. Napoleon expected that his invasion of the Iberian Peninsula would quickly crush a weak native resistance and finally destroy the British position in the extreme West of Europe. But the revolt in Spain and Portugal, fanned by a fanatical Catholic church, already a bitter enemy of the revolutionary and atheistic ideas spread by the French Army, was more determined and more self-sacrificing than the French or the English could have imagined. Britain, at last seeing an opportunity to strike at France on the mainland of Europe, from a base supported by a friendly population and from a position where overwhelming British naval superiority could be used to maximum advantage, wholeheartedly embraced the Spanish cause. Munitions and money were quickly made available to the insurgent forces and, from 1809, a British expeditionary force was permanently in the Peninsula to fight the long and heroic series of battles which was to take the British Army from Lisbon to Toulouse over the next five years. Battles that were to bring such a glorious reputation to the regiments taking part in the war that its operations would set a standard and an example for the next hundred years and more.

The Peninsular War

The Peninsular War has always been regarded as one of, if not the most outstanding and sustained feats of arms of the British Army of all times. Waterloo, seen as the culmination of Wellington's genius, included on the allied side thirty British battalions of which sixteen had been with the Peninsular Army. But the Allied Army, apart from the British, was made up of Hanoverians, Netherlanders and troops from Brunswick and Nassau who together outnumbered the British by two to one. The Prussian Army under Field Marshall Prince von Blücher was defeated on the 16 June 1815 but not decisively, and so it was able to rejoin the battle and, by the evening of 18 June, it was able to clinch Wellington's victory at Waterloo. Furthermore a corps of Prussians under Gneisnau was still fresh enough to take up what he called 'a hunt by moonlight', pursuing the defeated French as far as Frasnes. The Prussians were thus able to achieve what the Peninsular Army had never been able to bring off satisfactorily, the complete annihilation of a defeated French Army. The Prussian Army was twice the size of the Allied Army under Wellington of whom as we have seen, the British numbered only a third. Waterloo, although Wellington's greatest triumph, was anything but an exclusively British victory whilst most of the battles in the Peninsula could certainly be called that. British regiments fought as well at Quatre Bras and Waterloo as they had in Spain, despite the loss of so many Peninsular veterans and their replacement by green recruits from the British depots. But Wellington's army in Spain was overwhelmingly British and at its peak included fifty-two battalions from British regiments as well as fifteen regiments of British cavalry. Such a collection of British regiments would not be seen again for almost a hundred years. In the interval, they would show again (but this time in India) that they were at their best when providing an example and an inspiration to native ancilliary troops. In the Peninsula, the Portuguese Army (after it was reorganised by Beresford), Spanish irregulars (especially in the attack) and the British-raised King's German Legion, fought bravely alongside the British regiments. Indeed the Legion, with good reason, considered itself to be part of the British Army and appeared in the British Army List; eight battalions of infantry and five cavalry regiments served under Wellington at Waterloo. In Spain, however, it was the British who consistently held the centre of the stage whilst their ancillaries and allies found honour and glory enough in the supporting role.

What made the Peninsular War unique for the British Army was a combination of circumstances which may never arise again. Outstanding leadership in the person of Wellington was only one of them. Wellington's genius was the more apparent since his previous military experience had been in India only, where, although his spirited leadership of the Hyderabad Contingent in the invasion of Mysore and his brilliant generalship at the battle of Assaye in 1803, already demonstrated remarkable talent, both enterprises were undertaken against native armies. Wellington's achievements are put more fully in context in Chapter 5 but the scale of his victories in the Peninsula was of an altogether higher order and demonstrated his superiority over some of Napoleon's finest and most experienced generals. It is true that Wellington made the Peninsular Army in at least one sense but he was not the only British General for whom the troops would fight and die. The senior British regiments had been in existence for over one hundred and fifty years and had seen many Generals, good and bad, come and go. Despite a retreat that was perilously close to disaster, Sir John Moore was able to rally and organise his exhausted soldiers so that they were able to beat convincingly their French pursuers in the battle outside the walls of Coruna. The British were then able to embark on the waiting fleet unmolested. Already it was noted that British soldiers, however tired and disorganised, could be rallied, and the stragglers and strays would come together as though from nowhere, when the chance of battle offered. Sir John Moore was surely also one of the main architects of the successful new Peninsular Army through his model training of the embryo Light Division at Shorncliffe Camp in the first years of the nineteenth century. It is possible that had it not been for his untimely death in the battle in front of Coruna he might have commanded the British Army throughout the war in Spain and appeared finally at Waterloo. Unlike Wellington, who was a strong Tory and was related to important members of the government, Moore was Whiggish in his political leanings and could have expected only limited support from Castlereagh at the War Office and even less from later administrations. But Moore does impress as a more sympathetic character than Wellington and although his gallant death at Coruna may have silenced some of his critics, most of the contemporary evidence shows that he was popular almost to the point of veneration with his staff and with his soldiers.

Another Peninsular General, with his detached force from Cadiz, fought a successful but very bloody little battle at Barossa in 1811 whilst the main British Army was behind the 'Lines of Torres Vedras'. Thomas Graham commanded the British element of the Cadiz garrison. With his 4,000 British troops reinforced by a British regiment which had been detached from Gibraltar to hold Tarifa across the Bay of Gibraltar, he joined a much larger Spanish force in a sortie by sea against the rear of the French Army beseiging Cadiz. Because of bad weather the attacking force was landed in the Bay of Gibraltar about seventy miles from Cadiz. Graham had unfortunately conceded the overall command of the expedition to the Spanish General Lapena, known scurrilously but significantly to his own troops as 'Donna Manuela'. The Spanish troops outnumbered the British by two to one, so Graham had little option but to make a gracious gesture. Lapena led his mixed force, mainly at night, by an incredibly confused and zigzag route across country in the general direction of Cadiz. He finally arrived, much to his relief, in the rear of the French blockading forces. But his 'sortie' was strung out along three or four miles of coastal track with his baggage in the rear. Graham and his British contingent constituted the reserve and were acting as the rearguard. Victor, who commanded the French forces investing Cadiz, seized the opportunity presented by the widely dispersed Allied force to attack the rear of the long column. Graham, realising that the Anglo-Spanish force was in danger of being driven into the sea, turned his retreating force about, recaptured a low hill overlooking the coast and drove off the French with heavy losses on both sides.

Graham became both a popular idol and a soldier's hero and remained one for the rest of his life. He was rewarded by a grateful British government for a success they badly needed, with the appointment of Second-in-Command to Wellington. Graham had at first been an object of some suspicion to the troops and to his fellow officers, having come late to the Army. He was forty-seven years old when he first received a commission and, despite having raised a regiment for the King's service, the 90th Regiment of Foot, in 1794 with a second battalion almost at once, he could still only obtain a temporary commission. It was not until after Moore's retreat and death at Coruna in 1809 that Graham, who had acted as senior aide-de-camp during the campaign, was granted a full commission back-dated so that he was immediately promoted to major general. He was accounted by all to be an outstandingly loyal and brave officer. His very well deserved victory at Barossa was the result of being in the forefront of the action everywhere on the day. This may not have been the prime requirement for a British general even in the Peninsula but it gained the obedience and respect of the soldiers and the immediate understanding and compliance of his officers, not always an easy task even for Wellington.

The battle of Barossa, even though on a smaller scale than many of the other great combats of the war in Spain, in its confused events, garbled anecdotes, fatigue, gallantry and pathos provides a vivid picture of the war across the whole Peninsula. The many accounts of this comparatively minor action confirm the difficulty for the historian of being accurate about the opposing commander's intentions, the actual movement of troops before and in battle, the topography of the area involved and even of the final casualty states. It seems likely that Barossa was one of the few Peninsular battlefields that Fortescue did not visit. His clear description of the battle is somewhat belied by a visit to the area. He says that the battlefield was much more heavily forested in 1811 than at the time of his writing in 1917, but when visited in 1986 the cover appeared to be even sparser. The Cerro de Puerco, allegedly the key to the battle, sprouted only scrub and a few small trees. It was difficult to see Barossa Hill, as it is now called, one hundred and sixty feet above the sea, in gently rolling heavily forested country, as it was then, as such a dominating feature. There is also some underplaying of the distance between Barossa Hill and the so called ridge at Bermeja where Lapena's advance guard under Lardizabal was first engaged with Villatte's division of Victor's army barring the way to Cadiz. Lack of Spanish support for Graham was an accusation made after the battle but under the circumstances, with the Spanish engaged in an encounter battle with an unknown number of the enemy and separated by three or four miles of forested and possibly marshy country, early support could have been difficult. Fortescue notes that the two Spanish battalions which had been attached to Graham's force and which marched 'eagerly to rejoin him as soon as they were permitted to do so', arrived just too late to take part in the action which involved 'an hour and a half of sharp work'.[3] It is perhaps not improper nor ungenerous to consider that Graham may have had another motive in turning back to counter-attack the French. Graham's biographer[4] also seems to make heavy weather of the topography and suggests that Villatte's division was posted 'High up on the ridge of Torre Bermeja'. But a casual walk through what is now the new holiday village of Barossa shows that the 'ridge' is merely an elevation of less than fifty feet which, clad in trees, would have provided no great assistance against an enemy who could have approached under close cover. Graham's ardent nature and his understandable desire to make up for the time lost at the start of his military career may have persuaded him to bring on the battle that Lapena was clearly and pusillanimously doing his best to avoid. But whatever his motive, there can be no doubt that Graham's men had every confidence in him and fought as solidly and bravely as in any of the Peninsular battles. Graham never again really lived up to the promise he had shown at Barossa, despite a respectable if pedestrian handling of Wellington's left wing at Vittoria. But it must have been extremely difficult for any British general to shine in the shadow of Wellington's genius.

Barossa seems to have been particularly prolific of anecdotes and Fortescue refers to many of them. Lieutenant Colonel Browne of the Twenty-Eighth, who commanded a composite battalion made up from the flank companies of three other battalions, was forced down off Barossa Hill, overlooking the coastal track, in the first French attack. Graham rallied the remnants of the retreating British battalion and, despite their heavy casualties, sent them back up the hill to take part in its eventual recapture. Browne's men had retreated very sensibly in open or skirmishing order and commenced the return up the hill in the same formation. Graham is alleged to have ordered Browne to get his men into a compact body for the attack since at this time of crisis it was necessary to show something more serious than skirmishing. Fortescue doubts if Graham gave any such command since another battalion, attacking on Browne's left, advanced in extended order and produced far greater effect with far smaller losses. But Graham's biographer, Anthony Brett-James,[5] says that Graham first ordered the battalion to attack in open order then, changing his mind, gave revised orders for the men to close up into a compact battalion. Brett-James goes on to say that Browne acquiesced with pleasure saying, 'It is more in my way than light bobbing'. One has to admit that this comment has a ring of authenticity about it and probably conformed well with Graham's own rather orthodox views. Brown's provisional battalion made up from flank companies would have contained three companies of soldiers trained in light infantry (light bobbing) tactics. Nevertheless, Browne seems to have managed his mixed battalion very well, regardless of its composition.

Fortescue plays this incident down but he cannot resist a sly dig at the Guards and the Eighty-seventh Foot who could not, despite a heavy and destructive fire from the French guns 'file out of the

wood . . . without wrangles over precedence'. Fortescue can be sentimental over animals but rarely over men and he devotes a footnote
to the story of General Rousseau's dog.[6]

> The last named was found desperately hurt with his white poodle beside him; when
> the bearers approached to carry the general off, the dog flew at them, so that it was
> necessary to smother him with a cloak before they could touch his master. Poor Rous-
> seau died at midnight and was presently buried, but the dog broke loose and tried to
> dig his way down to him. With some difficulty the British soldiers carried the dog to
> General Graham, to whom the poodle, after refusing food for some days, finally
> attached himself, eventually coming back with Graham to England.

Sentimentality was not the exclusive prerogative of British soldiers
nor of British Generals. When the author visited the battlefield of
Barossa in 1986, the owner of the villa 'Santa Monica' in the grounds
of which the Torre Bermeja still stands, presented the writer with a
print of a painting of the battle of 1811. The painting by L F Lejeune
(1775–1848), who was a general in his own right and an ADC to
Berthier, is executed in the most romantic fashion. The Tower of
Bermeja is in the background and the battle is set on a hill overlooking
Bermeja and Cadiz which is clearly seen in the distance. All this is
plainly impossible in fact. In the foreground is a *vivandière* giving
water to the wounded, very much in the front line. The only thing
which seems to be missing from this composite impression of Lardizabal's first clash with Villatte at Bermeja and Graham's battle at Barossa
is General Rousseau's little dog. The painting is one of eight depicting
great Napoleonic battles now preserved at the Versailles Museum.[7]

The Leaders and the Led

General Beresford, Marshal of the Portuguese Army, which he
trained and re-organised, fought one of the costliest and most grimly
determined battles of the war only a few months after Barossa, at
Albuhera. The British troops comprised only a quarter of the allied
troops present, half being Spanish and the other quarter Portuguese
whilst of the enemy, William Maxwell in his life of Wellington, echoing
Napier's francophilia says, 'All were French troops; and consequently
admirable soldiers'.[8] The British troops performed magnificently and
undoubtedly took the lion's share of the action. As was the case with
Graham, where troops were detached under subordinate generals or
in independent roles under their divisional or brigade commanders,
they performed no less well than under Wellington himself. Many of
the British generals were of a notoriously independent cast but like
Crauford, who was often rebuked by Wellington for insubordination,
they could almost invariably get the best out of their men. It was in

his strategic vision, broad grasp of issues and in his ability to combine successfully large bodies of men to achieve a planned purpose that Wellington's true genius resided. Undoubtedly his presence alone inspired enormous confidence and merely by arriving at the scene of action, he was able to restore a seemingly lost situation. This gift contributed to the resolution and steadfastness of the British regiments in the Peninsula and was a powerful and lasting legacy which the regiments carried with them to Waterloo, and beyond into the countless numbers of 'small wars' in which they would be engaged throughout the nineteenth century.

To achieve his full potential, the British soldier needed leaders of both types. His regimental officers and most of his generals were recognisably of the old school; brave country gentlemen, squires and their sons and, except in a few regiments, unacquainted to any degree with the court or with the sophisticated life of the capital. Andreski[9] has suggested that where wars are short and comparatively gentlemanly, with a reasonable chance of loot and glory, as they were in the eighteenth century, officer recruiting tends to be restricted to a narrow ruling élite but where the war is long, dirty and total, as it was beginning to be in the early nineteenth century, it is necessary to open recruiting to a much wider stratum. There is evidence that this was happening in the Army, with more soldiers being commissioned in the field to replace battle casualties and as a reward for outstanding bravery. But this tendency never worked its way through to affect the background of the more senior officers until the Second World War and even then only to a minor degree. It never happened to the highest ranks with one notable exception.[10] Wellington was a well educated and cultured man and a member of parliament who had held office under Tory administrations. His often remarked upon dourness of manner and taciturnity stemmed, apart from a refusal to suffer fools gladly, from a genuine diffidence and shyness which made easy-going relationships and close friendships equally difficult for him. Nevertheless, he was not known to his officers as 'the Beau' for nothing and his elegant and disdainful manner set him apart from his more mundane colleagues. An interesting comparison is made between Wellington and the other great British hero of the Napoleonic wars, Horatio Nelson, in Esme Wingfield-Stratford's *The Making of a Gentleman*.[11]

> Sense and sensibility—is it not as if we had uttered the names of the two great heroes of the time, Wellington and Nelson! . . . sensibility may have had as much to do with the brilliance of the Nile as sense with the tactical artistry of Waterloo. But it is difficult to imagine Nelson turning his hand to diplomacy, and combining the judgment of the statesman with the tact of the courtier, like Wellington and like Marlborough before him. For Wellington was as different as possible from the rough and laconic Iron Duke

of popular legend . . . a ready and fluent talker, with just that quality of emotional astringency that had been prized in the salons; it was thoroughly in that tradition for him to have . . . replied to Lord Uxbridge's laconic announcement, 'By God, my leg's shot off!' with an equally laconic 'By God, so it is!' We may be very certain what he would NOT have said, if he had got his quietus from that same ball—and that is, 'Kiss me, Uxbridge!'

There is some evidence that Wellington played out a role in front of his soldiers. Elizabeth Longford in *Wellington—The Years of the Sword*,[12] repeats Donkin's story of Wellington leaving Portugal for the last time in May 1813. As he crossed the frontier into Spain, Wellington turned his horse, waved his hat in the air and said 'Farewell Portugal, I shall never see you again'. Flimsy evidence, but Longford goes on to point out in a footnote that Wellington had been an enthusiastic amateur actor in India. But whatever Wellington's personal contribution to the making of the British infantry tradition may have been, and it must have been a great one, there were other influences to be considered. As we have seen, several other British generals were able to conjure outstanding performances from their troops in the Peninsula and some, like Sir John Moore, seem to have been better trainers and all may have been better loved than Wellington. But all the Peninsular generals, including Wellington on his own admission, accepted that they were unable to control their own troops from time to time. Moore's retreat to Coruna increasingly became a shambles. Wellington's retreat from Burgos and even some of his advances were marked by indiscipline and disorders which could only be put down in the most serious cases by summary executions. Perhaps more to the point, some of Wellington's victories were put at hazard by the lack of control, lack of discipline and wild over-reaction to what might be a purely local and temporary success on the immediate field of battle. At Talavera, the uncontrolled pursuit over the Portina Brook by Langwerth's Germans and a Guards Brigade turned a praiseworthy defeat of the first line of Sebastiani's and Lapisse's French attacking force into a crushing defeat by the intact French second line. This incident on the second day of the battle, which might easily have lost the whole of the battle for Wellington, was typical of the over-enthusiasm of the British troops, and especially of the cavalry (although not on this occasion) who, in the heat of battle, appeared to be quite impervious to the commands of the leaders on the spot. The failure to follow up a defeated and demoralised enemy which was so often the disappointing outcome of one of Wellington's brilliant defensive victories, was in many cases due to the dispersal and confusion of the successful British. Much of this battlefield disorder could not be blamed directly on the troops, who were often joined in their runaway battlefield looting expeditions by their immediate regimental officers who should have been rallying their men in anticipation of a counter attack or the arrival of orders to pursue the defeated enemy. The French were no less avid looters but their officers seem to have had better battlefield control and their ability to rally and retire in good order often robbed the British of a significant victory.

But the point to be made is that British soldiers were not automatons in the manner of Frederick the Great's soldiers nor even in the modified style of Dundas. Their tendency to lose all reason and discipline in a wild wassail could be overcome. Above all, they needed to be well led at the company and battalion level and then they could bring something of their own to the battle. It was necessary for leaders and led to have confidence in each other. The first two battles in the Peninsular War, Vimiero and Rolica opposed a British to a Napoleonic army for the first time and it was a test upon which everything in the future depended. Maxwell, despite his hyperbole and purple prose, was present in the Peninsula and at Waterloo and in his *Life of Wellington* emphasises the importance of those early battles.

> There is no reminiscence of the Peninsula which the soldier recalls with more pride, than the small but brilliant action of Rolica . . . The moral effect of the combat of Rolica was of immense importance. It was the dawning of a glorious day; and its results were admirably calculated to confirm the wavering faith of doubtful allies, and remove the conviction of the French regarding their military superiority. It was a noble compliment paid by Napoleon to British infantry, when he observed, that they never knew when they were beaten; . . . while Rolica betrayed the fine properties of British soldiers to their enemies, it was not its least advantage, that it also confirmed the confidence of their leader in the troops on whom he depended for success.[13]

The mutual confidence gained in those early Peninsular battles stayed with the British regiments throughout the Spanish war. To return to Beresford's battle of Albuhera, fought almost three years after Wellington's first victories in Portugal, it was clearly a victory won by the regiments and the soldiers in them; a bloody and appalling victory won almost despite the commander. Beresford, whilst he had done well in reforming the Portuguese Army, was not a confident or decisive commander. Wellington was convinced that Beresford had mishandled his army at Albuhera and said so in no uncertain language. But the tactics employed by the French generals were also blameworthy and, in the end, the outcome of the battle rested upon the valour of the British infantry. Fortescue asks,

> Whence came the spirit which made that handful of English battalions—for not a single Scots or Irish regiment was present—content to die where they stood rather than give way one inch? Beyond all question it came from intense regimental pride and regimental feeling . . . Until recently the British Army was said, not untruly, to be no army at all but a 'congeries' of regiments; and there can be no doubt that our military organisation was imperfect and incoherent, until the virtual autonomy of every regiment a relic of the proprietary system, was finally broken down. But there

have been occasions when this very exaggeration of regimental independence has wrought miracles; and Albuhera is one of them. The regimental officers can hardly have failed to perceive that Beresford was making a very ill hand of the battle, but that was no affair of theirs. The great point to each of them was that his battalion was about to be tried, and that in the presence of other battalions, by an ordeal that would test its discipline and efficiency to the utmost. Sergeants and really old soldiers, of which latter there was always at least a sprinkling, took precisely the same view. Staff-officers might speak of general actions if they would; but, except to such inferior mortals, a battle was purely a regimental matter and must be treated as such. And hence it was when one man in every two, or even two in every three, had fallen in Hoghton's brigade, the survivors were still in line by their colours, closing in towards the tattered silk which represented the ark of their covenant, the one thing supremely important to them in the world. Regimental rivalry strengthened this sentiment; and therefore, when the French finally turned to flight, the Fifty-seventh, though but two hundred out of six hundred were still unhurt, dashed forward with the rest of their brigade in pursuit until recalled by the Commander-in-Chief. It was this regimental spirit which saved Beresford; and to do him justice, he acknowledged it to the full, for there was not in all the army a braver or more generous officer than he. Though eloquent neither with tongue nor with pen he wrote in his despatch a sentence which should never be forgotten. 'It is impossible by any description to do justice to the distinguished gallantry of the troops; but every individual nobly did his duty; and it is observed that our dead, particular of the Fifty-seventh regiment, were lying, as they had fought, in ranks, and every wound was in the front.'[14]

So much for 'The Die Hards' at Albuhera. The roll of honour of the British regiments at Albuhera is given by Fortescue: The Buffs, (East Kent); 7th (The Royal Fusiliers); 23rd (Royal Welsh); 28th (North Gloucester); 29th (Worcestershire); 31st (Huntingdon); 34th (Cumberland); 39th (Dorset); 48th (Northampton); 57th (West Middlesex) and 66th (Berkshire). He gives them in their order of regimental seniority, based on their date of being raised. Thus there are five regiments raised in the seventeenth century headed by 'The Buffs' who fought at Blenheim. The 28th (North Gloucesters), also a seventeenth-century regiment, fought equally well under Moore at Coruna, Graham at Barossa, Beresford at Albuhera and Wellington in five further battles in Spain, at Toulouse and finally against Napoleon at Waterloo. Three regiments raised in 1702 include the 39th (Dorsets) who had the honour of being the only 'King's' regiment to have fought under Clive at Plassey in 1757 and who took as their motto 'Primus in Indis'. The remaining three regiments were formed in the mid eighteenth century and include, of course, the 57th, The Die Hards, whose first battle honour was Albuhera and who were authorised to wear the 'Albuhera Badge' in 1816 in remembrance of the way in which they earned the honour. Of these last three regiments, only the 48th (Northampton) had gained battle honours before the war in the Peninsula. But there can be no doubt, as Fortescue says, the regiments with honours and experience stretching back over one hundred and fifty years, and in some cases like the 23rd (Royal Welsh Fusiliers) with men still serving who could just possibly have been amongst those immortal six regiments at Minden, would put the new regiments on their metal. Thus the youngest of the regiments 'died hard' and provided an example for their German, Spanish and Portuguese allies, and a challenge to their comrades in the, perhaps ostentatiously, senior regiments.

Even though Waterloo was different, in that the British formed a minority of the allies, it may have been the last occasion on which this peculiar form of mutal confidence between the men and their Commander-in-Chief and the rivalry of honour between the regiments operated in quite this way.

So much has been said about the battles of the Waterloo campaign that John Keegan's detailed analysis[15] must leave almost nothing further to say. But it is perhaps worth noting that even with the most recent writers, military history, apart from written orders, official despatches, ration and casualty states and war diaries, depends upon the memories and autobiographies of the participants and the views expressed are overwhelmingly those of officers. Where these accounts are not written or recollected by officers, they tend to be edited or 'translated' in a literary way and inevitably interpreted through a slightly alien eye. Keegan, who I believe comes closest to an authentic view of combat at Waterloo in the section of his book titled 'Infantry versus Infantry', relies almost entirely on officer memoirists with glosses added by academics. Whilst this may be the best we can do, it can only refine a partial view of events. Keegan and the modern school of writers who attempt a socio/psychological view of battle have so far been able to identify, with many reservations, the actual sequence of events which occur in battle and the re-active process which brings them about. As to the pro-active process, it is still almost impossible to make more than an inspired guess as to the 'why' of individual actions. Even for the later wars, despite all the official papers, recordings, films and on-the-spot television reportage, individual motivation is still an imperfectly understood area. It may be that Keegan's method of first setting up the constant or factual information in categories such as the historical situation, the physical circumstances and the viewpoint of the participant in the battle and only then applying the subjective reports may be sound. Certainly it will give a more immediately impressive and convincing picture of a particular battle. But in the end we are left with concepts of honour, for the officers, for the men, for the commanders and perhaps most importantly but also most mysteriously for the regiment. Without these concepts and without these shared beliefs, there could have been no battles and no victories. Keegan, echoing Fortescue, sums it up for Waterloo:

Napoleon had sent forward each of his formations in turn. They had been well led;

many of the British speak with admiration of the French officer's bravery. But they had not been able to carry their men with them the final step. Each formation had swung about and gone back down the hill. When at last there were no more formations to come forward, the British still stood on the line Wellington had marked out for them, planted fast by the hold officers had over themselves and so over their men. Honour, in a very peculiar sense, had triumphed.[17]

The Post-Napoleonic Reaction

So strong were the emotions engendered in the Peninsula and at Waterloo amongst the British Army, that the army that was sent to the Crimea forty years later was in all essentials the same institution. Fortescue may be correct when he says that the battle of Albuhera demonstrated the full flowering of the regimental spirit as against an identification with the army as a whole. But this feeling must have been even stronger after 1815 when Wellington was forced to hide the army away in 'penny packets around the world' in order to avoid what he saw as a disastrous reduction in strength. As late as 1840, the twenty-fifth anniversary of Waterloo and an occasion of great celebration, four fifths of the infantry from an army totalling 121,000 men were serving overseas. The brunt of overseas service fell upon the infantry but it was reported that with garrisons in Ireland and the main ports and bases, only between five and ten thousand men were available for deployment in an emergency. In fact, except from time to time in India, there was no British Army to which the soldier could feel a real attachment, or focus for his loyalty outside his regiment.[18] After Waterloo the Army in the United Kingdom demonstrated all those tendencies which we have already associated with conservative institutions under threat. Change of any kind was anathema to the large majority of officers and they were strongly supported in this attitude by Wellington. As a leading Tory politician, and Prime Minister from 1828 to 1830, he had been forced to accept Catholic emancipation and, as a leading member of the House of Lords, to allow the Great Reform Bill of 1832 to become law. In both cases he acted against the immediate interests of his party because his common sense allowed him to see that there was no other way of avoiding unrest and possible civil war. Unfortunately, whilst enjoying his support, few army officers had his breadth of vision or his ability to accept necessary compromise. Not only was change resisted in the Army but there was what amounted to a conscious withdrawal from many aspects of social and political life. The military found itself increasingly out of step with a society which was falling more and more under the influence of the Benthamite utilitarians. The industrialising and reforming tendencies which were growing equally and strongly with the advance of the Victorian era were seen as a threat not only to a privileged and obsolescent way of life but also to the discipline, cohesion and very existence of the Army itself. The Army in Britain retreated into its shell. On the part of some officers, especially in the more fashionable regiments, there was a manifestation of this retreat from reality in the practice of peculiar rituals and eccentricities of dress in military dandyism in an attempt to keep a rising lower class at a distance. The alternative was the colonies, and especially India where expenses were likely to be less and the amenities of a civilised life more easily obtained. India had become not only the military base for the bulk of the British Army but the main repository of the lessons and traditions of the Wellingtonian armies. Despite the large number of 'small wars' in which Britain was involved in the nineteenth century, they were mostly fought with native or 'company troops' supported by, at most, a battalion or two of 'King's troops'. The basis of soldiering abroad was still the regiment.

Whenever a sufficiently large army was got together to make it necessary, and this was usually only in time of war, an army might be divided into separate 'divisions', each under its own subordinate general but all still under the direction of a Commander-in-Chief. Although the divisions could have a tactical function even before the twentieth century, the breaking up of the army into groups was occasioned more by the necessity to use as many different lines of march as possible, and for some armies by the necessity to be spread over a wide area in order to forage and to 'live off the land'. In most respects, the division was and still is a small army in itself and has been recently defined as a grouped body of all arms that can be entirely self sustaining. Although, when a division has been in being for a number of years, an interest in its history is often rekindled, usually in the formation headquarters, the division is rarely a focus for loyalty in the sense that regiments and smaller military groups can be.

In the past, this ossification and, in some ways, direct abandonment of any attempt at higher control, left the regiments and their Colonels in a strong position. This meant that whilst the regiments were not lacking at their own level, the Crimean War and the Indian Mutiny broke upon British forces who found themselves almost completely unprepared for operations at any higher level. The nature of the Mutiny allowed individual commanders on the spot to make decisions and, when the commanders were competent, small composite forces were cobbled together as reinforcements became available. Eventually, the position was restored but only after a very large loss of life. In the Crimea, lack of an adequate staff and inexperience in handling the larger formations required had already led to misery and suffering on an unprecedented scale, even for the British Army. Both conflicts could in the end be counted as victories, but especially in the case of the Crimea, the campaign was fought out for the first time under the merciless gaze of the newspapers. For the first time the public was able to indulge in what it believed was an informed view of both catastrophes. Public opinion was at last a force to be reckoned with by an army at war. Outside those continuing 'small wars', the short-comings revealed in the Crimea and in the Mutiny provided a task in trying to understand and rectify them which occupied the higher direction of the British Army until after the end of the nineteenth century.[19]

4

The British Army Between Waterloo and the Crimea

1840 was the Silver Jubilee year of the Battle of Waterloo. It was 25 years since that decisive battle and more than 30 years since the beginning of the Peninsular campaign but the stirring events of those youthful days remained for the Army an inspiration, an excuse and for some a mental strait-jacket for more than another decade. *The Times* of 12 August 1840 reported that on that day there were still serving in the Army, 1 Field Marshal, 57 Generals, 204 Colonels and Lieutenant Colonels and 210 other officers who had fought at Waterloo. However, it was clear that the reputation and influence of the Field Marshal completely overshadowed the remaining veterans, and if the Army of the 1840's was still the Army of the Peninsula it was Wellington who was determined to keep it in its original image.

In almost every respect the Army at the beginning of the 1840's resembled its illustrious predecessor of the Napoleonic wars. The soldier's equipment and dress were almost unchanged except in some élite regiments. He still carried between 60 and 70 pounds on his back and his weapon was still usually the famous 'Brown Bess' musket which, after over 100 years' service, was only gradually replaced during the decade. The soldier's uniform was still based upon French designs, but 25 years after Waterloo many of the sensible refinements and rationalisations of dress developed and adopted under the hot Spanish sun in the Peninsula were forgotten. An inevitable tendency to return to what were regarded as the higher standards of a previous era meant that the 'Age of Folly' at the end of the eighteenth century, still set the pattern in military dress and equipment until the lesson was relearned in the Crimean War.[1]

Maria Ossowska has pointed out[2] that there was a noticeable change of fashion in Europe about 1835 and it is likely that the fashion was followed in Britain, but there is no evidence that the more sober dress influenced the uniform of the Army. In some regiments at least, commanding officers became more and more obsessed with military finery during the period. In this they were encouraged by the Prince Consort, who was not immune to the well-documented and wide-spread interest of European Princes in the design of lavish and impractical uniforms for their troops. If the finery could be traced to the French, some of the more barbaric survivals went even further back to Frederick the Great's father, Frederick William the 'Prussian Drill Sergeant'. The leather stock, worn round the neck under the tunic, forcing the soldier to keep his head up and thus to impress the enemy with his bearing and spirit, survived for a few more years.[3] But such was the ingrained habit of the veteran soldiers that even in India and Canada, where it was permissible to remove the stock on the march and in action, only the young recruits regularly did so.[4] The dress and equipment of the soldier had not benefited from the lessons of the American or Napoleonic wars. The introduction of the rifle and the use of lightly armed and equipped soldiers as skirmishers, the 'Light Bobs' of the Peninsula had pointed the way to new develop-ments. But Waterloo, where Wellington was probably misunderstood when he said 'They came on in the old way and we beat them in the old way', retarded until after the ponderous battles and painfully classical siege operations of the Crimea, the natural developments in tactics, equipment and military management foreshadowed so many years before. If the outward appearance of the Army had not changed much since the turn of the century, the men themselves had changed little either. The most sought after soldiers were still the agricultural labourers joining the Army as the only alternative to life in the new industrial towns. A report from a 'Mr. Marshal' in *The Times* of 25 March 1840 says, 'recruits from agricultural districts are more reliable than those from the manufacturing classes. Those from the agricul-tural areas join as a result of "family jar" whilst operatives as a conse-quence of idle and dissolute habits'. In the large towns most enlistments were made under the influence of drink, and the report goes on to say that, in some districts, between a quarter and a third of the rueful recruits 'pay smart money and all the other contingent expenses rather than complete the engagement they have entered into'. Inevitably, a proportion of the recruits were criminals since the Army did not ask too many questions and provided a cheap means of removal from the scene of the crime. Their presence would not have disconcerted Wellington nor many of his Peninsular officers, whose unshakeable belief in the efficacy of the lash was reinforced by the very presence of those brutalised men who were amongst the only ones able to survive for any length of time in such an environment.

The use of the lash continued for a further 25 years before the vicious circle could be broken.

Not all officers or indeed regiments were convinced of the value of the country yokel as a recruit. Field Marshal Lord Wolseley, writing much later but referring to his first years in the Army in the 1840's, said, 'slum recruits were numerous in Light Infantry and Rifle Regiments. They preferred recruiting in London to all other places. The sharpened wits of the city slum dwellers were necessary for the work of the Light Infantry. Country yokels were longer of limb but too stupid'.[5] He goes on to say, 'Discipline is essential in military training but the youth from Whitechapel understands and realises its necessity in the ranks far more easily and naturally than the stupid hedger and ditcher from rural districts'.

But it was not only the Light and Rifle regiments that recruited in the cities. The Royal Fusiliers (City of London Regiment) the old 7th Foot, whose honours go back to Namur in 1695 and who are second in seniority in Fortescue's roll of honour of the regiments at Albuhera, 'were raised in London . . . always recruited exclusively in that city and were truly a "London Regiment" throughout their separate existence.'[6] However, according to figures given by Dr Henry Marshall, Deputy Inspector of Military Hospitals and the same 'Mr. Marshall' of *The Times* report quoted above, the proportions by national origins of non-commissioned officers and men in the Army of 1840 were, English, 34 per 10,000 of population; Scotch, 51 per 10,000 and Irish 51 per 10,000. The predominantly agricultural areas must still at that time have provided a disproportionately high number of recruits.[7] Although there could be argument about the ideal temperament for a recruit there could be less argument about his physical condition. Health, or rather bad health, provided adequate grounds for the rejection of many volunteers in the first half of the nineteenth century. The Director General of Statistics published figures in 1844 showing that over one third of recruits coming forward were rejected on grounds of mental or medical deficiency; 6,026 recruits out of 17,540 examined were rejected in that year.[8]

The Military and a New Commercialism

Officers, were still traditionally from the landed classes and still predominantly from the rural areas. Officer recruitment was as yet comparatively unaffected by the rapid and visible rise of the business classes or by the civilising influence of the Public Schools, which were just appearing on the scene.[9] Indeed, it seems likely that the Army suffered particularly from what Esme Wingfield-Stratford describes as 'the decline in culture' in Britain after 1815.[10] He says that the

English landed gentry after 1815 became, in reality, merely nurseries of hereditary sportsmen, shunning classical learning and their great libraries, no longer indulging in the 'Grand Tour'. Even the High Regency was . . . 'Only a brilliant finale rather like the firework display that ends some stately ceremonial. After the bursting of the rockets and the coloured stars, and the massed bands thundering out the National Anthem, it was night, with only a shimmer of romantic moonlight fitfully penetrating the clouds'. There is evidence that the long period of peace in Europe from 1815 to 1854 produced an interesting paradox that goes some way to support Andreski's[11] thesis that in prolonged periods of peace the prospect of military service becomes more attractive to the nobility and upper classes. Whilst the rest of British society was beginning to exhibit rather less concern over social exclusiveness and businessmen and business interests were everywhere coming to the fore with the 'self-made man' beginning to emerge as the quasi-hero which he later became in the image of Isambard Kingdom Brunel and his fellow captains of industry, an opposite trend appeared in the officer corps of the Army and Royal Navy. In the period between 1816 and 1838 the proportion of commissions obtained without purchase in the Guards, Infantry and cavalry decreased from exactly one half to less than one quarter.[12] Razzell, similarly finds that there was a five-fold increase in the number of landed gentry entering the Army between 1780 and 1830. Taken with what Razzel categorises as aristocracy, in which there appears to have been some decline in representation, the overall effect was that the 'upper classes' increased their representation during the period from 40 per cent to 50 per cent of all officers. It would be interesting to know if this increase was spread uniformly over the fifty years in question or appeared more obviously after 1815.

Most of the middle class officer recruits were, in fact, the result of internal recruiting, Service families providing a steady flow of recruits right through the nineteenth century. Much of this internal recruiting would have been from the sons of the many soldiers who earned battlefield commissions during the Napoleonic Wars but by the middle of the century this type of commission would have been very rare indeed. The role of internal recruiting and its connection with the upward mobility of soldiers, officers and their families will be discussed later but it is clearly still a very prevalent and potent force in modern British military society.[14]

M A Lewis,[15] has produced two studies for the Royal Navy for the period between 1815 and 1849 which support the view that the officer corps during the long peace up to the Crimean War became more aristocratic in its origins and at the same time more reliant on internal recruiting. As with the Army, up to 1815 a modest but important group of naval officers commissioned from the lower deck, amounted to 6.7 per cent of all the officers commissioned between 1793 and 1815. After the Napoleonic Wars this group disappears completely and even commissioning from the business and commercial classes falls from 3.9 per cent over the war period to 0.4 per cent in the post war period. There is no army study for this period comparable to Lewis's work but his findings do support the suggestion that the Army was following a course at odds with the general social pattern. The officer class as a whole appears during this period to have become distinctly more exclusive, more withdrawn from society in general and much more inward looking. This exclusiveness was maintained in several ways. To obtain a commission it was first necessary to be nominated either by the Commander-in-Chief, or for entry to the Artillery or Engineers through the Royal Military Academy at Woolwich, from the Master General of the Ordnance. Most commissions, apart from those in the Artillery and Engineers, had to be purchased and this, taken with nomination, ensured in the Duke of Wellington's often quoted words that officers would be 'men who have some connection with the interests and fortune of the country'. An additional guarantee was built into the pay structure where the comparatively low emoluments ensured that few could serve without private means, treating their pay as a kind of honorarium, a useful but not essential adjunct to their private income, usually from family estates. Wellington's influence in this, as in all else to do with the Army before the Crimean War, is well known. He was able to convince many of his countrymen that the first stirrings of the spirit of reform, manifest for the country as a whole in 1832 and then gathering strength through the century, were not appropriate to nor desired in the armed forces. Perhaps of more importance, he was able to epitomise the feelings of resentment, suspicion and obscurantism which were largely typical of the officers of his last years. In return, the officers and many of the men, veterans and recruits alike regarded him with a veneration which would have been unthinkable twenty-five years before. The strength of this feeling is shown by the eulogies appearing everywhere in newspapers and journals. Typical of them all is an anniversary article printed in the May 1840 number of *The United Services Journal*. It concludes that Wellington 'serving a country jealous in an extreme degree of military rule, unwilling to bear any rule without constant murmuring and opposition is unfortunate in that he lived under monarchs who have turned aside, by various causes, from assigning to him the place for which he is pre-eminently qualified—a man to whom we owe it that we have a rightful monarch at all, and ourselves that we are not hewers of wood and drawers of water to an insolent and cruel oppressor'. The article, in a service journal, sums up the differences in attitude and outlook towards reform and democracy that were so apparent in the 1840s. The differences between the officers of the forces and the new business and commercial élite at its worst resulted in open hostility, at its best caused indifference and withdrawal from society. It took the disasters of the Crimean War to bring to prominence a new breed of young intelligent officers, dedicated to their profession but at the same time more attuned to the new society of the second half of the century.

The decade immediately before the Crimean War is seen by some as the beginning of that long period of peace and stability, the Victorian age which outlived Victoria and was ended only by the rumblings of the approaching First World War. For the military, however, the whole of the nineteenth century and indeed most of the present century has seen a succession of wars and disturbances no less bloody and no less painful for their being ignored or misreported, and only very occasionally glorified, at home in Britain. Thus, during the hundred years between Waterloo and the outbreak of the First World War, the British Army was involved in more than 100 small wars.[16] In the 1840's alone, British troops were in action in Afghanistan, Scinde, South Africa, China, New Zealand, Aden, Syria, Beyrout, Saint Jean d'Arc, Tahiti and Mauritius. The forces involved often amounted to only a battalion plus a few locally raised ancillaries but even when a larger force was involved, as it sometimes was in India and elsewhere, one or two British battalions would find themselves brigaded with 'Company' or other local troops or a 'Settler's Militia'.

At home, however, in addition to the real, albeit small, conflicts going on overseas, the 1840's saw a renewal of suspicion and fear of French intentions. Through the whole decade there was an agitation on the part of military writers and commentators for an increase in the Home Army and for increased fortification of the main ports.[17] Many of these reports and scares were directly inspired or encouraged by the military authorities, who were concerned not only about French intentions but pressed also for a larger army so as to be able to cope with the unrest and subversion which was so much feared during the 'hungry forties'. Sir John Burgoyne, Inspector of Fortifications in 1846, submitted a paper to the Master General of the Ordnance warning of Britain's new vulnerability resulting from the French decision to concentrate on a steel-hulled, steam-propelled navy. Palmerston, the Foreign Secretary, was sufficiently impressed to have the paper circulated to the Cabinet. Wellington himself wrote to Burgoyne approving of his paper and criticising the Government's inadequate defence measures.[18] Arising from this a number of new defensive works were constructed around the ports and dockyards. Whether out of anger at the expense or derision at the idea of a French invasion, the new forts were known locally as 'Palmerston's Follies'.

The French Revolution of 1848 and the advent of Louis Napoleon who was to become Emperor of the French, Napoleon III, raised the fear of invasion to panic proportions in some quarters. But events at home were themselves causing serious concern by now and when these had finally run their course, fears of a new French invasion, whether by Jacobins or Bonapartists, was seen in a less hysterical perspective and dismissed as the scare-mongering which it largely was. The agitation and troubles in England and Ireland which culminated in the Great Chartist Demonstration of 1848 had proceeded unabated through the whole of the 1840s. Bread riots inevitably followed the series of bad harvests which were typical of the period, and troops were used increasingly during the decade, usually to disperse mobs who were trying to prevent grain from being loaded onto ships for export. Troops were used in five different places in 1847 and were stood-to but not used during riots at Exeter, Wadebridge, Collompton and Saint Austell. Apart from food riots, the Army had been employed against Chartists at Newport in 1843 and on several other occasions up to 1848 when, although they did not have to be used in London, they were required to fire on rioting mobs in Glasgow and elsewhere. Wellington, at the age of seventy-nine, was called out of retirement to command the troops in London during the great Chartist procession and presentation of the charter. But in 1848 he saw no real danger in the Chartist agitation in England.[19] However, he took a different view of the situation in Ireland, where mobs were more likely to be armed. Throughout the decade and especially during the potato famine, agitation for the repeal of the Corn Laws and often of the Act of Union itself, led to repeated clashes between the troops and the Irish peasantry. Troops serving in Ireland were by no means safe from subversion and regulations and directions were continually passing between the 'Horse Guards' and the Commander-in-Chief in Ireland as a result of reports in the newspapers of soldiers in Ireland cheering for repeal, joining 'ribbon societies' and generally engaging in disloyal conduct.[20] The normal attitude of the troops appears to have been one of interested neutrality but there is no doubt that they regarded the putting down of mobs as legitimate employment.[21] An article in *The United Services Journal* of May 1840 gives a description of troops marching through Cirencester and Gloucester to Monmouthshire during the troubles of that year. The writer, an officer of course, describes the attitude of the troops as contemptuous of both Chartists and Special Constables. His report of the subsequent trial of Frost and the other leaders of the Newport Chartists, whilst showing his conservative sentiments, is not bigoted and gives a fair

and balanced account of the men on trial. As with the earlier disturbances in Ireland and those immediately after the Napoleonic Wars,
the Army was shielded to a certain extent from public condemnation
by the use of the Militia and Yeomanry to put down unrest. The
regular troops were usually held in reserve, as they were by Wellington in London during the presentation of the Charter in 1848.

The possible military dangers, or in modern terms the perceived
threat, at the end of the first half of the nineteenth century appeared
on three levels. First, there was the ever present possibility of being
called upon to support the civil power, often in England and continuously in Ireland. This duty was accepted by the troops as a normal
although unpleasant occupation, but by most of their officers as an
essential task in the preservation of a social order of which they stood
near the apex.[22] Secondly, with the bulk of the Army overseas, it was
impossible for the ordinary soldier not to be involved in the continuous succession of colonial wars which characterised the Victorian
epoch. Officers could, and often did, transfer out of regiments sent
overseas but for the soldier, and the officer living on his pay alone,
there was no escape.[23] For the hardy, abstemious and ambitious few,
India could be the making of them but for the majority, death from
disease, drink or wounds was inevitable.[24] The 3rd Light Dragoons
went to India in 1837 with 420 rank and file, when the regiment
returned to England in 1853 only 47 of its original men remained.
Some, at least, would have been discharged but the vast majority, as
Sergeant Pearmain makes clear, had died of drink or disease or were
killed in the ten wars which took place on the Indian sub-continent
during those sixteen years.

That the numerous colonial wars and expeditions were accepted as
a natural part of the soldier's lot did not mean that they were accepted
with equal indifference by the civil population of the United Kingdom. Even less were they indicative of an adventurist and expansionist
military policy. If an overall military or army policy existed, and this
is extremely doubtful, it was essentially a defensive one. Military
leaders and theorists, up to the Crimean War, and probably well
beyond it, were concerned almost entirely with the threat from the
Continent, and this meant from France. Caricaturists and lampoonists
made much of the traditional fear of the French, still a recognisable
legacy of the wars against the first Napoleon. Since most of the British
generals in the Crimea had learned their business under Wellington it
is not surprising that the British Commander-in-Chief in the Crimea,
Lord Raglan, who had lost an arm at Waterloo, in moments of aberration called the enemy 'the French' instead of 'the Russians'.[25] The
hundreds of small British military detachments scattered round the
globe were seen as drastically weakening the forces available for home

defence. Whilst the main threat was still seen as coming from France, the troubles in Afghanistan and India could perhaps be seen as the beginning of what Brian Bond describes in a later context as 'this protracted confrontation between Britain and Russia'.[26] Thirdly then, the threat of invasion presented itself to the military as real and imminent. Ironically, it was only because the Army could be hidden away overseas, and because the Army in India was paid for largely from Indian taxation, that it was tolerated at all by large sections of the British population. The European threat was not accepted by the new industrial and commercial classes and the Army itself, in its turn, was contemptuous and ignorant of those new forces which were providing it with a genuine role which was to become increasingly important as the century wore on.

If the military environment of the Army at mid-century caused the soldier some confusion, at least the problems which presented themselves were not new. 'Muddling through' was a traditional method which could still be applied, especially since Wellington was no longer young enough to keep a firm hand on all aspects of military policy. But the social environment was an area of which the Army was still remarkably ignorant and one from which it consciously chose to distance itself. Raymond Aron in his study of August Comte,[27] says that Comte, writing in the early nineteenth century, predicted lasting peace since war no longer had a function in industrial society. In 'War and Industrial Society' Aron continues the study of Comte's ideas.[28] Industrialisation and war were incompatible for Comte because he saw history as a unilinear movement from one type of society to another. He believed that in the early part of the century, a predominantly military type of society in Europe was being transformed into an industrial society in which war could play no part and must therefore decline. Many of the English reformers and especially the disciples of Jeremy Bentham, whilst not accepting the whole of Comte's philosophy, would have agreed whole-heartedly on the obsolescence of the military.

The Military Attitude to Reform

The electoral reform of 1832, the end of slavery in all British possessions in 1833 and the Poor Law and Municipal reforms of 1834 and 1835 may, in part, have been the work of humanitarians of various political hues, but overwhelmingly they were a practical expression of a belief in rationality, the power of industrial organisation and the need for individual responsibility. What David Thompson describes as the corrosive force of Bentham's utilitarian philosophy, inevitably found itself opposed to the military.[29] A military organisation, which was at best based upon an aristocratic paternalism, was to many observers the last stronghold of privilege and the instrument of oppression and obscurantism.

By the late 1840's the direct line of action advocated by the Chartists and other, even more radical, groups had failed to attract the mass support required to make any impression upon an entrenched ruling class loyally supported by an Army effectively quarantined from the newly emerging feelings of class consciousness. Increasingly, however, the reformers had moved into the field of administrative legislation. Frustrated by the unsatisfactory outcome of the 1832 Reform Bill, the utilitarians switched their attack to the areas of public health, the Poor Laws and judicial reform. In this last matter they came up against a code of military discipline based upon an exceedingly harsh, and barbarically public system of corporal punishment. *The Times* of 6 February 1840 reported: 'On Tuesday another of those disgusting exhibitions, the infliction of the lash, took place at Hounslow Barracks, on the person of a private of the 14th Light Dragoons.' The report goes on to say that the soldier, who had served for less than six months, had absconded with his own and a comrade's kit and was sentenced to 150 lashes. The punishment is described in considerable detail and in terms calculated to present the Army in a most unfavourable light. The flogging of Private White of the 7th Queen's Own Hussars on 15 June 1846, and his subsequent death brought about an enforced post-mortem and a great public outcry. Even so, only after constant agitation for a further forty years was abolition of the lash finally achieved.[30]

Paradoxically, Wellington was himself responsible for another situation in which the Army found itself dragging its heels. As Prime Minister in 1828, Wellington was faced with the election to Parliament of O'Connell, who was debarred from taking his seat as a Catholic. Giving way to the inevitable, Wellington persuaded George IV to accept Catholic Emancipation in 1829. But it was not until 1841 that Macaulay, then Secretary for War, in answering a question in the House of Commons,

> agreed to the principle that, whatever opinions they might hold with regard to religious establishments, there could be no doubt that if we would beat up for recruits in Catholic countries, and place men, strongly attached to the church in which they had been brought up, to fight our battles in the midst of pagans and barbarians and get wounded and killed in our service, it was our duty as far as we would to provide them with the comforts of their religion.[31]

By 1841, the Army enjoyed formally the same religious liberty as the civil population. Nevertheless, in November 1843, Military Headquarters in Ireland told commanding officers that Catholic soldiers 'must be removed from church immediately after mass and not allowed to stay on to hear exhortations etc'.[32]

Throughout the 1840's, the military found themselves more and more under pressure. Often the pressure was instinctive and incoherent rather than specific in direction. But the military reaction was equally mindless on many issues. The decade saw the end of the absolute dominance of the landed interests with which the majority of army officers identified themselves. The growth of industry and commerce had by now begun to make itself strongly felt, not least in Parliament where even those members directly related to the landed classes were more and more dabbling in business.[33] Army officers saw themselves exposed to an alien and materialistic philosophy which denied to the military a legitimate role in society and attacked as anachronistic all that the officer stood for. On the other hand, the very imperatives of the new society seemed to invite situations at home and abroad where a strong and efficient presence was essential. Wellington, General Burgoyne and many other naval and military leaders believed that not only had Britain's early industrialisation made her a rich and tempting prey to aggressive Continental nations but that the arrival of iron hulls and steam propulsion made an invasion across the Channel a much less hazardous operation.[34] What the rank and file thought of all this, if they thought of it at all, it is hard to say but it is likely that they followed the line of their officers and whatever they thought it did not seem to affect their steadiness or their loyalty in the Crimea.

The attitude of the industrial and commerical bourgeoisie, so despised by the frustrated and alarmed military, is summed up by a passage from a book called *The Defenceless State of Britain* by Sir Frances Head, published in London in 1850:

> I will, during every day of my life, enjoy cheap cotton, cheap silk, cheap linen, and cheap woollen clothes. I will warm myself in the evening at a cheap fire; I will sleep at night between cheap sheets and between cheap blankets; I will travel at 40 miles an hour at a cheap rate; I will read a cheap newspaper; say my prayers out of a cheap bible—all cheapened by steam: But if I am called upon to contribute to repair the only little injury to the defences of my country which at any hour may deprive me and my family of our property, our lives and our honour, I deliberately reply, 'I know nothing about your new inventions. I have inherited a good old English hatred to a standing army; the thing I tell you, is unconstitutional and besides this I can't and won't afford it'.

The Withdrawal into Ritual

The early 1850's saw the flowering of a society in which it seemed the Army could have no part. The success of the Anti-Corn Law

Movement and the introduction of free trade supported by the business interests was regarded by most army officers as another blow to their landed connections. It also attacked their traditional way of life and, they would say, was another threat to the self-sufficiency of the country in war time. That the Leaguers and Free Traders attracted to themselves radical support from a wide spectrum of anti-military groups merely confirmed the soldiers in their belief that all reform was inherently subversive. Hume, and Cobden who had said that the Duke of Wellington was in his dotage for advocating a larger army, were the heirs of Locke and Bentham whilst the army officer was *par excellence* the disciple of Hobbes. Huntington, who describes man as seen from the point of view of the military ethic as 'the man of Hobbes, weak, cowardly, needing to be organised and strengthened, civil and irrational',[35] goes on to say that 'the military ethic is pessimistic, collectivistic, historically inclined, power orientated, nationalistic, militaristic, pacifist and instrumental in its view of the military profession. It is in brief, realistic and conservative'.

The pessimism of the Army contrasted sharply with that peculiar brand of Victorian optimism and confidence which manifested itself so clearly in the Great Exhibition of 1851. The Exhibition signalled a new era of international trade and co-operation, an era in which the Army, and certainly many army officers, feared that they would find themselves isolated and redundant in an alien world. The reaction of the army officer was to withdraw even further from a world with which he had little sympathy and of which he had little understanding. At the same time, as we have seen, he attempted to erect or reinforce barriers which would maintain his own fast disappearing world.

We have said that for the greater part of the nineteenth century the normal route to a commission for the majority of officers, and especially those who set the 'tone' of the Army, was through purchase after nomination by the Commander-in-Chief. But in addition, promotion up to the rank of Lieutenant Colonel had to be purchased at each step.[36] Purchase by itself might not have produced a narrowly exclusive officer corps at a time when the upper classes were being increasingly infiltrated by *nouveau riche* Victorian businessmen. However, the effect of nomination was to restrict for several more decades the main source of officer recruits to the old aristocracy and landed gentry. This, in its turn, meant that most officers still based their beliefs and code of conduct upon those of the English country gentleman. In an age of reform, industrialisation and urbanisation, the remaining vestiges of feudalism, chivalry and a seemingly permanent social order, still visible in the countryside, assumed an added, if nostalgic, attraction. It was precisely these ideals and values, often in an exaggerated form, that the younger sons of the aristocracy took with them into the Army. But if the way of life was that of the country landowner, with its emphasis upon horse racing, hunting and other country pursuits and sports, usually of a cheerfully philistine nature, the underlying code was still that of service and honour based upon that of the medieval knight. The hunting field and race track may have been more congenial to them than the library but that they preserved a fierce and unbending code of personal behaviour, at least outwardly, is seen in their stubborn adherence to the duel as a means of settling affairs of honour.

Although the Articles of War for 1844 expressed Her Majesty's displeasure at duelling and set out several specific measures to prevent the practice in the Army, it was not eradicated until after the Crimean War. Like so many other features of the pre-Crimean Army, it could not really be ended until the 'Old Duke' died, especially since the Great Man had himself 'called out' the Earl of Winchelsea in 1829 to the general approval of the Army and much of the nation. As late as 1848, *The United Services Journal* published 'A Requiem Upon Duelling' in which it was stated that some method of settling disputes of honour would have to be found before duelling could be completely got rid of. Towards the end of the article, the point is made more precisely:

> 'Society very justly expects from all who move in a certain rank, and occupy certain stations a strictness of principle and an amenity of manners in the general intercourse of the transactions of life which no present law can enforce, under the extreme penalty of loss of caste. . . . The laws of honour comprise the whole of the universal "LEX NON SCRIPTA" comprehended under the significant designation of "good breeding" which materially mark the minor as well as the major virtues of thorough-bred gentlemen, who fear death less than dishonour.'[37]

That the duel was common in England is born out by regular references in the Annual Register.[38] Many of the military duels became *causes célèbres*. The public were quite prepared to be titillated and pleasantly horrified by the spectacle provided but were quick to seize upon the caste aspects of duelling and to condemn the illegality and barbarism of an exclusively aristocratic practice. If Lord Cardigan's duel with the unfortunate Captain Harvey Tuckett and his subsequent acquittal by the House of Lords is the best example of class solidarity during the period, there were other 'affairs' which did not turn out so well for either of the participants. In 1843 Lieutenant Colonel D L Fawcett and his brother-in-law Lieutenant A T Munroe fought a duel as a consequence of which Fawcett died of his wounds. Munroe was sent to prison but public outrage was not assuaged and, as we have seen, in 1844 the Articles of War were amended so as to express Her Majesty's displeasure. But even this was not considered sufficient and, significantly, it proved necessary to invoke the name of the Duke of Wellington. A statement made by the Duke in the Peninsula in 1810, emphasising that there was no degradation or dishonour in explanation and apology, was found in the files and circulated with the revised Articles. Wellington had nevertheless refused to intervene against Cardigan since he believed that this would lead to increased civilian interference in army affairs and to a general undermining of discipline. Even so, it was his Peninsular letter which was eventually instrumental in stopping the practice in the Army.

It was not impossible for the sons of the *nouveau riche* to obtain commissions but before the Crimean War it was a comparatively rare phenomenon. Whilst some writers, de Tocqueville for example, insisted that the British aristocracy was already in 1833 distinguished from its European counterpart by the ease with which it opened its ranks to riches,[39] others emphasise the struggle of the old aristocracy to preserve its peculiar style of life. Maria Ossowska[40] says, 'The decline of chivalry was accompanied by a very elaborate etiquette, a practice typical of a declining social class who, by observing complicated rituals tries to keep a rising lower class at a distance'. Stearns[41] says that the struggle in England led directly to 'dandyism' and the growing interest, in certain exclusive regiments of the Army, in eccentric uniforms, mess life, manners and culture. When Cardigan was carrying on his great public relations campaign with the London public, he had fifty men working on new uniforms for his regiment as well as the regimental tailors. *The Times* reported: 'The brevity of their jackets, the irrationality of their head gear, the incredible tightness of their cherry-coloured pants altogether defy description'. Cardigan paid for most of this display himself and he was estimated to spend £10,000 a year of his own money on the regiment.[42] The famous 'black bottle' incident was perhaps typical of the eccentricities designed to embarrass and exclude the supposedly less well bred officers.[43] That this eccentricity in dress and manner was in fact a pathological reaction and not merely a survival is supported, perhaps inadvertently, by Hobsbawm who says, speaking of the 1840s, 'The fundamental style of aristocratic life and art remained rooted in the eighteenth century, although considerably vulgarised by an infusion of sometimes enobled *nouveaux riches*; . . . A comparison of eighteenth century and post Napoleonic uniforms—the form of art which most directly expressed the instincts of the officers and gentlemen responsible for their design—will make this clear.[44] In fact the influence of the *nouveaux riches* in the design of military uniforms is by no means clear. It is quite likely that the genuinely aristocratic members of the dandyfied regiments were as capable of errors of taste as any enobled member of the *nouveaux riches*. Certainly the Prince Consort took a personal interest in military finery and had inspected and approved the new uniforms of his own 11th Hussars. But dandyism was confined in the Army almost entirely to the élite regiments and particularly to the cavalry, where the *nouveaux riches* were slow to penetrate even in the second generation.[45]

Within the Army, the reaction against change expressed itself not only in extravagant dress in some regiments but also in a desperate attempt to retain all the customs, harsh and sometimes mindless discipline and most provocative of all, the punishments of the past. The punishments especially were maintained in the face of public outrage and the growth of a rational reforming movement within the Army itself. One of the clearest ways in which this feeling of Tory, thick-skinned indifference to changing public sentiment showed itself was in the way in which many officers regarded the enlisted men. Most officers saw themselves as part of a natural hierarchy; their own position in that hierarchy, next below the Sovereign, assured by the natural order and their soldiers at the base of the pyramid of prestige and authority, because they were by nature base. For some officers, the military order extended right through society and the officer's epaulette was assumed to give authority in dealings with the many new officials and functionaries springing up in the age of reform. Happily, the situation never reached the stage of a society dominated by militarism as it was increasingly in Prussia and later in Wilhelmine Germany. An amusing encounter is related in *The Times* for 25 December 1840, between one Colonel Molyneux of the 8th Hussars and a village policeman who, on being rebuked by the Colonel for not saluting him, 'thereupon saluted him with a very vulgar expression'.

In Garrison Before the Crimean War

The self-fulfilling view of the soldier as a kind of sub-human, whilst it did not originate with Wellington was reinforced and supported in every public debate by pronouncements from him. The introduction of limited service in 1846 gave rise to one of these petulant interventions. The intention of the Limited Service Bill was to attract a better class of recruit and to make possible the discharge of some of the old soldiers who had survived so long in the service only because of the brutishness of character which allowed them to alleviate the frequent application of the lash with regular bouts of drunkenness.[46] Wellington objected on two grounds. In a letter to Russell, the Prime Minister, dated 18 December 1846, he said characteristically, 'There can be no doubt that every soldier in the British Army would be happy to have his discharge, excepting probably those serving in the Life Guards. He would desire from it an advantage if only by receiving a bounty and enlisting again'. He was, of course, referring to fraudulent enlistment which was certainly widespread but by no means as sought after as Wellington appeared to suppose. But not only did Wellington believe that there would be a mass exodus if discharge was free to all after ten years' service but he also felt that the backbone of the Army was made up of these hardened, brutalised old soldiers who somehow or other had survived countless campaigns under a harsh and repressive discipline. One would like to think that affection and respect informed his opinion of the value of the veteran soldier but there is absolutely no evidence for this. There can be no doubt that life in pre-Crimean Britain for the soldier offered an extremely coarse and brutish existence. Poor food and living conditions were perhaps not the main feature distinguishing the life of the soldier in garrison from that of the labouring poor. But the harsh discipline, brutal punishments and lack of almost any alleviation from the bleak routine except through intoxication was what made a previous civilian life idyllic in retrospect to so many recruits. Flogging was an issue which raised intense feeling, not only among the civilian reformers but within the Army also. The struggle for abolition was gathering strength by mid-century but to many senior officers, perhaps confusing cause with effect, there seemed to be no other way of enforcing discipline and preserving order amongst the unregenerate men who made up the lower ranks of the Army. The 1836 Articles of War limited General Courts Martial to the infliction of 200 lashes, District Courts to 150 and Regimental Courts to 100. But these restrictions had been accepted most unwillingly and to the accompaniment of dire warnings about the imminent collapse of discipline and a growing necessity to impose death sentences for violence to superiors in the absence of other effective sanctions.[47]

Branding had been introduced as an alternative to flogging for the punishment of desertion in 1840. In reality, branding was not as barbaric as it sounds being by then a form of tattoo rather than a burn mark. As late as 1864, William Gladstone, as Chancellor of the Exchequer and concerned about what must have been a very small financial loss, was able to justify branding by claiming that 'marking a man with a letter was not a cruel exhibition'. Its main purpose in 1864 was to prevent a discharged soldier or a convicted deserter from receiving a bounty through a second enlistment. The introduction of military prisons in 1844 provided a further alternative to the lash and over the following years imprisonment was increasingly combined with and substituted for flogging. Although the death penalty was commonly pronounced at Courts Martial, invariably in cases of murder and often for violence to an officer and sometimes for desertion, it was usually commuted by the Queen to transportation for life.

Transportation was for a minimum of seven years and roughly half the sentenced soldiers were condemned for this period, the other half being sentenced to fourteen years or for life. Whilst the punishments meted out to the soldiers reflected a view of them as something rather less than human, the records of officers' Courts Martial for the period, of which only the overseas ones are available, throw an interesting light on what was considered acceptable in the conduct of a gentleman. Assistant Surgeon G R Smith, accused at a Court Martial of 'Conduct unbecoming the character of an officer and a gentleman' in that he encouraged and entertained women of bad character within the precincts of the hospital of which he was in charge, was 'found guilty with the exception of the same being conduct unbecoming a gentleman'. Smith lost two years seniority and was Severely Reprimanded. On the other hand, Cashiering was the invariable punishment for officers who could not meet their debts. In almost every other case, an officer could hope that a sympathetic Court of brother officers would find for him. This frequently happened despite the obvious displeasure of commanding officers and The Horse Guards.[48] Fighting in or promoting a duel, even after the notice published with The Mutiny Act of 1844, was likely to result, overseas at least, in a Reprimand or Dismissal but never Cashiering.

Drunkeness was by far the most prevalent 'crime' in the pre-Crimean army and, as we have seen, the vicious circle of drink and harsh repression could not be broken until alternative punishments, better living conditions and a higher standard of recruit could be found. If drink was a traditional failing of the British soldier, desertion was common everywhere. *The United Services Journal* of 1842 calculated that the Army of the United States of America, only 12,500 strong at that time, lost one third of its strength annually from desertion. In the British Army the annual loss from desertion in 1843 was calculated to be about 3,000 from a strength of 43,000 in the United Kingdom only. Overseas the problem rarely arose, except in Canada, where it was easy for deserters to escape over the border into the United States where free land was an attraction, although an illusory one, to recruits who had been predominantly farm labourers.

Although there were many examples of bad treatment and mismanagement brought to light by the press, the military in the United Kingdom, even before the Crimean War, was held very substantially in check by the civil power. The Civil Courts and the Coroner's Courts were able to bring pressure to bear on the authorities even when the punishments inflicted were in accordance with military law and custom. Frederick John White whom we referred to earlier, died in July 1846 after receiving 150 lashes. The Coroner's Jury agreed that the punishment was legal but expressed their disgust in no uncertain terms and there was a great public outcry. The Army had tried to prevent an inquest, but after the facts were made known, the Commander-in-Chief had to announce some scaling down of corporal punishment to meet the popular sense of outrage. Similarly, in Ireland, as a result of action in the Civil Courts, the Commander-in-Chief had to send a circular to all the Military Districts regulating and limiting drills and parades.[49]

Whilst civil control and a critical press provided some safeguard for the soldier at home, it was overseas that the full weight of an archaic military system was felt, only intermittently relieved by the humanitarian efforts of those few officers who, like Wolseley, had begun to see the need for reform. Wolseley was particularly scathing about the invariable ration of salt beef or pork, biscuit and rum. This, he said, led to drunkenness and incapacity, and combined with inadequate clothing, often to sunstroke and death. That drunkenness and death were the usual lot of the soldier overseas is attested by the military memoir writers of the period.[50] Even at Home the mortality rate for the Army was well above the civilian figure. In 1828 it was calculated that the average annual mortality rate for males aged 20 to 40 years in England was about 10.7 per 1,000; whilst for the Army at Home it was about 15 per 1,000 and overseas 57 per 1,000. Overall, it was concluded that mortality in the Army in peacetime was a little higher than three times the civil rate.[51]

After poor food, harsh discipline, encouragement to over indulge in alcohol and the ever present possibility of death in one unpleasant form or another, the final brutalising influence was the impossibility, for the majority of soldiers, of marriage. Most sergeants were able to marry but only 7 per cent of the rank and file were officially permitted to marry and thus have accommodation and transport provided for their families. Even though provision for the official families was primitive in the extreme, usually a curtained off corner of a crowded barrack room, a further 7 per cent contrived to marry unofficially. The lot of these unofficial families is described repeatedly in Victorian literature in the most horrifying terms. The most important thing for the wives, official and unofficial alike, was to remain married so as to retain some protection for themselves and their children. The haste and frequency with which they remarried, especially in India, is almost unbelievable until one realises the fate of the unprotected.[52] Given all the evidence concerning the lowly status, the appalling conditions and the seeming indifference of most of the officers, it is not surprising that the Forces, and particularly the Army, were seriously under recruited throughout the nineteenth-century. Wolseley says that in 1837 the Army was 9,619 privates below establishment[53] Colonel Maurice Firebrace writing in the *The United Services Journal* in September 1845 complains about poor recruiting and the high desertion rate. He says:

> '. . . the official returns show every seventh man, woman and child in Great Britain and Ireland are either absolute paupers or partly subsisting on charity but we still find it difficult to keep our miserable peace establishment full . . . during the period of the Afghanistan disaster we were forced to give a bounty of twenty shillings to our own soldiers to volunteer their services to India'.

There can be no doubt that in the period before the Crimean War the ordinary soldiers were regarded by most of their officers as of a different species from themselves. The perceptible movement towards more humane and enlightened notions was regarded as at best weak and misinformed and at worst lunatic or subversive. When General Sir William Napier, writer of the most famous of all Peninsular War Histories, was approached by The Army Reform Association, he summed up the reaction of most senior officers by saying:

> If the persons composing the Society are military, their proceeding is an act of grave insubordination; if they are civilians, they are incompetent persons, perniciously meddling with what they do not understand.[54]

The soldiers themselves exhibited a stoical indifference for the most part both to their treatment by their officers and to the agitation for reform going on around them. Their discipline was not, for the most part affected, and drunk or sober they answered to the call of the drum and were prepared to march against the enemy, internal or external as they were commanded. The frustration felt by the reformers as well as the hard core of revolutionaries is well brought out in a letter from George Eliot to her publisher, J Sibree, in 1848, the 'Year of Revolutions'. She says, 'Our military have no notion of fraternising. They have the same sort of inveteracy as dogs have for the ill-dressed canaille. They are as mere a brute force as a battering ram, and the aristocracy have got firm hold on them'.[55]

Wellington would not have been displeased with that judgement. He died in 1852 having dominated the British Army for half a century and the country as whole for at least some of that time. The Crimean War, after his death, was fought in his shadow, and if he was responsible for the state of the Army that was sent to fight in it, there was very little wrong with the spirit or the courage of the ordinary soldiers. The regiments also, despite in some cases coming from the 'flesh pots' of London, where showy uniforms appeared to be more important than good training, acquitted themselves with honour. The Light Brigade was not the only formation to enter into the pages of history at Balaclava. The Heavy Brigade, led by Sir James Yorke Scarlett in an uphill charge against a much larger force of Russian cavalry which was bearing down on them, routed them completely and would have achieved immortal fame but for the romanticised disaster of The Light Brigade. The 'Thin Red Line' of the 93rd (Highland) Regiment of Foot, later The Argyll and Sutherland Highlanders, might have been fighting a battle straight from the Peninsula or the field of Waterloo. In a detached position, guarding an approach to the Allied landing place at Balaclava, Sir Colin Campbell ordered his men to lie down in a line two deep on a reverse slope under heavy bombardment. A very large force of Russian cavalry advanced without being aware of the Highlanders' position. As the Russians breasted the slope, the British infantry stood up in their thin extended line. Sir Colin rode down the line and shouted, 'Men remember there is no retreat from here. You must die where you stand.' The Highlanders expected to die but they faced the enemy with stern determination and their steadiness turned the engagement. The Russians would not close with them and withdrew in the face of the devastating volleys of the 93rd. Such was the spirit of the infantry that some of them wanted to charge forward and engage the Russian cavalry hand to hand. Sir Colin in another echo of the Peninsula restrained his men, calling out, 'Ninety-Third! Ninety-Third! Damn all that eagerness'. The same regiment, and no doubt with many of the same men, gained six Victoria Crosses at the Relief of Lucknow only three years later. The stand of the Thin Red Line at Balaclava is perhaps the best known of the exploits of British infantry in the Crimea but all three of the great Crimean battles, fought by the British and their French allies, the Alma, Balaclava and Inkerman, were soldiers' battles. The infantry soldiers and the cavalryman won them. Their steadiness and their grim tenacity and their determination not to let their regiments down made them unbeatable as they had been at Albuhera, despite generalship which would have made Wellington weep.

The conditions under which the Army existed between Waterloo and the Crimea were still very much the conditions of the eighteenth century but they had not sapped the fighting spirit of the soldiers, whose performance, especially under officers in whom they had confidence like James Yorke Scarlett or Colin Campbell, was quite outstanding. The regimental system was working well, in the regiments. However, at a higher level, disparagement of the staff and staff work and a tendency to despise professional competence as something not within the province of the gentleman led to the administrative débâcle which was so easily exposed by the press in the Crimea. A second great disaster followed, almost immediately, in India. We must now see how the regiments stood up to events in the great sub-continent.

5

The Regiments in India

Service in India was to play a very large part in the lives of the regiments of the British Army and their soldiers, particularly throughout the nineteenth century and the first forty years or so of the twentieth.

The story of Britain's rise to power and the end of the French threat to India begins with Robert Clive's victory at Plassey over the French-backed army of Suraj-ud-Daulah, the Nabob of Bengal, on 23 June 1757. It was then to be exactly one hundred years before British power was again under threat, in the Great Indian Mutiny of 1857.

Robert Clive, a former clerk in the service of the East India Company, who had contrived to transfer to the Company's army in the brevet rank of Captain in 1751, had met with his first resounding success in the same year in the capture of Arcot. Then followed a series of brilliant victories, achieved through his energetic and determined leadership, culminating in the recapture of Calcutta and the siezure of Chandarnagar in the Spring of 1757 and the triumph of Plassey in June.

Philip Mason, to whose classic account of the Indian Army I shall refer often in this chapter, deems Plassey to have been hardly a battle at all in purely military terms. However, the scale of Clive's success and the consequences of Suraj-ud-Daulah's defeat were such that it is hailed by many as one of the decisive battles of the world. Furthermore, it was remarkable for the courage shown in the decision to fight.

The European element in Clive's force at Plassey numbered only 950 infantry and 150 gunners. Of that total 200 were '*topasses*' (Christian Indians) and as many again were French prisoners who had changed sides after Chandarnagar. He had over 2,000 Sepoys but these included a Bengal battalion only three months old. His Madras veterans were still organised only in companies.[1]

Clive's small force was completely surrounded by an estimated 50,000 foot and 18,000 horse and his eight six-pounder guns and two mortars faced fifty-three pieces of artillery, all of them of heavier calibre than his own. All the senior officers except Eyre Coote, but including Clive, taking part in a Council of War before the battle were in favour of withdrawal. After more consideration Clive changed his mind and gave the order to advance across the river to his front in order to attack the enemy. This was the decisive issue since if he was defeated and pursued by the enormous mass of enemy cavalry, it would be impossible to escape back across the river without heavy loss. But the battle was won, largely through muddle and lack of leadership on the Indian side and because of the intrigue of Meer Jaffier against his Overlord, the Nabob Suraj-ud-Daulah. Clive had already agreed to support Meer Jaffier in his claim to the Nabob's position and possessions in return for his assistance in the battle. Meer Jaffier however, determined to end up on the winning side, came late in the battle and only to confirm his neutrality. The victory gave to the British, through the East India Company, the absolute possession of Bengal, Behar and Orissa, whilst Meer Jaffier was installed as a puppet ruler only.

The French had not been involved formally in the battle but Clive's success marked the end of their ambitions in India. More important however it opened the eyes of the East India Company and the British Government to the almost limitless possibilities of expansion into the Indian sub-continent.[2]

Although Plassey marks the beginning of British ascendancy in India, by 1757 the British had already been in India for over 150 years and were almost halfway to the time in 1947 when they would finally hand over power. Elizabeth Tudor, always ready to encourage schemes which might increase her revenue, granted a Charter to a London Association of Merchant Adventurers in the year 1600 and thus brought into being the East India Company. By then the Dutch and Portuguese were already busily at work trading from their factories on the Indian mainland and the islands of the East Indies. In the end, neither the Dutch nor the Portuguese proved to be great rivals to British supremacy but a French East India Company was formed in 1609. French military and commercial power built up slowly over the following century but, by the end of the seventeenth century, the British position was being overhauled and their trading supremacy threatened. It seemed too that the French had unfair advantages in the competition. Fortescue, in another of his splendidly vituperative passages explains what these advantages were:

> All Frenchmen had and still have a passion for interference with the internal politics of any barbarous or semi-civilised races with which they may be brought into contact, and will spare no pains to gratify it. The emissaries of the most insolent nation in Europe approached the Indian Princes with flattery of their self-esteem, deference for their authority, respect for their prejudices, conformity with their customs and imitation of their habits; while the French love of dramatic action and of display

brought them at once into touch with the oriental character. They gave sympathy, sometimes in reality, always in appearance; and they obtained in return not only toleration but friendship and influence. Mere trading was sufficient for the English; it was not so for the French. Their ambition rose above the mere bartering of goods to the governing of men and the swaying of them by subtle policy to the glory of France.[3]

The 'Company' and the Conquest of India

The British East India Company soon learned that trade followed the flag and that what used to be exclusively European wars would increasingly be fought out around the globe. The pattern was set as early as 1612 when a British fleet under Captain Best attacked a superior Portuguese fleet in the Bay of Surat, North of Bombay, and defeated it so completely that the reigning Mogul King broke the Portuguese monopoly of trade with his dominions and granted important concessions to the English, consenting at the same time to receive an ambassador from them at his court. In March 1644, the Company sent out 30 English recruits to Fort St. George its Madras headquarters. These were the first soldiers, native or European to be enlisted directly into its service. Eventually they became the Madras European Regiment.

With the Restoration of Charles II came a new Charter for the Company, allowing it to send ships and men to defend its factories and, more important, allowing it to make peace or war with any people who were not Christians. In 1661, Bombay as well as Tangier came to the British Crown as part of Catherine of Braganza's dowry. We have seen that Tangier proved to be a short-lived British possession but Bombay had an altogether more lasting and profitable history under the British flag, becoming the headquarters of the East India Company in 1683. In 1668 the Crown had made over the whole of its interests in Bombay to the Company for a rent of ten pounds a year. At the same time, the King's troops in India were allowed to transfer to the Company Army. By 1683 Bombay was heavily fortified, mounting over one hundred guns on its walls and having a garrison of 600 European soldiers with two ancillary companies of Rajputs. From then on the Company's Army took the place of the Royal troops in India, completely at times but always as the largest contingent of British troops in any combined army. Indeed, from about the 1680's until 1754, the Company was left literally to fight its own battles without help from the British Army which had been withdrawn from India. After almost a century of indecisive campaigning against the French in India, the British Government decided to act in support of the Company. Three British warships carried out recruits to reinforce the East India Company's Army and a small party of the Royal Artillery plus, most important of all, His Majesty's 39th Regiment of Foot. This arrival in 1754 allowed the regiment, later the Dorest Regiment, to earn its motto, '*Primus in Indis*' (First in India). Three years later, in 1757, the regiment won the battle honour 'Plassey', as the only King's regiment to fight in that decisive battle. The 39th was one of the five regiments to defend Gibraltar successfully during the Great Siege of 1779–83 and, as we have seen, was one of the British regiments at Albuhera in 1811.

There were no more Royal regiments in India again between 1765 and 1780 but in 1787 four regiments of foot were raised, two in England and two in Scotland, especially for service with the Company in India. The new regiments were numbered 74 to 77. The 74th (Highland) Regiment of Foot was known later as The Assaye Regiment because of its outstanding performance there in 1803 under Wellesley. It was also awarded an Honorary Colour by the East India Company to commemorate the fact that all the officers of the regiment were killed or wounded at that battle. Three colours are still carried on parade by the successors of the 74th, now The Royal Highland Fusiliers. The Regiment, as indeed did all four of the regiments created for service in India, succumbed to the amalgamations of 1881, joining the 71st Foot to become The Highland Light Infantry and then in 1959 joining The Royal Scots Fusiliers to become The Royal Highland Fusiliers.

The second of the new regiments to be raised in Scotland in 1787 was the 75th (Stirlingshire) Regiment of Foot, amalgamated in 1881 with the 92nd Foot to become The Gordon Highlanders. The 76th Regiment of Foot was also known as The Hindoostan Regiment until 1812, being the only British infantry regiment engaged in Lord Lake's campaign in Central India, 1803–5. In 1881 it was amalgamated with the 33rd (Duke of Wellington's Regiment) to form The Duke of Wellington's (West Riding Regiment). The 77th Regiment of Foot, later the 77th (East Middlesex Regiment) amalgamated in 1818 with the 57th (West Middlesex Regiment) to form The Duke of Cambridge's Own (Middlesex Regiment). Despite being raised for service with the Company in India, three of the four regiments found themselves in the Peninsular War. The 76th was in time to take part in Sir John Moore's retreat to Coruna and to fight in the battle there. After being evacuated to England they soon returned to fight under Wellington. We shall return to the amalgamations of 1881, noting meanwhile that however disruptive they were, there was nothing new about disbandments and renumbering, they had gone on almost from the first establishment of the Army. These four gallant regiments with their honours and special awards were to lose their original identity and be absorbed by equally gallant regiments with whom they enjoyed equal status on the field of battle. However, where the prestige of their patrons, the capture of public attention through the newspapers and the intervention of political considerations were involved, they could only come second in the race to survive. This situation could only become worse in the present century and, as we shall see, has now reached the stage where the very existence of regiments as such can be called into question.[4]

To return to the situation in India. Eventually it came to be accepted that there would always be a mix of King's troops, the Company's European soldiers and the Company's native troops. By the last quarter of the eighteenth century, all the Company's European troops were British, usually transferred or discharged British soldiers. It was no longer necessary to employ French deserters or the 'topasses' who contributed to Clive's victory at Plassey. Each of the three Company 'Presidencies', Bombay, Madras and Bengal maintained its own army. Whilst the 'ideal' of the native Indian army was based on the philosophical and religious work the 'Arthashtra' and favoured a mass of elephants surrounded by a horde of cavalry, the British, drawing on their European experience were firmly attached to the concept of rock-like bodies of infantry. In both cultures, the cavalry enjoyed the most prestige but horses were expensive to obtain and maintain and cost was of paramount importance to the Company. At first it was usual to look to the native rulers with whom the Company was in alliance to provide the cavalry as their contribution to a mixed force. Mason suggests that the mainly middle class merchants, traders and business men of the Presidencies, were reluctant to introduce the essentially aristocratic figure of the cavalry officer into their tight little circle.[5] Whatever their reasons, expense was almost certainly the overriding one. However, commanders in the field continually stressed the unreliability of the cavalry supplied under treaty and eventually the Presidencies reluctantly gave way and regular cavalry units were formed piecemeal.

By 1799 the army which was assembled to invade Mysore and depose Typpoo Sultan was made up of two King's cavalry regiments, four native cavalry regiments from the Madras Presidency, three King's infantry regiments, eight battalions of Madras native infantry, three battalions of Bengal native infantry, two companies of Bengal and two battalions of Madras artillery and finally one thousand Madras pioneers. In addition Sir Arthur Wellesley later the Duke of Wellington, commanded a separate force, the Hyderabad Contingent, made up of six native battalions and some cavalry and a French battalion, all provided by the Nizam of Hyderabad. Wellesley was also given His Majesty's 33rd, his old regiment, later to become The Duke of Wellington's Regiment, as the backbone of his force. The main invasion force approaching Mysore from the East was made up from the Company's armies in the Madras and Bengal Presidencies. The Bombay Presidency contributed yet another force made up of His Majesty's 75th and 77th regiments and the 103rd Bombay Europeans, (Company troops) plus six Bombay native infantry battalions. This army invaded Mysore from the west.

The two-pronged attack was successful and Typpoo Sultan was killed at the battle of Seringapatam, after which Mysore became a 'protected' state, losing its independence. This left the Marathas States to the North of Hyderabad as the main threat to the Presidencies. In the two years after Seringapatam, Wellesley fought and beat the Marathas at Assaye and Argaum and General Lake struck them successively at Deeg, Aligarh and Laswarree but the final crushing of the Marathas power had to be postponed. In 1804, the British, in face of the imminent breakdown of the Peace of Amiens and determined to forestall action by Napoleon, renewed hostilities against the French. The King's regiments in India and elsewhere were urgently needed. They were first used in ill-managed and unsuccessful expeditions in Northern Europe and then in more successful but highly expensive campaigns in the West Indies. Finally, like the 76th, they took part in the campaigns in the Peninsula, first under Sir John Moore and then, triumphantly under Wellington.

The East India Company's policy had always been to avoid armed encounters as far as possible since these were bad for trade. But as the Company collected rights and property and jurisdiction, the need for some kind of force, if only for self-defence, became apparent. However the real pressure to build up the armies of the three Presidencies came from the war with the French. From 1688 until 1815 there was intermittent war between Europeans on the Indian subcontinent. The French were the first to drill, train and equip the Indian armies and they were the first to demonstrate the importance of the initial, unhesitating attack, a doctrine used so brilliantly by Clive and Wellesley and one taken up whole-heartedly by British commanders in India and elsewhere against barbarian and semi-civilised foes. The Company's armies proved to be well-organised and highly successful in the Mysore campaign of 1799 and so the pattern remained more or less the same, including the division into three separate armies until after the Mutiny of 1857. The three armies were not combined into a unified Indian Army until 1895. In the early nineteenth century, the Presidency armies were each made up of three or four brigades and each brigade would include one battalion of European infantry, one regiment of native cavalry and up to seven battalions of Sepoys. In addition, each army would have its own artillery, which by the time of the second Maratha War (which started in

1803) included some troops of horse artillery. Each army had its own Sappers and Miners and these tended to become élite troops, both from the point of view of their discipline and technical training and for their high morale, loyalty and fighting spirit.

Commanding officers, who were responsible for obtaining recruits for their units, tended usually to favour a particular caste, a personal liking being re-inforced by the convenience of having, at least in each separate company, men who ate the same kind of food and who would eat it together. Mason explains[6] that it was the usual practice to send the men back to their own villages where they would recruit and return to their units with their sons and cousins. In this way it was possible to maintain a certain homogeneity. In the early days, the British in the Madras and Bombay Presidencies were more confident than their colleagues in Bengal and recruited regardless of caste and it seemed to work. The sepoy was said to 'put down his religion when he picked up his knapsack'. In the Bengal Presidency, on the other hand, only the highest castes were admitted to the Company's Army and great care was taken to avoid breaches of caste restrictions. Ironically, Oudh provided most of the mutineers in 1857 and they were almost exclusively in the Bengal Army. There were no mutinies in the Madras Army and only two battalions of the Bombay Army were involved. An interesting sidelight on caste is given in Mason's account of the Madras Pioneers, later The Madras Sappers and Miners who, as we have said, were an élite corps appreciated and praised right up to Independence in 1947. The Pioneers were all low caste Madrassis, a despised group. In Bombay and Bengal, on the other hand, the Sappers and Miners, whilst being equally distinguished, were recruited like the other branches of the armies in those Presidencies, that is to say, on a caste basis.

After the Mutiny, the Bengal Army was reconstructed, but still on caste lines. However it was, and still is, customary to have mixed battalions but with the individual companies recruited from one caste only. Mason suggests that the British after the Mutiny were still prepared, perhaps even more prepared, to accept caste as a basis for the reformed armies because of the late Victorian feeling for the importance of heredity. The prejudice in favour of certain castes in recruiting for the Army was re-inforced by Darwinian theories, not always fully understood, about the predominance of the Europeans in general and the British race in paricular. After the trauma of the Mutiny, and the uneasy suspicion of all the Indian races which it generated, British interests and attention switched towards the North of India where the growing awareness of Russian expansion and a pre-occupation with Afghanistan made recruiting in the North particularly convenient. The advantages of recruiting from the northern areas fitted happily into the theory of 'the martial races'. Some races were said to provide natural soldiers and others not. After the loyalty displayed by the Gurkhas, the Sikhs, Pathans and Baluchis, it made sense to accept that they were the 'best' soldiers and to recruit increasingly from them whilst decrying the effete, disloyal and unsoldierly southerner. The fact that the early battles were fought and won largely by Sepoys from the south, standing bravely and loy-ally alongside their British comrades was too easily forgotten.

The impact and influence of the British on India is still everywhere apparent and nowhere more than on the Indian Army. Apart from the obvious signs in uniforms, titles, signposts, customs and cer-emonial, the attitude of almost all the senior officers has been fixed in the mould of a public school dominated Sandhurst. So much is this so that it is possible to conceive of the Indian Army being run on late nineteenth century English 'class' lines, leading one might hope to the demise of the caste system. Alas this still seems to be some way off, even if it could be seen as an improvement on present arrangements. The Indian Navy, to some extent, and the Indian Air Force, entirely it seems, manage their business without paying regard to caste, but not so the Army. Whilst on a visit to India in 1986 the author had a conversation with a senior officer on the staff of the Indian National Defence College. The officer was from a very prestigious Indian Infantry Regiment. He explained that the Indian Army found it con-venient, if not absolutely necessary, to maintain the caste system and to continue to favour the 'martial races' in recruitment. When the author suggested that the Indian Air Force seemed to manage quite satisfactorily without these distinctions, the Indian Colonel replied with a twinkle 'what would you expect?' The point could not have been made more clearly, nor with more humour, in a contemporary British Army officers' mess.

The point has already been made that 'the man on horseback', in most societies enjoys a position and a prestige which is denied to mere mortals on foot. In earlier chapters we have suggested that the military ideal is based upon chivalry and the code of behaviour of the horsed knight, however much this has become overlaid and obscured by the more mundane middle-class virtues. The East India Company resisted whilst it could the formation of cavalry units but an early development was the taking over of native cavalry to form, under British officers, irregular cavalry regiments. Some of the best known and most romantic of Indian Regiments arrived on the scene in this way and in some cases are still numbered in the Indian, or where they were comprised mainly of Muslims, in the Pakistan, order of battle. Skinner's Horse, the 'Yellow Boys', perhaps the best known of all Indian irregular cavalry regiments, was formed in 1803 and by the

time of the Mutiny was the 1st Bengal Irregular Cavalry. Although
they were of the same class and origin as the 3rd Regular Bengal
Cavalry, with whom the Mutiny had started at Meerut, they remained
loyal and are now the senior cavalry regiment of the Indian Army.
The irregular cavalry units were recruited under the '*silladari*' system
by which a contractor, a native officer or minor feudal lord, would
agree to provide and sometimes lead a number of troopers, together
with their horses and equipment, at a fixed price per head. In another
variant of the system, the trooper would buy his horse and equipment
from the regiment and sell it back again when he left the Service. The
sillidari system was popular because each trooper was provided at
between one half and one third of the cost of those in regular cavalry
units. Another reason given for its popularity by Mason was that the
British confused the *sillidar* trooper with the English yeoman class,
believing by analogy that this kind of recruit would make the best
soldier.

M M Kaye, a best-selling novelist in her own right, descended from
a line of distinguished Indian Civil Servants and a kinswoman of the
Sir John Kaye, who wrote standard works on the Mutiny and the
First Afghan War, has edited the diaries of Emily, Lady Clive Bayley,
under the title of *The Golden Calm*.[7] In her diary, Emily, who was the
daughter of Sir Thomas Metcalfe, the Resident at the court of the last
Mogul Emperor in Delhi until just before the Mutiny, describes life
in the larger Indian cities for the senior British expatriates who lived
there. As Kaye says, in the quarter of a century that preceded the
Mutiny, there were still famines, risings, and mutinies, the disastrous
First Afghan War and the First and Second Sikh Wars but for many
of the European inhabitants of Bombay, Madras, Calcutta and even
Delhi there really did seem to be a 'Golden Calm'. So calm was this
period that many of the victims of the Mutiny were quite unable to
see the changes that were taking place around them. Mason identifies
three elements in all the mutinies in India of which that of 1857 was
the most serious of a long series. First, he suggests, there was usually
a disturbing element from outside, like news of bad crops. Secondly,
rumours are spread, often concerning religion and finally, the officers
have grown old or slack or both, or were newly arrived and ignorant
of the native language, customs and religious beliefs.[8]

Lady Bayley's diary does illustrate and support many of Mason's
points. He suggests that by the 1840s, even before the opening of the
Suez Canal, the advent of steam ships combined with the overland
short-cut from Alexandria to Suez, reduced the travelling time from
India to Britain from sometimes as long as nine months to less than
that in weeks. The effect of this was that officers began to take leave
in Britain, marry there and bring their wives out to India. In addition,

it became possible and even fashionable to visit relations in the East and many young ladies were invited or were sent to India to find husbands. Lady Bayley describes her own return journey to join her father in Delhi after several years in England as a child. Her overland journey across the isthmus of Suez took less than two days and the onward voyage to Calcutta took a further three weeks. Indian Army officers and civil and Company servants no longer resigned themselves to a life spent entirely in India until the final return on pension. They no longer took native wives or mistresses, mixed less with Indian society and found the native languages more difficult and less rewarding to learn. Officers became out of touch with their native troops and joined less and less in their games, celebrations and ceremonies. Of course this was not true of all officers and especially not of those in the 'irregular' units which had only a very small proportion of British officers. But with the increase in white British families, there was a natural tendency to turn inwards and to develop a British type of Victorian upper-middle class society with all its prejudices, inhibitions and taboos. Lady Bayley mentions the family of Colonel Skinner, the founder of the irregular cavalry regiment and builder of St. James Church which still stands in Delhi. Skinner, although of mixed blood and married to an Indian lady, was a close friend of her father. Lady Bayley's comments on the Skinner family allow one to believe that the easy intercourse and understanding between the races, enjoyed by her father and his generation, was coming to an end. After the Mutiny, which naturally re-inforced so many existing prejudices, the situation was not improved by the new Victorian idealism and sense of duty which brought about an influx of missionaries, some of whom concerned themselves with questions of education, health, social conditions and women's rights as much as with religious questions. Religion has always held an interest for some army officers and whilst instances of overt attemps at conversion were rare in India, the influence of the religious revival in England and in the Army was strongly felt. Benighted heathen meant exactly what it said for some officers and their wives, perhaps even more for the officers than for the soldiers, who would use the term as one of mild abuse rather than as a condemnation of the non-Christian to eternal damnation.

The Great Mutiny and Its Aftermath

The immediate causes of the Mutiny were, as they always are everywhere, to do with allowances, petty grievances and personalities aggravated by a lack of reliable information. Badly handled by unsympathetic officers, against a background of the long-term discontent outlined by Mason, men of spirit encouraged by a few hot-heads found themselves in a position from which they could not withdraw without loss of honour amongst their comrades. Despite a realistic view of the outcome in many cases, the mutineers partly now from fear of the consequences but partly also from a fatalistic attitude which seems to develop under these circumstances, pressed on to the bitter end. There had been many signs which pointed to the coming of the Mutiny and it is likely that firm but just action taken in good time could have averted the tragedy. But many officers were immobilised by their disbelief in what was actually happening and by a reluctance to admit, in time to take the appropriate action, that their own troops were involved. This was not unlike the gap in comprehension which existed between some officers and their men in England before the Crimean War. A similar gap seems to have opened up between the officer and society in both countries.

Of course, India could count on many good soldiers and administrators at the time of the Mutiny, some of whom had warned of the coming catastrophe, but few of the outstanding men were in the actual trouble spots. Henry Lawrence, one of a famous family of brothers, had formed 'The Guides' in the Punjab in 1846 where it quickly became one of the most prestigious and spirited irregular corps in India and the inspiration of every romantic story, and later film, about the 'Frontier' for the next one hundred years. Lawrence was shut up in Lucknow at the beginning of the Mutiny and he commanded the beseiged garrison bravely and efficiently until he was killed by a cannon shot. His much loved wife, Honoria, had died three years earlier and he was more than ready to die. Whilst they were in the Punjab, Henry and Honoria had built between them a 'Soldiers Garden' in Lahore where the British soldiers and their families could play games, frequent the coffee shop, look at a menagerie which included two or three tigers and relax in pleasantly laid-out surroundings. They had also spent much of their own money on providing a school for 'the poor white barrack children' opened at Sanawar in 1847 and called 'The Lawrence Military Asylum'.[9] Henry's brother John was Administrator of the Punjab at the time of the Mutiny and, despite the recent Sikh War and the subsequent annexation of the state, he stripped the Punjab of troops to send to the trouble spots. He was the first to emphasize the importance of the recapture of Delhi and did all that he could to bring this about. He had always been the most ambitious and practical member of the family and became Lord Lawrence and Viceroy in 1864. The third of the brothers, George, had accompanied General Macnaghten on his disastrous mission to Kabul in 1840, as his ADC. He was present at the treacherous murder of the General and was kept in captivity with Lady Macnaghten and others for a year until they were rescued.

John Jacob was another trainer of irregular cavalry who not only raised and commanded two regiments which later became the 14th Scinde Horse but also had strong views on the organisation of native forces which influenced the shape of the armies in India as they were reformed after the mutiny. Like so many of the soldiers and administrators in India, he took a strong moral line. Only the very best and most committed type of Englishman should be brought into contact with native troops, and to this end he believed that three British officers was enough for a native regiment or battalion. Jacob looked towards the Cromwellian 'New Model' for his inspiration and consciously sought to implant a kind of moral fervour in his soldiers and native officers which would support and compliment the lifelong and absolute devotion demanded of his white officers. Another famous figure in mid-nineteenth century India was John Nicholson, who marched the Punjab Mobile Column to Delhi in record time to join the investing British forces. Nicholson had been one of Henry Lawrence's specially selected young administrators in the Punjab and, like the Lawrences and John Jacob, he had a moral driving force which could be uncomfortable for less energetic and less dedicated men. Fortescue says that until Nicholson arrived, there was no direction or leadership evident amongst the heterogeneous collection of units assembling for the assault on Delhi. Nicholson quickly ended that and provided the example and driving force which initiated the storming of the city. He maintained the momentum of the attack even from his death bed. It is said that after Nicholson was mortally wounded in the assault and Wilson, the nominal commander of the British forces, was contemplating withdrawal from the city in the face of fierce opposition from the mutineers behind the walls, Nicholson rallied in his dying agony and said 'Thank God, I still have strength enough to shoot that man'.[10]

All the political officers were seconded from the Army and most of them chose to remain in this special employment until the end of their service. Apart from Nicholson, and perhaps Henry Lawrence, Fortescue had no time for them, believing them to be professionally incompetent and sometimes mischievous. Few of the British generals in India at the time of the Mutiny are treated with much respect either and, perhaps with justice, are lumped together with the Crimea Generals. Fortescue reserves his praise for General Sir Hugh Rose who had been hurried to India to take command of the Central India Field Force. Rose, who had been the British representative at French Headquarters in the Crimea, had no previous experience of campaigning in India but he combined great personal charm with enormous energy and a very strong will. The Central India Force advanced north-east from Bombay into Central India. Between January and June 1858 they marched more than 1,000 miles, fighting

battles against the rebels wherever they made a stand, capturing and
reducing rebel towns and fortresses and harrying to death most of
the remaining rebel leaders. Rose's campaign was a model of its kind.
Sir Colin Campbell who brought final relief to Lucknow and successfully completed the destruction of the rebels in the North and East
of India is afforded less praise. Whilst it is dangerous to question
Fortescue's judgement, one wonders if he might not have been applying a slight historical corrective. Campbell's reputation could have
appeared a little 'overblown' only two years previously, although
through no fault of his but by the national hysteria over 'The Thin
Red Line'.

Whatever is said of the Generals, by common consent, the troops
behaved magnificently. But the end of the Mutiny, excluding Company troops, there were eight British cavalry regiments and sixty-
eight battalions of British infantry in India. This force was almost
twice as large as the army we had sent to the Crimea and probably the
largest assembly of British troops in one country until we come to the
mass armies of the First World War. But the hard fighting and much
of the hard marching was done by the few battalions already in the
country in May 1857. At the outbreak of the Mutiny, there were only
twenty-one battalions and five British cavalry regiments. Four of the
British battalions and two of the cavalry regiments took part in the
siege and capture of Delhi and thirteen battalions and three cavalry
regiments were part of Sir Colin Campbell's Lucknow relief force.
The 32nd Foot were at Lucknow at the start of the Mutiny and provided the mainstay in the defence of the Residency. The 9th Lancers
seem to be the only regiment who gained honours for Lucknow as
well as Delhi. There were many other regiments and battalions which
took part in the suppression of the Mutiny. Four of the East India
Company's European regiments were involved in the early fighting.
With the other two Company regiments, all the white regiments were
transferred to the Crown in the post-Mutiny reorganisation, being
numbered 101st to 106th Regiments of Foot. The irregular cavalry
regiments, most of which remained loyal, were particularly valuable
during the Mutiny because of the acute shortage of regular British
and Indian cavalry. Although only a minority of the native regiments
took part in the Mutiny, it was some time before the extent of the
disaffection could be gauged and so a much higher percentage of
European troops was involved at Delhi and Lucknow than was normal
in India. It soon became clear that the Punjabi Sikhs and Muslims
could be relied upon as well as the other northern troops. The Gurkhas had not only remained loyal but a force from Nepal under Jung
Bahadur joined Campbell and took part in the relief of Lucknow.
Once it was found that the armies of Bombay and Madras had

remained loyal, their regiments were quickly incorporated into the various striking forces and Sir Hugh Rose's Central India Field Force was largely made up of troops from the Southern Presidencies.

However, as we have said, the British troops who were already in India bore the brunt of the fighting and perhaps this was as it should be. There were few British troops who were not thirsting to be revenged for the massacres and outrages that had occurred at the start of the Mutiny. For the majority of the troops involved, the battles with the rebel armies, the assaults and the street fighting in the capture of Delhi and Lucknow, the marching in intense heat over extraordinary distances at a forced pace, thirst, heat-stroke and cholera were only more severe rather than different from their common experiences of India. Even after the Mutiny, 64 out of every 1,000 soldiers quartered in Bengal and 44 out of every 1,000 wives died annually. Amongst officers the mortality rate was three times higher than in London.[11] We have seen from Sergeant Pearmain's Memoirs referred to in the previous chapter, the high mortality rate from drink, heat-stroke and disease in the pre-Mutiny army but Private Waterfield in his memoirs[12] gives an equally harrowing account of his life with the 32nd Light Infantry in the Sikh wars and on the North West Frontier. Waterfield complains bitterly of the harsh discipline, of the corruption of the Quartermasters, the reliance on strong drink to make life bearable and the aimlessness and infinite boredom of life in cantonments. Whilst he seemed to manage well enough, the long marches caused the death of many of his comrades through heat exhaustion and excessive drinking of native spirits. He is particularly scathing about the women of the regiment, condemning their hasty marriages and their general immorality. Interestingly, Waterfield, who was a native of Leicester, had several friends from that city, including his brother, serving with him in the regiment. They met frequently and sustained each other with news of home and no doubt they passed on news of their doings in the regiment to friends and relatives in Leicester. It is this close comradeship, linked with families at home which is put forward as one of the strengths of the British regimental system. The regiment did not seem to engage Waterfield's loyalty to any great extent but it is likely that he was sensitive to his comrade's good opinion of him and was heartened by their familiar presence at times of stress. Perhaps as a non-Cornish member of a Cornish regiment (later The Duke of Cornwall's Light Infantry) this is all that could be expected, expecially from one described by his editor as a prickly character. By 1856, he had had enough of soldiering and returned to England after ten years in India, to an honourable discharge. His regiment, as we have already seen, went on to take part in the heroic defence of Lucknow.

In the reorganisation after the Mutiny it was first proposed that many more British troops should be based in India than the one Briton to about nine native troops which was the rough ratio maintained before 1857. It was even suggested that native Indian troops should be dispensed with altogether. But as order returned, the cost of keeping European soldiers in India became a more important consideration than absolute security.[13] The reorganisation committee finally recommended a figure of 80,000 British troops to 190,000 Indian. In fact, the actual numbers from 1863 onwards were about 62,000 British to 125,000 Indian. This ratio of about one to two remained the guide until 1914.[14] Memories and myths of the Mutiny maintained this high ratio but it was also accepted in the second half of the nineteenth century that the cost of maintaining a large force in India was a proper part of 'the white man's burden'. Our administrators and soldiers were performing a mission to protect, civilise and, where possible, to Christianise the Indians and only incidentally, it was suggested, to guarantee the unimpeded flow of trade and commerce. The growth of the new public schools with their emphasis on games and Christianity produced a new breed of young officers and administrators who really did believe in 'the Great Game' and who became better than ever before at leading and organising their men, whether they were Indian civilians or soldiers, black or white. The new schools, with their cult of muscular Christianity, did all that was required of them until after the First World War when a new phenomenon appeared on the scene.

Esme Wingfield-Stratford in *The Making of a Gentleman*, referred to earlier, questions whether character training alone is sufficient for the requirements of modern civilisation. Writing in 1938, he said the public school system had paid a high price for the standardisation of its output in terms of the discouragement of intellect and the crushing of individuality.

> The *'fin de siècle'* gentleman was magnificently qualified for any straightforward task of leadership that did not require subtlety of intellect. As an officer, though he might be abysmally ignorant of military science, he had no equal in getting the best out of the men under his personal command; he may have known little, and cared less, about modern developments of scientific agriculture, but he was seldom without the knack of achieving popularity as a landlord; in the process of imperial expansion that was taking place in the last quarter of the century, he was without a rival in dealing with natives, providing that these were only of a mentality even more primitive than his own. When the native happened to be educated and imbued with the traditions of an ancient civilisation, there might be a different tale to tell; one of blank prejudice and incomprehension.[15]

Between the wars, an educated, radical group of young Indians emerged, in many cases better educated than their masters and often able to use the old Victorian ethical precepts to devastating effect in both India and England.

In the 1860s, it was still possible to erect a tablet in the Cawnpore Memorial Church which read 'In memory of Mrs Moore, Mrs Wainwright, Miss Wainwright, Mrs Hall and forty-three soldiers' wives and fifty-five children', without a suspicion of irony. To this extent, social conditions for the soldiers and their families in India merely reflected the situation in Britain. Senior officers were in the forefront of all attempts to impede improvements in conditions of service and living conditions for a group of people who had suddenly become the focus of attention because of the Crimean War and the Indian Mutiny. In both conflicts, the British soldier had again become the hero that he was for a short time after Waterloo. This no doubt helped to increase and enhance his self-pride and strengthen his loyalty to his regiment. At the same time it enabled him to take a proprietary interest in the burden of Empire which he was largely shouldering. Mason has a list of eleven expeditions outside India which took place after the Mutiny and in which the reconstructed Indian Army took part. In addition, before the First World War, there were several campaigns within or on the Indian frontier some of which, like the Malakand 'affair', dragged on for a year and involved the equivalent of four divisions. It was in these hard fought 'little' wars that the Indian and British Armies, coming sometimes from India and sometimes directly from Britain, learned the kind of soldiering that epitomised the regimental system so admired by the late Victorian and Edwardian poets. That the lines were often more redolent of the drawing room than the battlefield didn't seem to matter. 'Cannon to right of them, cannon to left of them' would have been recited in many a Victorian officers' mess as would 'The Colonel's dead and the gatling's jammed'. The sergeants too and the soldiers at their 'smokers' in a slightly more critical or cynical vein might have listened to 'O it's thin red line of 'eroes' when the drums begin to roll', and found a wry pleasure in it. Even when the real events commemorated in verse were so glamorised and romanticised as to be unrecognisable to many of the participants, they still served a purpose. The view from a distance, even when expressed with sickly sentimentality and more than a degree of hypocrisy, coloured the soldier's image of himself and boosted his confidence in the same way that the short-lived hero-worship after the mid-century catastrophes provided a slightly bogus but very welcome elevation of the spirit.[16]

Despite the insularity of mess and barrack life, Indian and British troops still managed to establish a kind of friendly rivalry, especially when campaigning together. The fact that the proportion of British to native troops was higher now and that the Indian troops were more likely to be fighting a 'foreign' foe made something like the old inter-regimental rivalry, so highly rated by Fortescue as a morale builder, a real possibility between British and Indian units. Apart from regimental rivalry as a source of honour for the Indian regiments, another influence which we have observed operating in the British Army was also present and was perhaps even more important in the Indian Army. Private Waterfield shows in his memoirs that home contacts were important for the British soldier and we have suggested that this became one of the main planks of the regimental system especially after the localisation which followed Cardwell's reforms of 1872.

A similar influence was at work among Indian soldiers much earlier in the century. A tract published in Calcutta in 1841 with the title 'On The Spirit of Military Discipline in The Native Indian Army', by Sir William Sleeman, stressed the importance of family opinion in influencing the sepoy's behaviour. Sleeman had hunted down the malign but widespread Indian religious fraternity known as the Thugs. He had practically destroyed the organisation by the classic method of infiltration. In his tract he pointed out that three-quarters of the Bengal infantry came from Oudh, north of the Ganges and were Rajput and sometimes Brahmin by caste. They visited their families every two or three years and the good feelings of their families exercised a salutary influence over their conduct as men and soldiers. They knew, he said, that misconduct or cowardice would be reported at home because so many of them came from the same neighbourhood. This tended to produce a general and uniform propriety of conduct which was based on a veneration of parents who are cherished through life.

Sleeman was not the only Briton to appreciate native virtues and to compare them favourably with the habits and customs of his fellow countrymen. Sergeant Pearmain who, like Private Waterfield served in India just before the Mutiny and who also, like Waterfield, used his diary to record complaints about the harsh discipline and appalling conditions under which he lived, had this to say about the caste system as he saw it: '. . . But the white man will eat anything, do anything (but serve God). Our caste is never broken'.[17]

After the Mutiny there was without doubt a drawing away from native Indian society by the British, partly caused by the increased number of British wives in the stations and their tendency to set up and remain within a narrow insular group organised strictly on class lines. There was also a more pronounced division between the military and government functionaries. The public school ethos was beginning to have a very real influence on the administrators of the Empire. Haileybury, opened in 1862 in the first great wave of reformed and reconstructed schools on the Rugby model, was established in the defunct East India Company College. Whilst it did send a number of boys to Sandhurst and Woolwich, its main and continuing purpose was to provide recruits for the Indian Civil Service. Peter Parker in 'The Old Lie'[18] says that Government and Colonial Service were preferred as careers by public school men. 'The schools were just not equipped to provide an education suited to a boy who wanted to enter the Armed Forces'. He goes on to say that some schools had Army and modern 'Sides', but these were often used as dumping grounds for the least intelligent pupils. 'Most boys who wanted to enter the Army were syphoned off—the Harrovian Winston Churchill amongst them—into special military crammers'. In a footnote, he points out that of the 375 candidates at Sandhurst between 1858 and 1861 only 23 came directly from their public schools.[19]

Philip Mason describes the pre-Mutiny conflict of opinions between the progressive, reformist 'levellers' in the Government Service who tended to favour the peasants against the landlords and native aristocracy and the others, 'Warmer of heart, less sure they were right and more tolerant of Indian ways'.[20] It was a similar difference of view which divided many army officers from their civilian colleagues in the later part of the century. It might be said also that, on one level at least, the titanic row between the classical, olympian Viceroy Curzon and the pragmatic, commonsensical but devious Commander-in-Chief Kitchener had its origins in the same kind of mental divergence. It would be a mistake however to accuse either Curzon or Kitchener of undue warmth of heart.

The conflict between Kitchener and Curzon, which eventually brought about the downfall of the Viceroy, obscures the important differences between the Commander-in-Chief and his predecessor Field Marshal Lord Roberts. Roberts took up command of the Madras Army in 1880 and then became Commander-in-Chief of the Bengal Army in 1885 with supervisory powers over the Madras and Bombay Armies. He was strongly prejudiced in favour of the northern 'martial' races and on his appointment to Madras he was in a good position to confirm his already strongly held prejudices. He was, however, able to find much to praise in the Madras Sappers and Miners without seeing any inconsistency in this. Roberts also disagreed with many senior officers and members of the Indian Government about the commissioning of Indians. He said that there was an inveterate feeling in all British ranks on the moral and physical inferiority of natives. Kitchener was anxious to build up the Indian Army, which had finally been brought together under a Commander-in-Chief in 1895. This meant that native officers would be required for at least some of the newly raised units. Roberts and Kitchener also disagreed about the brigading of native and British battalions. Roberts, who had taken part in the suppression of the Mutiny, believed it was still necessary to brigade one British battalion with two Indian battalions whilst Kitchener thought it would be more efficient and good for Indian morale to have exclusively Indian and British brigades. Kitchener saw an enlarged Indian Army as part counter-balance to the enormous conscript armies of the European continent. His attitude to the 'Indianisation' of the Indian Army was, at a time of high imperialism, remarkably liberal and he consistently preached the message that there was no danger of another mutiny. The reorganisation of the Army in India, begun by Roberts and continued by Kitchener, involved a much higher ratio of British to Indian troops and a full utilisation of the extensive railway network to increase mobility. This made a large-scale mutiny much more hazardous for the mutineers than it was in 1857. In 1905, said Kitchener, dread of mutiny was an anachronism. He set out a seven point memorandum amounting to a code of conduct for behaviour towards all Indians but particularly towards Indian soldiers. The code was meant to show respect and confidence and all officers were required to study native customs and prejudices. Perhaps most important of all, officers were to set an example to their men in their relations with Indians: 'All were subjects of his Majesty'.[21]

The Indian Army and the World Wars

Kitchener's view was vindicated in the First World War when 1,302,394 Indian troops served overseas. Indian units were in action in France by the end of September 1914 and altogether 138,000 Indian soldiers served there. The campaigns in Mesopotamia were almost entirely Indian operations involving 675,000 men, and Egypt absorbed a further 144,000. All these men were volunteers and Mason has some little difficulty in deciding what it was they thought they were fighting for. With very few exceptions, they fought bravely and loyally. In France, the Indian units who were early in combat were decimated in the first winter of the war like their British comrades of the original Expeditionary Force. They endured the appalling conditions of trench warfare and the cold and wet of two winters and complaints only appeared in letters home to India from soldiers who, wounded once and recovered, were to be sent into action again and saw no possibility of a second survival. In Mesopotamia again, they fought gallantly and performed all that was asked of them but here, through bad generalship, they suffered defeat and the shame of surrender. To make matters worse, they were surrendered to a brutal and incapable Turkish Army which allowed the majority of the prisoners to die in captivity whilst their British Commander was carried off by train to Istanbul to be fêted and made much of by the Turkish Generals.[22]

There were some minor failures of discipline and some desertions, but mainly by the troops recruited from outside the Indian frontiers. Even with the mutiny of the 5th Light Infantry in Singapore in 1915, the disturbances in the Indian Army were much smaller, even by proportion than those in the French and British armies. What did emerge quite quickly in the 1914–18 War was that all the theorising about the so-called martial races was so much mythology. The mutiny in Singapore involved a situation in which most of Mason's preconditions, despite warnings and example, were again present.[23] In the 1915 mutiny however the mutineers came from a regiment which had remained loyal in 1857, they were entirely Muslims recruited from the Punjab or they were Pathans or Baluchis,[24] they were not from the despised southern races. The Marathas, despite Roberts' low opinion of them, strikingly vindicated their worth as soldiers in Mesopotamia and Palestine and the Garhwalis, whom Mason describes as not having been famous before the war either as a class or a regiment, performed magnificently in France. The Garhwalis were brigaded with the Leicesters and struck up a friendship with them which continued long after the war.[25] The trend away from recruiting mainly from the 'martial' races was continued by General Auchinleck as Commander-in-Chief when he opened up recruiting in Madras and Behar in the Second World War. Roberts and many other Generals had been obsessed with the necessity for good breeding without ever understanding the Darwinian philosophy on which their ideas were based, nor having any clear notion of how warriors evolved and declined. But as the more extreme interpretations faded, or the original theories became better understood, the views of Wolesley and Kitchener and even Sir John Moore came into fashion. It began to be accepted that race was not all and that the most unlikely material could be made into good soldiers and even into good officers with adequate training, good leadership and inspiring examples to emulate.

In the Second World War, the Indian Army was again expanded but it was also mechanised and armoured and the resulting expansion of the technological and industrial base, although no doubt long overdue, was to provide a sound footing for the new industries of India and Pakistan after partition. The Army, under its leaders Auchinleck and Slim, increased from 189,000 to over 2.5 million, the largest non-conscripted army the world has ever seen, and the number of Indian officers increased from 1,000 to 15,740. Although Indian divisions fought in Africa, the Middle East and Italy, their main theatre of operations was on the Eastern frontier of India, in Malaya and later Burma. By 1944 there were Indian battalion commanders and since

Independence was already in the air, within a very short time officers were being groomed for the highest appointments. The Indian Army, and the Pakistan Army which emerged from it on partition, were lucky in their last wartime commander. Slim was an outstanding representative of the Indian Army. Above all he admired and respected his Indian soldiers. He gave them every chance to succeed and they never let him down. As Mason says, he went back to Kitchener's ideas and towards the end of the war in Burma, he brigaded Indian with Indian battalions and British with British. He believed they were not only easier to supply like that but that they fought better also. Gone were the days when it had been supposed that the example of British troops was needed to fire Indians to valour. British battalions in Burma were generally under strength and Slim thought they had sometimes been reinforced from other units to such an extent that they had lost much of their old regimental spirit. Cross posting, mixing of reinforcements and the failure to ensure that returned casualties, leave men and stragglers get back to their original unit has always been a cause of low morale and we shall return to it later. Slim went on to say that, after the battle of Imphal, divisional commanders called for Indian battalions in place of British. In comparison with British troops, Slim thought the Asian fighting man, Indian, Gurkha and Japanese, was at least equally brave, usually more careless of death, not so moved by slaughter and mutilation and more like the British soldier had been in the eighteenth century.[26] It is easily said but perhaps for the first time since they became part of a 'British' Indian Army the Indians were fighting for something which, however dimly, they perceived as being their own country. Perhaps, as well as being a little war weary, many British troops were not too certain of why they were fighting the Japanese in the Burmese jungle with the help of Indian soldiers. Cromwell would have understood their dilemma.

Towards the end of his study of the Indian Army, Mason, thinking particularly of the horrors of the First World War, asks himself what the Indian soldier thought he was dying for. There were no war memorials in Indian villages as there were all over Europe. It was unlikely he thought, that their regiments would remember them for more than a short while and in any case the regiment was not part of a national tradition or at least not an Indian one. Furthermore, the time was not far off when the allegiance of the regiment would be transferred from the King Emperor to the President of India. In the end, Mason rejects the regiment as the cause for which men died. Surely, what they had really died for, he says, was honour, 'The good name in the world of their kin and clan and village, their own good name among those who knew them, and last of all personal honour, that vindication of integrity which is involved in faithful perseverance in a path once chosen'.[27] There is a coded message here which may have some bearing on our attitude towards and relations with non-British troops in British employ, especially perhaps, one of the remaining jewels in the British military crown, the Gurkhas. Perhaps too it was personal honour of the kind which Mason talks about which persuaded the British mercenaries in front of Breda and those serving with Gustavus Adolphus, in the sixteenth and seventeenth centuries, to fight and die for a foreign power on a distant shore.

6

The Great Age Of Army Reform

The over-riding impression given by the Army in Britain between Waterloo and the Crimean War is one of stagnation and reaction. The Crimean War and the Great Mutiny are rightly seen as the watershed between the years of obscurantism and obstruction which were largely responsible for the debacles in India and Russia and the genuine movement towards reform and increased professionalism in the half century which followed. However, there had been some attempts at reform even before the Crimean War and some of these attempts had been supported and occasionally inspired from within the Army itself.

It is obvious from the heated correspondence in the Service journals of the period that those few officers who were genuinely concerned to introduce reforms into the Army were more feared and hated by their military colleagues than were the civilian reformers who could be dismissed as un-informed meddling busy-bodies.[1] Although there can be no doubt that the military reformers were influenced by humanitarian and religious motives and that there was a tacit alliance between them and the 'Army Movement' which was the military branch of the religious revival going on at that time in Oxford and elsewhere, the main impetus for reform within the Army was the desire to increase military efficiency.[2] The arguments for reform were, almost without exception, stated in rational, utilitarian, Benthamite language which stressed the concern of the reformers with improving the standard and number of recruits; with better organisation, equipment and training and with the introduction of professional standards into the Officer Corps. Those improvements which were reluctantly accepted concerned only the enlisted men. They were designed to improve the 'image' of the Army and thus improve recruiting at a time when the 'French Scare', referred to in Chapter IV was still growing.[3]

The introduction of branding and the setting up of military prisons could be accepted as reform measures in that they allowed for a reduction in flogging. However, the introduction of Army school-masters, reading rooms and a small, carefully selected library[4] could be seen more realistically as an extension of the Church's growing concern with education and personal improvement rather than with increased military efficiency. The first Army schoolmasters were recruited in 1846 although there had been Regimental Schools since the formation of the Regular Army. But the early schools, like so much else in the British Army, depended upon the interest and good-will of the Regimental Colonels. When G R Gleig became Chaplain General in 1844, he accepted as a reality his responsibility for Regi-mental Schools whilst previous Chaplains General had accepted the role as a formality.[5] As a result of Gleig's pressure and his exposure of the general imcompetence of the untrained sergeants and warrant officers who were employed as teachers, he was appointed Inspector General of Schools in addition to his duties as Chaplain General. He recruited and trained a Corps of Army Schoolmasters, entry to which was open only to qualified teachers. After 1846 there was central control of all Army Schools, regular inspections and competent instruction but, in reality, during the 1840's at least, very little pro-gress was made in the eradication of illiteracy amongst the soldiers or in the improvement of the educational standards of the non-com-missioned officers. As late as 1858, an analysis made by Colonel John Lefroy, then Inspector General of Military Schools, showed that one fifth of the troops could not read or write whilst another fifth could read but not write. This lack of progress was due to the general dis-trust of education in the Army felt by most of the senior officers and echoed readily by many of the junior officers and men. A disastrous legal judgement of 1811 in the case of 'Warden v Bailey', where on appeal the judge ruled 'it is no part of the military duty to attend a school, and to learn to read and write' bedevilled education in the Army for over half a century and provided sanction for the apathy with which it was regarded.[6] The Inspectorate of Schools was set up in 1846 by Sidney Herbert the Secretary at War, and given the distrust and rivalry between the civilian and military heads of the Service, this was probably enough to arouse the suspicions of the Commander-in-Chief, giving rise to the apocryphal remark attributed to Wellington, 'If ever there was a mutiny in the Army, these new-fangled school-masters will be at the bottom of it'.[7]

The Education of the Soldier

Thirty vacancies were advertised in 1846 for the new posts of Regimental Schoolmaster. Applicants were to be between the ages of 19 and 25. They were to complete their education at the Royal Military Asylum Chelsea, and then to be posted to the infantry and cavalry. They were to be uniformed but would have civil appointments ranking with sergeants major. Their pay was to be 17s 6d per week plus lodgings, coal and light. There were 200 applicants for the 30 posts and the 'Observer' described the new Corps as 'A grand step towards the advancement of the moral and intellectual condition of the British Soldier'.[8] Unfortunately the step was not so grand as it may have seemed at the time, and, for the reasons already outlined, many of the first Army Schooolmasters had a rough passage in their new appointments. James Thompson, who was perhaps not untypical of the early Army Schoolmasters quickly became a radical after meeting Charles Bradlaugh in the Army, was in constant trouble with the authorities and was finally dismissed the service in 1862 for disobeying orders.[9] Like the Surgeon's Mate, the Army Schoolmaster occupied an ill-defined position in the Service, and even without radical tendencies his lot was not an easy one.

The attitude of some senior officers towards the education of soldiers and towards the educational services as a whole was compounded of three elements which are still alive and can be seen at work even today. First, there was the inevitable resentment of yet another service to be added to what was widely believed to be the unproductive and parvenu 'tail' of the fighting forces. This exclusivism was none the less painful in that it had from time to time ostracised many of the other arms and services including even the Gunners and Engineers, whose traditions of gallantry and devotion were not surpassed by élite regiments of cavalry and infantry. Secondly, education which first blossomed in the Army under the aegis of the Church was regarded as a 'morale' service rather than one concerned exclusively with military efficiency. This meant that despite its increasing role in the direct support of training, where it answers in formations to the Training and Operational staff, overall army education is controlled in The Ministry of Defence by the Adjutant General. This has limited to a certain extent the role and effectiveness of the modern Army Educational Corps in the sphere of management training and even of training technology which the Corps was largely instrumental in introducing into the Army. More sadly, in recent years the Army Department has virtually removed the higher education of officers from its own uniquely trained body of post-graduate army officer tutors. Despite Napoleon's elevation of 'Morale' into one of the most important principles of war, the 'morale services' take an inevitable back seat. Finally, the association in the early nineteenth century of universal education with criticism of the status quo, with reform and subversion has never been completely laid to rest. Thus, whilst a largely classical education confined to a small minority has been accepted as a harmless eccentricity, serious education for the professions, including the Armed Forces, and especially as a qualification for entry to them has, until comparatively recently, received only half-hearted support.[10]

Recruitment and Short Service

During the 1840's, there was a steady, if thin, flow of suggestions for military reform. In 1841 there was a proposal that the cost to the recruit of 'buying himself out' should be reduced from £20 to £5 on the grounds that many recruits enlisted under the influence of drink or despair. The idea was at first taken seriously by the authorities, especially since a condition of the new cheap discharge was to be a transfer to the Militia, but the scheme was shelved eventually since it was felt that it would be bad for the Militia and would cause discontent and an undermining of discipline in the Army as a whole.[11]

In 1842 Sir J E Alexander, commanding the 14th Foot, suggested that regiments which bore County names should recruit from that County only. Further, that men should be given an extra penny a day after seven years service, twopence a day after fourteen years service and a free discharge and a pension of a shilling a day after twenty-one years.[12] These suggestions were prompted by the very high rate of desertion from his regiment, stationed at that time in Canada. Alexander went on to say, 'These advantages, together with a medal of service and uniform good treatment ought in National or Country Regiments make men content to serve their turn . . . especially since it is notorious that British private soldiers are better fed, clothed, lodged and paid, and attended to in sickness than any other troops in the world'. Localisation had to wait until after the Cardwell reforms thirty years later. However, in 1845 the Meritorious Service Bill did allow soldiers an extra penny a day for each five-year period of service with good conduct. Although this was a very modest sum, it was no doubt appreciated by the old soldiers with long service whose basic pay, fixed at 1/- per day in 1797, was not increased until 1867 and then only to 1/2d per day.

The one Bill that was successfully introduced or, as we saw in Chapter IV, imposed upon the Army despite strong opposition from Wellington, was the Limited Service Bill of 1846. Although the Secretary-at-War's Bill was weakened in the process of persuading the Army to accept it, it really did begin to affect the composition of the Army and the life of the ordinary soldier. In a small way it did begin to show that it was possible to get rid of some of the hardened old criminals from the ranks without destroying that steadiness in action which was so praised by admirers and enemies alike.[13] The objects of the Bill were threefold. First by offering a ten-year engagement instead of virtually unlimited service it was hoped to attract more recruits and reduce desertion. Secondly, it was hoped that the new engagement would attract a better class of recruit and this was coupled with the provision that serving soldiers who had been in the ranks for a minimum of ten years could apply for an immediate discharge without payment. Some at least of the long-serving bad characters would be discharged to the benefit of the new young recruits and the sadly worn image of the Army in the public eye might be improved. Thirdly, it was proposed that all soldiers discharged after ten years would be enrolled in local companies with a reserve liability and regular training in order to earn a pension of six pence per day at the age of fifty-five years.

In the hope of gaining more recruits, most senior officers were prepared to accept the ten-year engagement for new entrants but they were not prepared to see their battle hardened veterans allowed a free discharge if they had already served for ten years. Wellington from retirement, and the Adjutant General, Sir John Macdonald, led the protests. Wellington insisted that he had never been consulted. Macdonald was prepared to have men on short service, for ten or fourteen years, but without pension or reserve liability and both of them insisted that to allow serving soldiers a discharge after ten years would denude the Army of its best soldiers and non-commissioned officers, leaving the country defenceless in the face of French ambitions. The Secretary-at-War, Lord Grey, was overwhelmed by the opposition and informed Somerset, the Commander-in-Chief, that the Act as it applied to serving soldiers was suspended. Figures were now produced by supporters of the Bill to show that there were not all that many soldiers with ten years service. About 7,000 out of the 30,000 soldiers in the United Kingdom had more than ten-years service and this included the Guards, who had a disproportionately large number of veterans. It was also shown that in the infantry, at least, there was no danger of too many soldiers seeking an early discharge.

A scheme already existed which allowed soldiers with twelve years service and two good conduct badges to claim a full discharge, but very few did, except from the cavalry where a knowledge of horses and the habits of the aristocracy provided better employment prospects. Eventually, the Bill, as it emerged in March 1847, allowed infantry soldiers to enlist for ten years whilst the remainder of the Army could enlist for twelve years. After this period, and only on recommendation, an infantryman could enlist for a further eleven years or a non-infantryman for a further twelve years. After the second period of service, a soldier on discharge could, by joining a local reserve unit, qualify for a pension. Something at least was achieved and the Bill laid the foundation for all future measures aimed at making military service a respectable trade acceptable to the Victorian middle classes.

Officers' Pay and Conditions in the Mid-Nineteenth Century

Except in so far as their initial situation was immeasurably better, reform of the officer corps during the first half of the nineteenth century presented an even sorrier picture than the half-hearted and emasculated attempts to improve the lot of the ordinary soldier. Of the three reforms conducive to the establishment of a more professional ethos embarked upon during the period, only one, the question of military duels, as we have noted, showed any signs of progress. In 1840, a commission was set up to report on naval and military promotion and retirement. Disquiet had been expressed over a long period in both Services as well as amongst the public over the stagnation into which the Armed Forces had sunk. After the Napoleonic Wars, very large numbers of officers were available and with the reduced establishments many officers were put on half pay where they remained for twenty years or more until, in the case of the Army they eventually sold out or, if they were naval officers, just died off. Naval officers were even worse off than their army colleagues. Many naval captains who continued to serve until well into the 1840's never got another ship after 1815.[14] But even in the Army, the almost complete absence of promotion in some corps and regiments merely intensified the competition when a more senior post became available for purchase and in its turn pushed up the price of commissions and subsequent 'steps' above the regulation price.[15] However, the Commission, either from conviction or outside pressure, did not regard the 'purchase system' as open to more than cursory investigation and, on grounds of cost, prompted inevitably by Wellington, rejected any change which would increase the charge to the public. Indeed, in evidence to the Commission the Adjutant General, Sir John Macdonald, confirmed his reputation as an opponent of all reform by suggesting that the condition of officers could best be improved by actually increasing the price of purchase so that officers would be encouraged to sell out at a profit.

On the question of pay, the Commission declared that in the inter-

ests of the Service as well as of the country, expenses should be kept
down because:

(a) The moment the Service becomes burdensome to the country or that prejudice be
created against it because of high pay its efficiency would be reduced, its strength
curtailed and its capacity for service annihilated . . . it would languish from wanting
that popular support which is essential not only to its vigour and efficiency but to
its very existence.
(b) High pay would mean a small Service, promotion diminished and many would be
without hope of employment and prospects.
(c) Steady and certain employment for the efficient with due encouragment of promotion and sufficient reward for those who may be worn out in the Service can
only be possible if remuneration is not unduly liberal.

The Commission also felt that 'Service should be performed well,
but cheerfully also. Severity of duty should not harass or overtask'.
This was no doubt a rebuff to those critics who strove to introduce a
fully professional Service in place of one regarded by many officers
as a part-time occupation for a few years only whilst waiting to inherit
their patrimony. Furthermore, the dangers and tedious nature of the
occupation could be avoided by transfer to another regiment if one's
own was warned for a foreign campaign or a garrison duty too far
from London or Bath.[16] Beau Brummel, it will be recalled, resigned
his commission on finding his regiment posted from London to somewhere north of Watford.

If the purchase system was dismissed by the Commission as unimportant in the problem of lack of promotion prospects and inadequate
pay, it was not so regarded by the reformers in and out of the Services.
Through the next thirty years the scandal and abuse inherent in the
buying and selling of commissions became the '*cause célèbre*' of military
reform. The final abolition of the system, which did not occur until
1871, was regarded by many people including politicians, writers,
reformers and by then, many officers as the decisive victory of military
professionalism over the loose-knit organisation, local loyalties and
ethos of a feudal officer corps. Sir John Fortescue links the final
sweeping away of long service for the soldier in 1870 with the ending
of purchase in 1871 as marking the end and ringing the knell of the
old British Army. He ends his monumental History of the British
Army at that date saying, 'Some other hand must record the vicissi-
tudes of the New Army . . .'. But 1870 was by no means the end of the
story and much canvassing and campaigning had to be undertaken to
arrive at that comparatively successful juncture after the disappoint-
ments and the obscurantism of the 1840 Commission.

Philip Abrams, writing in the *Archives Européennes de Sociologie
1965*[17] suggested that the period immediately following the abolition
of purchase was the high point of military professionalism in Britain

since when it has declined markedly. Using the indicators of professionalism chosen by Abrams, this may appear to be so and we shall return to the problem in a later chapter. Meanwhile, to return to the nineteenth century struggle for reform, it is clear that before the weaknesses in the officer corps had been exposed in the Crimea and exploited in *The Times* and other newspapers, opinion in the Army was almost unanimously in favour of purchase except in the Royal Artillery and Royal Engineers both of which were exempt from the practice. In 1842 the Editor of *The United Services Journal* wrote an article with the title 'Purchase Defended' in which he was able to put forward reasons for its retention on grounds of humanity and military efficiency. He makes the point again that purchase filled the ranks from those classes with the highest stake and neutralised the inherent evils of all standing armies 'which are dangerous to freedom in proportion as they are composed only of professional adventurers'. The writer of the article dismisses the only alternatives to purchase, not even considered by the Commission of 1840, as promotion by routine or by selection. The evils of routine promotion were said to be shown in the Royal Artillery, Royal Marines and the Army of the East India Company, where promotion was said to be even slower than in the purchase corps. Promotion by selection was to be abhorred because of the favouritism and jobbery said to be involved. Political interest was alleged to be irresistible in Britain as evidenced in the corrupt system in the Navy until just before the writing of the article. The interesting point is made that non-purchasing officers could be less well educated than purchasers because of the expenses of education at schools and at Sandhurst.[18] A minimum of service in any rank before purchase, it is insisted, should ensure professional competence. But finally the writer nails his colours to the mast in his concluding passage where he puts forward the principles of purchase, hereditary wealth, primogeniture and the established church as necessary 'to shield our institutions from the inroads of democracy'.

After pay and purchase, the third great question of reform, that of duelling, was, as we have already said, bound up in the conflict between a medieval code of personal honour, which would not accept that officers were bound by the normal laws of the land, and the growing movement towards rationality and humanitarianism which it often saw as characteristic of an inferior class. It was with the object of supressing duelling as 'sinful, irrational and contrary to the laws of God and man' that the Anti-duelling Association was formed in May 1843. The Association boasted 15 Baronets, 30 Admirals and Generals and many more junior officers among its early members and no doubt it was instrumental in getting the Articles of War for 1844 to express Her Majesty's displeasure at the practice of duelling. By

1848 *The United Services Journal* was able, as we have seen, to publish, perhaps a little prematurely, its 'Requiem Upon Duelling'. The next year the same Journal printed two articles on 'The Need For Regeneration' and on 'The Army Movement'. These articles dwelt on the need to develop Christianity in the Army through the medium of special chaplains, and on the reforms necessary to render marriage for the soldier respectable and dignified. Also included in the published dogmas of the movement was 'the diffusion of Education in the Army especially of the officers'. Even it was added, 'at the risk of driving out the aristocracy'. Sympathy and support was expected from the 'Scientific Corps', the Engineers and Gunners, and it was in this coincidence of interest between the requirements of the increasingly technical arms and the ambitions of the professionally orientated army reformers that they saw the possibility of future progress.

The extremes of opinion on both sides set the general tone of the acrimonious debate. That there was a role for the Armed Forces in the protection and policing of Britain's rapidly expanding trading interests abroad was obvious to many critics of army arrogance and obduracy. There were also serving officers, especially on the District and Command staffs and also at 'The Horse Guards', who were aware that the Army was seriously out of tune with the 'Spirit of the age'. But the real lack of common ground was between the radical, reforming politicians and newspapers and the Regimental Colonels and their officers, whose way of life really was under threat and who still thought of all change and all reform in terms of the French Revolution which had eventually brought Napoleon Bonaparte to power. There is plenty of evidence that the senior officers at the Horse Guards and even Wellington himself, when in the capacity of Commander-in-Chief, were well aware that control of the forces rested with parliament. They might expect the Sovereign to exert influence on their behalf and indeed to win some battles over appointments and promotions but, in the last resort, the will of parliament would be supreme. Despite the Civil War and the Glorious Revolution it was still difficult for the Regimental Officer to accept that this was so.

Contrary to the often expressed belief of the Duke of Wellington, a land-owning, partly paid and wholly unprofessional officer corps can be and often is far more independent of public opinion and a parliamentary paymaster than the 'soldier of fortune' whom he feared would take over the Army if purchase was abandoned.[19] Wellington was no military bully and although he defended Cardigan in public, and refused an enquiry into his administration of the 11th (Prince Albert's Own) Hussars, since he believed this would weaken military discipline, he censured Cardigan severely in private. It seems unlikely that had Wellington still been alive Cardigan would have been given command of The Light Brigade in the Crimea. There are instances of martinet Colonels and bullying junior officers who might seriously have perverted the course of justice in the military courts in which they wielded considerable influence, but who were restrained and frustrated by the more humane attitude of the confirming authorities. A typical case was that involving Lieutenant Colonel Sir Gaspard le Marchand. Le Marchand provoked a soldier until he was assaulted. The charge of assault carried a possible death penalty. Headquarters in Ireland, where the incident took place, knew Le Marchand as a bully and was aware of the provocation. The Headquarters was most concerned, in the event of a conviction, that the death penalty should not be carried out and wrote to the Horse Guards to say so. The soldier was eventually sentenced to transportation and Le Marchand was severely censured.[20] Most regimental officers, whilst not condoning bullying and provocation, were not prepared to accept that anything less brutal than the harsh regime then in operation would suffice to maintain discipline and efficiency in the Army. Even more, they were not prepared to admit the competence of civilian critics or the sincerity of their more enlightened brother officers. But, in the course of the next few decades after the Crimean War, it became obvious to all but the most bigoted officers that changes would have to come. The trickle of army reforms began before the war against Russia, grew as a result of public concern aroused by the war and by the Mutiny in India, and turned into a flood as the century progressed. However, the presence in Parliament of a large number of officer members was never a guarantee of a majority for reform measures. Quite to the contrary, as we have seen, most officers were in favour of 'purchase' almost up to the time of its abolition. As late as 1878, there were eighteen Guards officers in the House of Commons and there must have been many other Members of Parliament in the Services as well as a large Service representation in the House of Lords. However the cataclysmic and utterly unexpected defeat of the French in 1870 by the combined German armies, so shook the British civilian and military establishments alike that the hunt was immediately on to strengthen and improve the efficiency of the British Armed Forces. The new and alarming events in Europe broke the barriers of indifference and blatant class interest. Through the newspapers and parliamentary agitation, opinion was refocussed so that moves towards a genuinely professional officer corps and an efficient, well equipped army could procede with only a minimum of obstruction.

The Austro-Prussian War of 1866 had already alerted many military thinkers to the changes that were taking place. The Prussians' use of their strategic railway network following the lessons of the American Civil War and the devastating demonstration of the power of the breech-loading 'needle gun' at the battle of Sadowa had already anticipated the events of 1870.[21]

By 1870 it had finally become clear to the Government and a majority of senior officers that new and more objective criteria would be needed in the selection of officers and that better training, a new organisation and new institutions were necessary to compete with the highly trained mass armies of the continent. The abolition of purchase was one necessary measure; the new improvement of instruction in the Cadet Colleges and in the new staff courses for field officers was another, but what was really required above all else was a new attitude of professional dedication on the part of all officers. The tremendous impact of the Prussian-inspired defeat of France in one swift campaign, brought about this change of heart and justified that small band of professionally oriented officers who had been calling for changes and reforms. The events in Europe also gave to those senior officers who, like Wolseley, were thoroughly convinced of the need for change, the opportunity to be selected for the highest posts in the Army. This enabled Wolseley to counter the reactionary views of The Duke of Cambridge who, as Commander-in-Chief, modelled himself on Wellington without having his famous predecessor's experience or genius. Wolseley, who eventually succeeded The Duke of Cambridge, was able to gather round him and favour in their careers a group of outstanding young officers, dedicated to their profession who were able to shape decisively the British Army of the late nineteenth century.

An indication of the changed attitude of army officers from 1870 onwards can be seen in an analysis of the contents of the professional journals of the period. A comparison of the contents of *The United Services Journal* for the decades of the 1840s and 1870s shows the extent of the changes taking place. A detailed analysis is given at Appendix III. The most obvious change over the period in the interests of the officer, admittedly not an entirely typical sample for either decade, was in the increase in articles published on matters which could be broadly categorised as 'Professional Studies'. In the 1840s less than 25 per cent of articles on average were on professional matters whilst in the decade of the 1870s they had increased to 60 per cent. As we have said, the authors may not have been typical of the officer corps of their respective periods but the fact of their being chosen for publication and therefore judged as of interest to their fellows is in itself significant. Articles on Military Technology, although not numerous in either decade, had increased by almost 50 per cent whilst the most popular subject in the 1840s, Memoirs and Military History, had declined from 37.5 per cent to 22 per cent. Even a subject one would expect to have lasting appeal, Exploration and

Travel, declined from 15.5 per cent to 7.0 per cent, and interest had switched mainly to Central Asia. Unlike the Journals of the 1840s, which were still full of articles on the Napoleonic Wars, the 1870s Journals contained almost nothing on the Crimean War, then Britain's most recent major war.

Even before the impact of the Franco-Prussian War had made itself felt, the innovators and reformers had begun to publicise the lessons from the American Civil War and from the earlier Prussian Campaigns. At this stage, the suggestions for change and improvement were mainly concerned with technical matters and as was to be expected came almost entirely from the 'Scientific Corps'. Jay Luvaas in his 'The Education of an Army',[22] points out that the most enlightened of the contributors to the Service journals in the 1860s and 1870s appear to have been from The Corps of Royal Engineers. Luvaas rescues the reputation of one of the most famous military engineers, Field Marshal Sir John Fox Burgoyne by reminding his readers that although Burgoyne, who died in 1872, opposed the abolition of purchase and had somewhat reactionary views on military education, his official account of the siege of Sebastapol testified to his breadth of vision. Although he was officially concerned primarily with fortifications, his interests included tactics, strategy, military organisation and administration, and new weapons and equipment. Except for his views on promotion and military education, Burgoyne's outlook was undeniably progressive. Luvaas mentions the contributions of five engineer officers to the professional journals, all of whom wrote on technical matters, but perhaps the most influential article published in 1871 addressed itself to broader issues and was written in what could only be called sensational terms about the invasion of England.

The Cardwell Reforms and Afterwards

The Cardwell reforms introduced the most far reaching changes ever inflicted upon the British Army in peace time. The introduction of short service, the abolition of the purchase of commissions and the reorganisation of the War Office were the basic measures upon which Childers and others were able to build over the next thirty-five years. Cardwell brought in his first reform and it was accepted like a lamb but the later reforms required the loud roaring of a lion from the continent to convince the House of Commons that further reform was necessary. Gladstone's first ministry, in which Cardwell was Minister for War, carried into action the Liberal theory of military reform; any changes could be made as long as they resulted in retrenchment. Gladstone demanded economies and Cardwell won him over by promising that the Army estimates would be reduced.[23]

Cardwell kept most of his reform measures out of the fire of political controversy and was able to reduce the Estimates in 1869 and 1870 as the introduction of 'Short Service' in 1870 almost eliminated the need for pensions. Support for Cardwell reached its zenith in February 1870 when even *The Times* became quite lyrical in its approval of Government retrenchment and that might well have been the end of Cardwell and his reforms. He had finally managed to abolish flogging but this had not satisfied the radicals and had upset certain sections of the Army. Many Liberals and most of the Tories saw no further need for reform and an air of complacency seemed to settle upon civilian and soldier alike. Even the Duke of Cambridge saw no clouds on the horizon when he said 'There is no reason why the Army should not become a vast industrial school, where men could get the best training for the various employments of civil life'.[24]

Then came the swift defeat of the French at the hands of the Prussians, shattering the complacency of Victorian England. The French were no longer to be a model for the British Army and it was necessary to look elsewhere if Britain was to defend itself and its rich possessions and its highly profitable overseas trade against the new mass armies with their new weapons and their industrial-military organisation. The second shock occurred in May 1871 by which time the immediate furore had died down and the public, getting a little tired of the reform topic, in its usual way was beginning to question the cost of Cardwell's latest proposals. The follow-up to the Prussian shock was an article published in *Macmillan's*. General Sir George Chesney, a provocative and imaginative writer, wrote an account of a supposed German invasion of Britain. A successful landing on the South Coast led to an advance on London which was only defeated at 'The Battle of Dorking', the title of the article. But the moral of the story was that the regular British forces had been unable to defeat the enemy and only the patriotic volunteers and reserve forces were able to save Britain's honour. Public opinion, and at last specialist opinion was engaged once more and Cardwell was able to further jusify his reforms. Despite opposition from Disraeli over expense and the piecemeal nature of Cardwell's reforms, purchase was abolished during the 1871 session of Parliament. After abolition the great passions it had aroused began to die down and it was possible to discuss army affairs without radical bugbears and hysteria. Following the great excitement of 1871, the rest of Gladstone's ministry seemed almost an anti-climax. Having re-organised the War Office, ending the dual system of control by bringing army administration entirely under the Secretary of State, he had fought and won the battles over 'Short Service' and purchase and was at last able to address the problem of creating an adequate Army Reserve and a sound system of reinforcement.

Garnet Wolseley and George Cambridge

The uneasy relationship between The Duke of Cambridge and Sir Garnet Wolseley which existed for the last four decades of the nineteenth century epitomised the struggle going on in Britain between the representatives of the old order and the new breed of progressive, professionally orientated officers. The Duke of Cambridge was born in 1819 in Hanover. His father a son of George III, was brought up in the courts of Hanover and England and educated his son in Germany for a military career. The young Prince was brought to England by his uncle Clarence on his accession to the throne in 1830 as William IV. For a short time after Victoria came to the throne in 1837, Prince George, the young Cambridge, was regarded as a possible consort for the Queen but it seems that neither party was more than lukewarm. It was probably with some relief on both sides that the young Queen found her consort elsewhere.

After a series of military attachments, including the staff of the Governor of Gibraltar and an appointment as Lieutenant Colonel to the 12th Lancers, he was gazetted Colonel of the 17th Lancers and sent to Leeds to command the regiment where he was quickly engaged in suppressing riots in the town. From 1843 to 1845 Prince George commanded the garrison of Corfu and, at the age of twenty-seven, he was promoted Major General and held command appointments in Ireland until 1852. His father died in 1850 and he was sponsored by the Duke of Wellington and the Duke of Beaufort when he took his seat in the Lords. When Wellington died in 1852, it was necessary to appoint a new Commander-in-Chief. Wellington and the Queen had both wanted Prince Albert to become Commander-in-Chief but the Consort, wise and sensitive in all constitutional matters, rejected the suggestion and advised against selection of the young Duke of Cambridge. Cambridge at thirty-three was judged to be too young and, as a Major General, too junior in rank but it is likely that the Army would have been pleased to accept him as a 'Royal' Commander-in-Chief, despite his lack of seniority. Lord Hardinge, a veteran of the Peninsular and Waterloo campaigns, a former Secretary at War and a Governer General of India was, with Queen Victoria's obvious approval, chosen to take Wellington's place. Meanwhile, Cambridge had already been appointed Inspector General of Cavalry. Between the death of Wellington and the outbreak of the Crimean war, a short period of reform was inaugurated, at least in spirit and on paper, if not in practical terms. Under Lord Hardinge, Cambridge produced several papers proposing minor reforms mainly in army organisation but also, ironically, in view of later events, suggesting that sixty was far too advanced a period of life to commence upon the arduous duties of active military command. Cambridge had discovered that almost all the generals in the Service were aged sixty or more. He was to forget this youthful enthusiasm when, at the age of seventy-six, he clung on to his own appointment! To his credit, he advocated large scale manoeuvres and had supported Hardinge in his acquisition of nine thousand acres of Hampshire moorland from which was formed the great camp and training area at Aldershot.

Despite his youth and lack of seniority, he was appointed in the following year, on the outbreak of the Crimean War, to command one of the four divisions in the expeditionary force. Partly through the influence of the Queen, he was given command of the First Division, the senior division of the Army made up from one brigade of the Guards under General Bentinck and a brigade of Highlanders under Sir Colin Campbell. With stern advice from his brigade commanders, the Duke performed bravely if not brilliantly at the Battle of the Alma. At Inkerman, the Duke's behaviour was described as uncommonly gallant but after that he seems to have been unable to cope with the rigours and alarms of the campaign. He was eventually ordered home on sick leave and, despite some calumnious reports in the papers and many letters from friends and others advising him not to return until the war was over, he returned to England in January 1855. The Queen was far from pleased but, by the middle of 1856, all was forgiven. Lord Hardinge, attending the Queen at a review at Aldershot of troops returned from the Crimea, suffered a stroke and died in September. It was Queen Victoria's view that Hardinge, who was held in part responsible for a debacle in the Crimea, was killed by the Press. The Prime Minister, Palmerston, received an 'opinion' from the Queen concerning the vacancy now created which suggested that George was almost without a competitor. Since the Army was said to expect and wished for a Royal Commander-in-Chief, that is how it turned out. However, like the unfortunate Lord Hardinge, the Duke of Cambridge only received a title of General Commander-in-Chief. As in Hardinge's case, this was said to be in deference to the memory of the great Duke of Wellington but it was also because Cambridge was junior to many of the generals over whom he was preferred. To his often expressed chagrin, Cambridge had to wait a further thirty years until 1887, Queen Victoria's Golden Jubilee year and his own fiftieth year of army service, to be created by Letters Patent, Commander-in-Chief.[25]

When Wolsely took over from the Duke of Cambridge as Commander-in-Chief of the British Army in 1895, it was the culmination of a close relationship which had existed for twenty-five years. It would be foolish to characterise this association as a love-hate relationship but there can be no doubt that, despite bitter exchanges, their different backgrounds, temperament and outlook, they feared, envied and respected each other. Wolseley, fourteen years younger than Cambridge, had already served with distinction in Burma before going to the Crimea where Cambridge as we have seen, in his first and only campaign, was commanding the 1st Division as a Major General. Wolseley never missed a campaign that he could get himself involved in. Even in his War Office appointments, he was frequently called upon to lay down the pen and pick up the sword to command some expedition or other which the Government of the day, the British public and its popular press and certainly Wolseley himself, believed that only he could bring to a successful conclusion.

By the 1880s, he was popularly known as 'our only General' and even Lord Roberts VC, the 'Hero of Kandahar', who was eventually to succeed Wolseley as Commander-in-Chief in 1900, had to be content with the Music Hall title of 'our only other General'. Wolseley was lucky to have made his name in the comparatively bloodless Red River Campaign in Canada from which he returned to a Knighthood and to Secretary-at-War Cardwell who required an Assistant Adjutant General who would be sympathetic towards his great programme of military reform. Wolseley had already indicated his interest in reform in his military writings and particularly in his 'Soldier's Pocket Book', first published in 1869 and reprinted subsequently through the whole of his service. The Pocket Book was a remarkably liberal and progressive tract which, in its first part suggests the underplaying of caste differences in the army. 'Let us sink as far as possible the respective titles of officers, sergeants and privates, merging them into one great cognomen of soldier, . . . Let us give up the phrase "officer and gentleman" substituting that of "soldier" for it. Let the word "officer" be used as little as possible, so that the private may really feel that there is no gulf as at present between them, but that they are merely separated by a ladder, the rungs of which all can equally aspire to mount'. Cambridge was not impressed and nor was his cousin the Queen who was soon prepared to accept Disraeli's estimate of Wolseley as 'an egoist and a braggart'. Disraeli had added 'So was Nelson' to his description but it is not known if the Queen also accepted the Prime Minister's flattering comparison.[26]

Wolseley was lucky in that from Gladstone's first administration and from the time that he joined Cardwell at the War Office, public opinion was moving more and more in favour of army reform. The impact of the Franco-Prussian war was so strong that Wolseley was able to defy the Commander-in-Chief and, when necessary, although

Wolseley would have denied this, to appeal directly to his political chief. On occasions, he was suspected of appealing, even after becoming Adjutant General in 1881, directly to the general public through articles in the press in which his identity as the author was only barely concealed.[27] He bitterly resented being called a radical and whilst the two great series of military reforms carried through by Cardwell in the seventies and Childers in the eighties occurred in Gladstone's first and second administration, Wolseley disliked and distrusted the Liberals. He particularly blamed them for the fatal procrastination over the Gordon Relief Expedition, and more so because Gordon, whom Wolseley had first met in the Crimea, had remained a close friend and heroic model for him until his death in Khartoum. Despite the Liberal passion for reform, especially where it could be combined with internal economy or the withdrawal from an overseas interest, Wolseley, like the Duke of Cambridge, believed that the long-term future of the Army was safer with the Conservative party of Disraeli and Lord Salisbury. Wolseley was fortunate in his friends and supporters in both parties.

The Beginning of the End for the Regiments

It was the Childers Military Localisation reforms of 1881, strongly supported by Wolseley, that can now with hindsight be seen as the beginning of the end of the regimental system. The regiment was originally the property of whoever was authorised by Royal Warrant to raise it for the King's service or sometimes for service overseas with a foreign power. The Colonel of the regiment drew all the monies due to his men and paid them from time to time. He was responsible for clothing his men and usually expected to make a profit out of it. It was not a system which automatically guaranteed devotion to duty or bravery in battle. That certain inspired leaders were able to command that devotion and bravery cannot be doubted but the system which grew up, whilst it depended upon the example of brave officers in battle, was also compounded of personal honour. This honour cited and described by Fortescue and by Philip Mason in their histories of the British and Indian Armies, combines several intrinsic factors such as a personal sense of worth, understanding and belief in the rightness of the task in hand, the approbation of one's fellows and the approval and regard of one's superiors. The regiments of the late eighteenth and nineteenth centuries, despite the sordid conditions under which the men lived, seemed to provide an environment in which this honour could flourish. Perhaps the Company of eighty to one hundred men formed the ideal seat of honour and there is evidence that personal knowledge and contact is necessary for the intrinsic factors mentioned above to bloom. Of course the larger regiment or battalion with its Lieutenant Colonel, colours and battle honours must have provided a wider and more colourful focus but, it is suggested, the unit of up to 1,000 men was the largest military group to which a soldier could give any real allegiance. The smaller face-to-face group of friends and acquaintances provided the cement which held the ranks steady and ready to die rather than destroy the close bonds which are forged in all successful armies.

In so far as there was a spirit encouraged by and directed towards a larger group, it was the battalion-sized regiment with which Fortescue has made us so familiar. Clearly, the officers of the regiment felt themselves as one with their fellows and it would be natural for them to regard the regiment as their focus of loyalty and affection. To some extent this must have been true also of the long-serving sergeants who, like the officers, had learned to keep their distance from the men under their immediate control. It is possible to say that the establishment and maintenance of separate officers' and sergeants' messes was, and still is, essential for this kind of regimental loyalty. Despite the lofty phrases in his 'Soldiers' Pocket Book', Wolseley was able, seemingly without a qualm, to support the Duke of Cambridge in his opposition to Childers reported intention to 'do away or regulate by authority the Officers' Mess'.[28] Childers' localisation or territorialisation measures, which had first been proposed in 1877, and rejected by Disraeli, alarmed the Queen and, needless to say, the Duke of Cambridge as well as many senior serving and retired officers. The plan, to combine two or more regular battalions with units of the Militia and Volunteers to make a single regiment, with five or more battalions based upon one exclusive geographical locality, was sufficiently audacious. However, what appeared to be even more unacceptable was the doing away with the old numerals which were the honoured titles of the old regiments and the distinctive coloured facings of their uniforms by which they recognised each other on parade and, until recently, in battle. To belong to a regiment composed of five or more battalions and to share their honours and prestige with what would previously have been regarded in many cases as a pretentious rabble, was seen by many as a serious blow to the *esprit de corps* of the Regular Army. That morale was not badly affected, or at least that it recovered quickly, was shown at Tel-el-Kebir in 1882 and even more in the Boer War, at the end of the century, where, despite faults in leadership and planning, there was no lack of spirit or determination in the British regiments taking part.

Perhaps in the end it is true to say that most reforms affect the ordinary soldier to a remarkably small degree, at least consciously that is. Reforms may increase the efficiency of the organisation, especially

its 'business efficiency', which is what Cardwell saw himself as bringing
about. Wolseley too saw value for money as one of his prime objectives.
On the other hand, unlike Cardwell, he was not committed to nor
rigidly controlled by a government pledged to retrenchment. Short
service could be seen as an attempt to introduce business methods,
planning, cost effectiveness and scientific management to the Army
and Wolseley certainly saw it in that light, but the effectiveness of the
reforms of both Cardwell and Childers depended upon the commitment of the government to something more than saving money.[29] By
1883 Wolseley was complaining that the Army's share of national
revenue was falling, (From 21.45 per cent in 1863/4 to 17.36 per cent
in 1883/4). He raised again the constant complaint against the Liberals
that economy was always at the expense of the Army, 'The
Government's excuse [which] was always that they could not obtain
good recruits, was preposterous. What would they think of a railway
manager who failed to get workmen?'[30] Hamer, in his, The British
Army, (Civil-Military Relations 1885-1905,)[31] speaking of the reforms
says:

> The linked-battalion system did not work because it was not allowed to work. No doubt
> the campaigns of the 70s did place a great strain on the Army, but there were no
> inherent defects in the Cardwell scheme that were beyond remedy, provided Parlia-
> ment was willing to pay for the needed expansion and thus allow the system to work
> as it had been designed. The government, however, refused to ask Parliament to
> embody the militia or to pay for the increase in battalions to keep abreast of the
> expanding defence requirements. Of course, at the heart of the problem were the
> recruiting difficulties of a volunteer system. There seems to have been a limit beyond
> which voluntary recruitment could not be expanded under the terms of service the
> government was willing to offer.

Despite the limitations imposed by finance, and there was nothing
new in this, Bond[32] is able to sum up the achievements of the reforms
as: the creation of a reserve and a rudimentary mobilisation scheme,
localisation and a more thorough and humane recruiting system. Perhaps the more humane approach and a number of small improvements in matters like dress were all that could be said to make an
impact on the soldier. The reforms, as we have said, certainly did not
improve recruiting, or at least did not increase the number of recruits
the Army was prepared to accept. The Recruiting Report, C2832 of
1880 showed that the number of recruits rejected increased from
6,662 in 1875 to 15,477 in 1879 and the optimistic height standard
set in 1870 at 5 feet 8 inches had been reduced by 3½ inches by the
end of 1873. Standards, as they still do, varied with the availability of
recruits and they changed ten times between 1873 and 1880. However, what could not be disputed was, that by the end of the century
the Army had got rid of the teenagers and older men from the active

battalions. Sir A Haliburton published a pamphlet in 1898 titled 'A Short Reply to Long Service' in which he gives the following table:

Ages and Proportions per Thousand of NCOs and Men in Infantry Battalions

Year	Under 20	20–25	25–30	30–35	35–40	Over 40
1846	176.6	342.6	277	98	84.3	21.5
1866	132.4	275.2	356.2	150.8	74.4	11
1897	— *	322.3	483.6	179.9	11.2	3

*Note. By 1897 trained recruits had to be twenty years old before they could join a regiment or battalion serving overseas.

Despite the euphoria occasioned amongst the reformers by the abolition of long service and the purchase system, and eventually of the lash, there were some critics who insisted that the seeming progress was only illusory. It has been pointed out,[33] that the end of purchase and the requirement for officer entrants to have attended the Royal Military College merely replaced the stupid rich by the intelligent rich and the base of officer recruitment was no wider after purchase was abolished than before. But this was not all. In the 1870s, the annual average of first commissioned appointments in the Army was about 360;[34] of these, about 130 were filled by Militia Officers, NCOs etc. who were not required to attend a course at the College. In other words, there was a back door to a regular commission which was kept open in one form or another until the Mons Officer Cadet School course was merged with the revised and shortened Sandhurst course in 1972. The abolition of transfers from the Militia was considered in 1870 but was not agreed because of the bad effect it was likely to have on the Militia.

An interesting point on reform was made by Captain C E Callwell RA, in a book called '*Small Wars*' (*Their principles and practice*), published by Her Majesty's Stationery Office in 1896. Callwell, who was serving in the Intelligence Division of the War Office, says that, towards the end of the century, there was a reversion to old tactics in fighting against savage foes. Close order lines, squares and volley firing were re-introduced in the campaigns in India and Africa at a time when the use of breech loading rifles and artillery, and even more the machine gun, had completely ruled out such tactics in Europe. He says that the renewed emphasis on drill movements and close order tactics helped to retard reform. The slow pace of reform and the difficulty of arriving at a logical conclusion, even for a dedicated and energetic officer like Wolseley, are illustrated by three other issues which emerged towards the end of the century.[35]

In advocating the setting up of Aldershot Camp in 1852, Lord Hardinge pointed out to The Prince Consort that, by using the railways, it would be possible to concentrate a large military force on the chosen site. The importance of railways was largely ignored by the Regular Army after this, despite evidence of their great strategic value in the American Civil War and the Austro-Prussian War of 1866. Articles in the United Services Gazette of December 1864 and in the *Daily News* on 23 April 1867, saw the railways only as a source of employment for ex-servicemen who would help to increase travelling safety. The Volunteers, on the other hand, were keener on railways because they were more technically conscious and had to move large bodies of troops for their reviews. A Volunteer Railway Engineer group was formed in 1865 but it was not until 1882, after Wolseley had been let down by the railway facilities available in the Tel-el-Kebir campaign, that he insisted upon the Army having its own railway operators. It was announced in the House of Commons, two months after the battle, that some companies of Royal Engineers would be converted into a Railway Corps with permanent cadres which could be rapidly expanded when required for active service. This was a late but welcome decision. On the other hand, the problem of military correspondents for the newspapers has never been satisfactorily solved, as events in the Falkland Islands campaign have recently shown us.

Russell's despatches from the Crimea, and those of other less well known reporters, were crucial in exposing the muddle, incompetence and military buffoonery going on there. The Services have never forgiven the correspondents and the correspondents, with some few honourable exceptions, have never understood the preoccupation of the Services with the battle in hand rather than with the civil population at home or indeed with the correspondents themselves. Wolseley was very well able to use the press for his own purposes and he made sure in the Ashanti campaign, for example, that at least one of his hand-picked officers was sending reports directly to a London newspaper. Even so, in the first edition of his 'Soldiers' Pocket Book', he described newspaper correspondents as 'those newly invented curses to armies, who eat the rations of fighting men and do no work at all'.[36] In 1878 a confidential memorandum from the War Office on war correspondents[37] seems to represent modern military opinion as much as the opinion of its time. 'The presence of newspaper correspondents with an army in the field is an evil of modern warfare which cannot be avoided'. The memorandum goes on to advocate strict control of correspondents who should preferably be ex-officers subject to military discipline and who should operate under conditions of severe censorship. However from this early memorandum it was possible to draw up rules for the guidance of editors which were eventually accepted. The Duke of Wellington had spoken out in 1810 against his

officers writing for the newspapers or journals and that was sufficient
for the next hundred years.

The third point on which the Army or rather the War Office was
required to have an opinion for which previous experience had not
prepared it was the question of the Channel tunnel. Gladstone's
Government had given general approval to the project in 1871 but it
was not taken up till 1881, when it became one of the first matters to
arrive on the desk of Wolseley as the new Adjutant General. In 1875,
War Office opinion had been vaguely in favour of the scheme but
Wolseley wrote the first reasoned military objection to the tunnel. His
main grounds for opposing the tunnel were that it was impossible to
guard against surprise attack and seizure in war and secondly that
human frailty was such that it was impossible to guarantee that the
tunnel could be blown up at the right time to prevent it falling into
enemy hands. None of this sounds very much like Wolseley but it was
sufficient to confirm the Duke of Cambridge in his prejudices and the
Tunnel Defence Committee Report of 1882 insisted on the dangers,
minimised the advantages and suggested some extremely elaborate
precautions. Blowing-up, drowning, crushing and asphyxiating were
advocated against an invasion attempt through the tunnel and the
report was re-inforced by a memorandum from Cambridge pointing
out the expense of the defensive arrangements and the danger to
passengers in the tunnel. The whole military intervention ended in
farce but it did establish the War Office line of opposition, at least
until after the First World War.

It is easy to look at these three questions as evidence of the continuing policies of obscurantism and muddle in the War Office towards
the end of the nineteenth century. But, by any standards, it would
seem that in two of them, railways and war correspondents, the correct
conclusions were, perhaps belatedly, arrived at. In the matter of the
tunnel, it is difficult to dismiss Wolseley's opinions as easily as those
of the Duke of Cambridge and sadly, if wrong, he was in good company with the many senior military figures who were mistaken in their
misappreciation of the quickening pace of scientific and engineering
progress. A better assessment of what had been achieved between the
Crimean and Boer Wars is perhaps afforded by the criteria defining
professionalism. It is possible to define any occupation from the mer-
est trade to the highest calling as a profession but Samuel Huntington,
following Max Weber, has produced a list of five key institutions
against which it is possible to gauge progress towards full professional
status for the officer corps.[38]

The first of Huntington's key institutions is entry requirements.
There can be no doubt that after the abolition of purchase and the
requirement for most, if not all, aspirants to have attended the Royal

Military College, considerable progress had been made along this measure of professionalism. The second criteria of professional status concerns the means of advancement. Again, the abolition of the purchase of 'promotion steps', which led to promotion through a mixture of seniority and merit was surely a move in the right direction. The character of the third requirement cited by Huntington lies in the nature of the military educational system. Whilst the British military authorities have never insisted on a high academic standard as necessary for all officers, there was a perceptible movement towards higher standards of entry and achievement at the military colleges and on the staff and technical courses organised by the scientific arms. It is likely that the British military educational system did not approach the German, French or American systems in terms of university status or in the combination of military technology with more liberal aspects of a general education but, coming from a very backward position, considerable progress had been made by 1900.

The fourth area of judgement lies in the nature of the military staff system and here, compared for example with the German Staff Corps system the British officer corps might be found to be lacking. Certainly the move towards an efficient and properly trained staff was not helped by the outspoken antipathy of the Duke of Cambridge towards all staff trained officers. His comment on Staff College Officers, 'I know those Staff College Officers. They are very ugly officers and very dirty officers, ' must have rung round all the military headquarters in Europe. Wolseley, who was beaten into second place for the Wellington Prize in 1872 by a Lieutenant F Maurice, held no grudge and took Maurice with him on the Ashanti campaign in 1873 as his private secretary. The Prize was inaugurated by the second Duke of Wellington for an essay on the 'System of Field Manoeuvres Best Adapted For Our Troops to Meet a Continental Army'. The competition was a by-product of the anxiety aroused by the sudden and unexpected defeat of France by Germany in 1870. As a member of the 'Wolseley Ring' Maurice accompanied his master on all his campaigns until 1885 by which time Wolseley was Adjutant General and he was able to appoint Maurice to be professor of military art and history at the Staff College. Wolseley made sure that at the end of his appointment to the Staff College, Maurice was followed as professor by Colonel Henderson another military intellectual. Between them, Maurice and Henderson instructed almost all the British leaders of the First World War and to a level not below that of their European counterparts.[39]

Finally, Huntington suggests, professionalisation must be judged by the degree of ésprit and competence displayed by the officer corps. There can be no doubt that, throughout the nineteenth century, the officer corps and the British Army as a whole displayed a spirit, in the many campaigns in which it was involved, which was the envy and admiration of the world. The dash and bravery of the officers was matched by the devotion and energy of their men. Even in the comparative disasters of the Crimea and South Africa, the regiments were able, through their steadfastness, to emulate their great predecessors and retrieve many an apparently lost situation despite the incompetence of the higher command. It would be fair to award full marks for ésprit but rather less for competence. On balance, and taking all five attributes of professionalism together, there was a very clear move towards a better selected, better trained and better staffed and led army in the second half of the century. There had never been a problem with the spirit of the Army and, given the intensive effort to reform and improve under Cardwell, Wolseley and Childers, it is tempting to say that the mediocre quality of the higher leadership displayed by the British in the Boer War was against justifiable expectations.[40]

What can be said is that after the watershed of the Crimean War, the British Army, and particularly its officer corps, metaphorically reentered society. The movement within the Army for organisational and social reform, especially amongst the younger officers, grew year by year and it is likely that Gladstone's two great reforming governments were supported on much of their programme by a majority in the Army as well as outside it. If the strategy of the Army before the Crimean War was one of withdrawal from society in order to maintain cohesion and identity in a rapidly changing world, this was no longer so after the war. The reformers and the military educationalists' growing influence, the shock of the French defeat by the Prussians and above all, perhaps, the example of Wolseley, brought about a growth of professional interest. A new strategy to deal with change could be seen at work.

If, as Hamer says, the reforms introduced by Cardwell and Childers failed, they failed because they were designed to prop up an obsolete system. They were meant to provide, at last, an adequate garrison for an Empire which was already showing signs of old age. Furthermore, the garrison was to be produced from a 'short-service' army which would ensure a higher standard of recruit and increase enlistments. Finally, the reforms were meant to produce a reserve of trained soldiers which would remove the embarassing necessity to pay a special bounty to persuade troops to re-enlist for overseas service, or the reliance on volunteer formations which were not entirely popular with many senior officers. In most of these objectives the reforms failed, mainly through government parsimony.

The new system did not work in the South African War, where volunteer and colonial forces made up for the shortage of regular units from the United Kingdom. The set-backs in South Africa were frustrating, not least for the British regiments which expected to make the kind of impact they had made in India and elsewhere in the Empire, but they did serve a purpose. For almost the first time, and from within the Army itself, reformers and military thinkers began to look outside the regiment for a model on which to base a new force. Haldane's Territorial Army, early in the new century, was still based on local associations and connections and looked to the Regular Army for help and guidance. In one sense it was just more of the same, but other military leaders looked elsewhere. Perhaps for the first time in the history of the British Army a conscious effort was made by some senior officers to think and act positively. In the face of the mass continental armies, social withdrawal seen in the first half of the nineteenth century as a tactic to dissociate the army from an unsympathetic and largely uncaring public seemed hopelessly inappropriate. However the friendless state of Britain after the Boer War and the unmistakeable challenge of Germany's fast growing commercial and naval power convinced many officers of the necessity for action.

Between the Franco-Prussian and South African wars, there had been a technical and scientific surge in the arming and equipping of the British Army and Navy which amounted almost to a revolution. But the new thinking had not addressed the problem, shortly to arise, of how to shape an army which would help to re-forge alliances and serve to re-establish a basis of trust and co-operation with a major continental power. Haldane produced the nucleus of an expeditionary force and the means of reinforcing it. He was also largely responsible for bringing the British and French military staffs into a close and secret understanding but, as we shall see, the military tempo had increased almost spontaneously. From within the army, and supported by some very senior officers, there were those who demanded a large conscripted force. At the same time, efforts were made, consciously or unconsciously, to change what was still a predominantly anti-militarist population by the setting up or the encouragement of a whole host of patriotic and quasi-military clubs and youth organisations. Finally, a new-found assertiveness could be seen in a military attitude which, whilst it may not actually have encouraged mutiny in Ireland in 1914, was nevertheless sufficiently confident to bring on a political crisis which could only be put on one side by the coming of the First World War.

7

The Aberrant Corps

After the Crimean War, during the great debate that went on in
Parliament and across the country on the purchase of commissions,
the Royal Artillery and the Royal Engineers and the Royal Marines
were referred to by an exasperated Member of Parliament as 'the
Aberrant Corps'. They were aberrant because, unlike the rest of the
Army, their officers received their commissions without purchase. In
these three corps, because they were not raised by Colonels who in one
sense owned them, but answered directly to the King or Parliament
through the Board of Ordnance or the Board of Admiralty, officers
received their commissions free. Before the Indian Mutiny, which led
to the abolition of its armies, The Honorable East India Company's
armies were also officered by 'non purchase' nominees of the Court
of Governors of the Company. Officers of the Gunners and the Sappers were nominated by the Master General of the Ordnance whilst
Marine officers were nominated directly by the Admiralty. The technical nature of their work and the need for training, linked to a rigorous system of selection, meant that it would be inappropriate to make
entrants to the Artillery and Engineers pay for their commissions. For
the Marines, once the original regiments raised as soldiers were taken
over and paid for by the Admiralty, the same conditions applied to
them as to Naval officers, in other words they were 'non purchase'. In
the case of the East India Company it was probably a matter of making
the service as attractive as possible rather than having something to
sell. Unlike the majority of officers in the rest of the Army, officers in
these four corps were not only not required to purchase their first
commissions but were not required to pay for each step up the promotion ladder like their unfortunate colleagues in the cavalry and
infantry regiments.[1]

The Royal Artillery and the Royal Engineers were the two corps
regarded as the arch-villains in the controversy over purchase. Officers who had purchased were afraid that the reformers would have

the system abolished without compensation and, given the vastly inflated prices of commissions, they would have been considerably out of pocket. At the same time, because of the high prices paid for commissions in the purchasing regiments, the officers obtaining free commissions in the Gunners and Sappers were considered to be socially inferior. This point was rarely if ever made against Marine officers, no doubt because of their close association with the prestigious 'Senior Service'. However, such are the vagaries of human nature that Admiral Jacky Fisher, when First Sea Lord, was convinced that the Marine officers of his day looked down on Naval officers as their social inferiors and devised training schemes to eradicate this supposed snobbery.

The Royal Regiment of Artillery, like the Corps of Royal Engineers was quite separate from the rest of the Army under the Board of Ordnance until the Board was abolished in 1855. Both corps then came directly under the War Office and the Commander-in-Chief. The two corps share a great deal of military history and this is exemplified by their shared mottos, 'Ubique' (Everywhere) and 'Quo Fas et Gloria Ducunt' (Whither Right and Glory Lead). Neither corps carries Colours and they therefore display no battle honours although both have served with distinction in practically every campaign fought by the British Army. Known as the 'Scientific Corps', their cadets received their early training together at the Royal Military Academy, Woolwich, 'the Shop'. The Shop, as it was affectionately known, had been founded at Woolwich in the grounds of the Royal Arsenal in 1741, expressly to prepare young men for commissions in the artillery and engineers and throughout its almost exactly two hundred years of existence, it was always commanded by an officer from one or other of those two corps. As is so often the case with military institutions, it fell victim in the 1930s to mistaken views about economy. Rather than embark on a long overdue rebuild and extension at Woolwich plans were produced to combine the Royal Military Academy with the Royal Military College at Sandhurst. These plans were 'fought off' until 1939 when, at the start of the Second World War, the Shop was finally closed. After the war, cadets for the 'scientific corps' joined cadets for the other corps at Sandhurst.

Although there was probably little formal teaching at Woolwich in the early days, it is known that money was allocated for mathematical instruction for gunners and engineers and for the teaching and practices of ordnance. Initially, there was no age limit and cadets as young as twelve or as old as thirty were frequently admitted. Instruction could go on for five years or even longer. During the 1760s, the Academy began to improve its standards under the influence of the Marquis of Granby, who reorganised the classes and raised the entrance requirements. By this time, the Academy had 100 cadets on its roll, living in very overcrowded accommodation. Like cadets everywhere, their behaviour left much to be desired and the townsfolk of Woolwich suffered much from their hooliganism. Some of this was fortunately confined to Woolwich Common, especially during the holding of the Royal Artillery Races, which took place on the Common until the 1860s when the meeting was moved to Eltham and the cadets were forbidden to attend. General Gordon, a famous sapper 'old boy' of the Academy, and one whose subsequent career would not have led one to believe in his youthful indiscretions, whilst at the Academy in 1848, was banned from Woolwich Common for his persistent pranks and, on one occasion, was rusticated for a whole term.

Both Gunners and Sappers had and still have a strong local connection with Woolwich. Indeed Graham's *History of the Royal Regiment of Artillery*,[2] says that the first two companies of artillery were formed at Woolwich in 1716 and were housed in the 'Warren' site which also accommodated the Arsenal and later the Academy. Today, the Headquarters and Depot of the Royal Artillery occupy a very grand site, still in Woolwich, looking across the Common. The Sappers had meanwhile made Chatham their home with the opening of the 'Royal Engineer Establishment' in 1812 to consolidate the lessons learned by them in the Peninsular War. The third of the British based 'aberrant corps', the Royal Marines, were also early members of the Woolwich Garrison. Founded in 1664 as infantry regiments raised especially to serve at sea with the fleet, the Marines then moved to Chatham in 1775. In that year a permanent force, with the title 'The Marine Corps', was established and distributed in three 'Grand Divisions' between Chatham, Portsmouth and Plymouth which were the main fleet bases and the sites of the Royal Dockyards. Marines, Sappers and Gunners have been involved in actions together all round the globe. Like the other two corps, the Marines list no battle honours and their motto, like the 'Ubique' of the Sappers and Gunners, *'Per Mare Per Terram'* (By Sea and Land) reflects their worldwide theatre of operations. Their badge, selected by King George IV in 1827, repeats the theme with a globe encircled with laurel.

The Innovators from the Scientific Corps

Today the Sappers and Gunners are seen chiefly in close support of formations in the field but historically they have had an even more important role. In the days of fortresses and fortified towns, the Gunners specialised in defending the fortifications built by the Engineers who, in their turn, aided the Gunners in reducing the fortifications of the enemy by their sapping and mining activities. An epic struggle which illustrates this interdependence was the Great Siege of Gibraltar. The four year siege, which was already the fourteenth recorded attempt on the Rock, lasted from 1779 until February 1783. The Rock had been captured from the Spanish by a force of British and Dutch Marines in 1704 during the War of the Spanish Succession. Possession was taken of the Rock in the name of Charles III, who was the contender for the Spanish throne, supported by Britain, Holland and Austria. Although Charles III was not successful in his ambitions, Britain hung on to the Rock and, as we have seen earlier, gained a much disputed title through the Treaty of Utrecht in 1713. The Spanish attempted to regain the Rock through a siege in 1726 but this was unsuccessful and Britain's possession was confirmed by the Treaty of Seville in 1729. Gibraltar experienced peace for the next fifty years, despite war with France in 1756 in which Minorca was lost. The loss of Minorca resulted in the death of Admiral Byng, who was executed by a firing squad after a Court Martial for cowardice. This infamous incident and its fatal outcome owed much to the obtuseness of George II. Byng was found not guilty of cowardice but guilty of a lesser charge which also carried the death penalty. The King refused an appeal after the verdict, which gave rise to Voltaire's much quoted aphorism, 'In that country they shoot an admiral from time to time to encourage the others.'

During the Great Siege, both of the outstanding military personalities on the Rock had been students at Woolwich. Colonel Green, Chief Engineer on the Rock and later a General, was a trained gunner as well as an engineer. He had been wounded at the taking of Quebec and was posted to Gibraltar in 1761. He found the defences of the fortress in a very run down state and had to go personally to England to persuade the Government to pay for his plans for improvement. By 1772, he had replaced the civilian artificers on contract from Britain and the continent with a military company of soldier artificers. He described the civilian artificers as 'indolent, drunken, disorderly and overpaid'. They were also free to leave the Rock whenever they wished, regardless of local need or peril. The new company of artificers, forerunners of the Royal Engineers, who only included officers at that time, were drawn from volunteers from the regiments in garrison, of whom sixty-eight were selected. Sergeant Ince, an immortal figure in Gibraltar, was the senior 'Other Rank' and he and his company quickly made an impact on the sapping, mining and construction problems of the Fortress.

In 1777, a new commander was appointed to Gibraltar, just in time to lend his indomitable spirit to the defence of the Rock. General George Elliott was educated at Edinburgh and Leyden Universities and spoke several languages. He was trained as a field engineer, receiving his first military education at the Royal Military Academy, Woolwich. He was wounded at both Dettingen and Fontenoy and retired in 1776. However, he was offered the Governorship of Gibraltar in the following year. Born in 1717, he qualified as an engineer in 1737 and as an artilleryman in 1739, in which year he was gazetted a cornet in the Horse Grenadier Guards. He raised the 15th Light Dragoons in 1759 and served with them for two years after which he went off with Albermarle's expedition against the Spanish in Havana. By the time Elliott came to Gibraltar, he was a most experienced officer and this, added to his enlightened attitude and qualities of leadership, made him absolutely the right man in the right place at the right time. His personal qualities were perhaps the most important single factor contributing to the British victory in the Great Siege. The advice of Colonel Green, his Chief Engineer, together with his own knowledge of artillery matters, initiative and energy, was of inestimable value to General Elliott.

Green and his wife Miriam were typical of the many military families in Gibraltar during the siege who, through their courage and high spirits, sustained the lives and hopes of the inhabitants. Miriam Green kept a journal during the siege a printed copy of which, under the title *A Lady's Experience in the Great Siege of Gibraltar (1779–1783)* is kept in the Gibraltar Garrison Library.[3]

Many famous regiments took part in the defence of 'Rock'. The Suffolk Regiment and Hardenberg's Regiments of Hanoverians, who had fought side by side in the historic fire fight at Minden, took part together in the overwhelming sortie of the 27th November 1782, when half the garrison attacked the Spanish batteries to the North of the Rock. The sortie, during which General Elliott, who was meant to be an observer of the attack but appeared leading on the front ranks, caused great damage in the Spanish lines and effectively prevented any significant intervention from the landward side during the last great Spanish attack. However, the main battle for Gibraltar took place between the opposing gunners, and even the last attack, which was by sea, was a battle between the floating batteries of the Spanish, towed in against the western side of the Rock and the British batteries placed there to prevent a landing.

Between them, the Commander and the Chief Engineer planned and constructed a series of batteries one above the other at the North end of the fortress making a successful attack from that side almost impossible. The eastern side, because of its steepness and lack of beaches for a landing, was rightly considered impregnable. The British felt so secure that, after waiting for three months for the Spanish to start the land attack, they decided to force the issue. The first cannon shot was fired into the Spanish lines by the wife of a member of the garrison on the signal 'Britons strike home'.[5] The batteries, positioned up the flank of the Rock were extended and strengthened throughout the siege and quite early in the siege a gun was hauled up to crown its highest peak at 1,300 feet. This became known as Rock Gun and is still a well recognised landmark. Eventually, the North Front was covered with batteries and most of the enemy siege works could be enfiladed from the British positions.

Sergeant Major Ince, as he had now become, solved the last problem of military engineering during the siege by suggesting that galleries could be carved out of the rock from which fire could be directed on to the only remaining section of the Spanish lines which was not enfiladed by British batteries. By September 1782, five guns were positioned high in the Rock and by the end of the seige the gallery was pushed to the 'notch', a prominent landmark on the North face. A battery was established there and it was distinguished by the name of St. George's Hall. The hall is so grand and lofty that for a time it was customary for visiting dignitaries to be given a banquet there. In Gibraltar there is a photograph of Theodore Roosevelt being dined in this great chamber of the Rock, which overlooks the whole of the landward approaches. Today, St. George's Hall is a tourist attraction containing a tableau showing guns and gunners of the siege period and a model of Sergeant Major Ince looking out from his master-piece.[6]

Gibraltar presented two problems to the Gunners, apart from having to haul very heavy guns up the side of the Rock, something they would have done elsewhere, in any case. Explosive shells were in use by 1779 but it was found that when they were fired at targets on the sandy isthmus they buried themselves before exploding and did very little damage. An infantry officer, Captain Mercier, a member of the garrison, suggested the use of a short fuse to produce an air burst, and this proved to be very effective. It so happened that a Lieutenant Shrapnel was also serving there during the siege and it is quite likely that his 'shrapnel' was based on Mercier's short-fused shell. The second problem was caused by the difficulty of firing the guns at a steep angle down into the enemy positions. Lieutenant Koehler, the Governor's aide-de-camp, invented new carriages which enabled the guns to be trained at extreme angles of depression and which were later used widely elsewhere. An interesting reconstruction of Koehler's gun carriage is mounted in Casemates Square and is a great attraction to visitors. Before leaving Gibraltar and this brief glimpse of two of the 'aberrant corps' in action, it is worth mentioning that the Fortress of Gibraltar remains, at least for the time being, an encapsul-ation of British military archaeology of the eighteenth and nineteenth centuries. Together with the collection of historical documents in the

Garrison Library, the tunnels, emplacements and general fortifications represent a unique illustration of one aspect of our military past which should be seen before it is swamped by the inevitable Mediterranean development.

The Gunners and Sappers, because they were officered by men who had received a scientific training and because they habitually had to solve the many problems connected with sieges, both as defender and attacker, tended to be great innovators, and the popularisers of military novelties many of which came to be an accepted part of army equipment or of army life. The Royal Engineers spawned a whole series of military activities with a scientific basis which, in some cases led to the formation of a whole new Corps to ensure their proper development and utilisation. We shall see in a later chapter how Colonel Capper from the Royal Engineers Balloon School at Aldershot encouraged William Cody in his early aeronautical experiments on Laffan's Plain and could be said to have inaugurated Army Aviation. Laffan himself was a Royal Engineer officer who was given the task of drawing up the plans for the first permanent barracks at Aldershot. He was later Chief Royal Engineer, Member of Parliament for St Ives in Cornwall and finally Governor and Commander-in-Chief of Bermuda, where he died in 1892. We shall see also that Capper went on to become closely connected with the early history of tank warfare and became the first Colonel Commandant of the Tank Corps. No doubt many other Royal Engineer officers were associated with the tanks and took part in the first great tank attacks in the First World War. The Royal Sappers and Miners, who were to be incorporated into the Royal Engineers at the conclusion of the Crimean War, laid the first field telegraph ever to be used on active service. The line covered twenty-five miles and had eight signals stations. By 1914, after further expansion during the Boer War, there were thirty-one regular and territorial signal units which were to expand to 531 units by the end of the Great War. In June 1920 a separate Royal Corps of Signals was formed which, in an earlier century, would itself have been an aberrant corps. General Sir Garnet Wolseley, who was a great encourager of innovation, made use of the telegraph to signal his victory from Tel-el-Kebir and later, during the Gordon relief expedition, to signal the news of his failure to save Gordon. Wolseley also took a keen interest in railway transportation and, after some trying experiences with Egyptian organised railways, was instrumental in the formation of Royal Engineer railway units. The Royal Engineers were also involved in the development and introduction of searchlights; survey work, which dates from 1746 following the Battle of Culloden, when a full survey of Scotland was undertaken for military purposes, and Postal and Courier Services.

Engineer officers were also responsible for the design and construction of several well-known public buildings, including the Royal Albert Hall.

It is interesting to note that the Royal Engineers has the highest ratio of Lieutenant Colonels to major field units of any Corps or Regiment in the British army. Appendix II shows that the Sappers had a ratio of one major unit for every 8.25 Lieutenant Colonels in 1986 whilst the Guards only mustered seven Lieutenant Colonels per battalion and the infantry, including the Guards, could only find four per battalion. The Gunners and the Royal Armoured Corps (RAC), whilst they do less well in this calculation than the Sappers or Guards or the Army Air Corps, with the RAC at 5.5 Lieutenant Colonels per regiment and the Gunners at 6.3 certainly come out better than the infantry. However, by the time one arrives at the rank of Major General, and it is necessary to say that at this level and above the figures change abruptly from year to year, the Sappers in 1986 could only count four, all at Major General level, as against ten for the RAC, thirteen for the RA and thirty-five for the infantry of whom the Guards could count five, all of them Major Generals.[7]

The New Corps After the First World War

By the end of the First World War it was obvious that it was not only the signallers who required a corps of their own if they were to develop satisfactorily. The tanks needed their own environment and became first a 'Tank Corps' and then an 'Armoured Corps' in which the tank regiments joined the regiments of mechanised and armoured cavalry. As we shall see, the early enthusiasts of the first Tank Corps bungled their opportunity to influence decisively the development of armoured tactics in Britain but an Armoured Corps was formed and still remains. Another Corps that was formed in the First World War was the Royal Flying Corps but it separated from the Army after the war to become the Royal Air Force leaving the Army with the painful and expensive and still not completed task of building its own Army Air Corps. Despite the Army's early involvement with Army Co-operation Squadrons of the Royal Air Force, the establishment of Air Observation Post Flights manned by the Royal Artillery and the emergence of the Glider Pilot Regiment during the Second World War, it was not until September 1957 that the Army Air Corps, as we now know it, was officially established. In the Second World War other needs emerged of a specialist and technical nature which required a different organisational framework from that of the traditional regiment or one of the older Corps in order to carry out the new tasks efficiently. The Royal Electrical and Mechanical Engineers were formed in 1942 to cope with what was seen as a failure to recover and repair weapons and fighting vehicles damaged in action as expeditiously as possible. Tasks and personnel were taken over from the Royal Ordnance and Royal Army Service Corps and from the Royal Engineers and concentrated in the new Corps where they could operate under a Directorate with unity and purpose. In 1965 the Royal Army Service Corps, which had existed in nearly the same form since before the Boer War, was disbanded and its transport duties were taken over by a new Royal Corps of Transport. The new Corps picked up relevant responsibilities from the Royal Engineers for the control of all army movements. The old Service Corps' duties to provide rations, fuel, barrack services and an Army Fire Service were taken over by the Royal Army Ordnance Corps. Rationalisation had become very important by the 1960s but the need for specialisation had become even more important. From the beginning, with the original 'aberrants', specialisation has implied the special selection and training of personnel, special traditions of service and a separate 'modus operandi' which has often been at odds with the long-standing traditions of the infantry and cavalry regiments.

This separateness of method and outlook, occasioned sometimes by a difference of background and education, which tended towards the technical and scientific rather than the classical, does not necessarily mean that all the valuable and well-tried components of the regimental system had to be abandoned by either the old or the new Corps. Indeed, as we have seen in some of the Corps which can trace their ancestry back as far if not further than most of the regiments, their ésprit, morale, gallantry and loyalty cannot be faulted by any standards. However, they have generally managed to avoid a narrow, self-regarding parochialism. Attachment to a particular locality, which did not become very important to the Army until the latter half of the nineteenth century, has never been important to the Corps. The genuine tribalism of the Celtic areas of the British Isles had to be placated when their fighting men were incorporated into the national army but it becomes an odd explanation of the separatism and exclusiveness of say one of the three regiments of Royal Anglians or of the Greenjackets or of a Lancer Regiment. The Corps manage to operate within a larger framework than the conventional regiment, and seemingly they do it without sacrificing any essential soldierly qualities. When regiments appeal against amalgamation into a larger entity, as they have increasingly had to do over the last hundred years, they pray in aid their longevity, their record in battle, their family and local connections and finally the colour of their uniforms and the shape of their cap badges. As we shall see, even very senior generals are concerned about the survival of their old cap badges. With forty-one generals out of seventy-seven in the 1986 Army List coming originally from an infantry or cavalry regiment, those regiments have powerful although sometimes embarrassed allies in high places. However, it is clear that the latest round of amalgamations into 'big regiments' and even larger and more disparate divisions will necessitate the emergence of new loyalties, customs and traditions. To convince oneself that this can be done successfully, it is only necessary to examine the Parachute Regiment, which is arguably the best fighting force in the British Army today.

The Regiment was formed less than fifty years ago with volunteer members, and only became a corps in its own right for soldiers in 1953 and for officers in 1958. Before these dates, soldiers and officers were seconded from their parent regiments on a more or less temporary basis. The Regiment already has impeccable battle honours, an interesting history, its own list of VC heroes, a nickname, a motto *'Utrinque Paratus'* (Ready for Anything) and a Regimental March composed by Wagner. Its performance in the Falklands Campaign, where its members were awarded two Victoria Crosses, is sufficient guarantee of its quality. Nevertheless, there is something vaguely uneasy about the relationship of the rest of the Army to the Parachute Regiment which probably stems from the Second World War suspicion of 'Special Forces' rather than from any doubts in the regiments about their own ability to measure up to the high fighting standards set by the Parachute Regiment. An important point about the Parachute Regiment, however, is that, as with the Gunners and Sappers, the Regiment is almost infinitely expandable and is not localised, except that regimental depots tend to attract a disproportionate number of recruits from their immediate locality. In 1986, the Regiment was composed of three battalions but it could double in size at short notice. The only problem then might be that (as with the Falklands, where it was necessary to hire suitable sea transport for the invasion force), a plan calling for a full scale parachute landing might reveal that no suitable aircraft were available. The *Canberra*, whilst not ideal, functioned reasonably well as a troopship in the circumstances of the Falklands but suitable aircraft for parachutists are few and getting fewer. The advent of the helicopter can be seen as limiting the requirement for parachute troops but it is unlikely that they can be eliminated entirely from the order of battle. The training of paratroops, in itself, seems to produce the high morale, fitness and determination to close with the enemy which is essential in shock troops and whilst this should remain an ideal standard for the rest of the Army, it is nevertheless essential to retain the model. Parachuting is only one of the special skills practised by the Special Air Service, formed like many other 'Special Forces' units in North Africa during the Second World War.

During that war, the SAS expanded into a brigade which, by 1944, included French and Belgian regiments. Along with many other 'unorthodox' units it was disbanded in 1945. It was not until the Emergency in Malaya was at its height that the deep penetration role of the SAS was revived to contribute to the ultimately successful fight against the communist guerilla bands from deep within the jungle. The increasingly serious threat of terrorism, including hijacking and hostage taking, has secured a more permanent role for the SAS which became a Corps in its own right in the early seventies and now includes territorial units as well as its regular regiment. It now seems possible that its increasingly specialised role may lead to its being removed completely from the Army Order of Battle and its transfer to direct Home Office or Cabinet Office control.

The Royal Marines and Commando Forces

The 'Aberrant Corps' which has probably caused the most controversy in its more than three hundred years of history, and still continues to be a subject of contention, is the Corps of Royal Marines. Reckoning their history from the raising in 1664 of The Duke of York and Albany's Maritime Regiment of Foot, they have, like every other British regiment, been subject to disbandment, amalgamation and expansion as wars commenced, waxed and waned. By the middle of the eighteenth century, it was clear that a permanent body of soldiers was necessary in the Fleet to take part in its typical close quarter actions and to be available for the land operations which our dominant naval position and aggressive forward maritime policy dictated. Until the 'Marine Corps' was established in 1775, the Fleet was manned, whenever there was a manpower crisis, by sailors who in the main had been seized by the press gangs, and supplemented and overawed by embarked regiments of the Regular Army. The special Maritime Regiments were never sufficient to guarantee a full complement for the Fleet. The increasingly severe demands on the Army during the eighteenth century meant that fewer and fewer soldiers could be spared to serve afloat. It would be consistent to think also that duties afloat and the requirement to be ready to take part in opposed landings, carrying with them heavy naval ordnance and other heavy equipment would call for a specialist corps especially trained for this exacting role, but there is little evidence of this kind of thinking in the early days of the Royal Marines.

Another important duty of the Royal Marines, and some say the most important duty right up to the twentieth century,[8] was to stand between the Naval Officers and their men who, in addition to pressed men, would include a high proportion of men released from prison sentences to serve at sea. In Admiral Bacon's Life of Lord Fisher he says that the chief function of the modern Marine Force established in 1775 was to keep mutiny in check. The Marines, he says, were 'sworn men' whereas the seamen swore no allegiance to anyone. Writing in 1929, he goes on to point out that 'to this day, the custom is maintained of having the rifles and other arms of the seamen kept near the officers' quarters, and of placing the living quarters of the marines between the officers and the remainder of the ship's company'. Early in the nineteenth century, artillery companies, which later became the Royal Marine Artillery (RMA), were formed and in 1855 the remainder of the Corps was designated Light Infantry (RMLI). For a time the Royal Marines began to assume a completely self-sufficient role in which they could operate like a detached army corps without the need of further support. By 1923, however, the usual post-war economies, helped inevitably by inter-service rivalries, led to the RMLI and the RMA being amalgamated under their old title, the Royal Marines. During the First World War, the majority of marines served afloat with the Fleet and took part in all the important naval actions of that war. In addition, they were involved in several land actions and in the famous raid on Zeebrugge, which was planned to block the way out to the sea of the German U-Boats from their submarine shelters at Bruges. The raid on Zeebrugge provided a blueprint for the equally famous raid on St. Nazaire in the Second World War which aimed to deny the dry dock facilities of the port to the German battleship *Tirpitz*. This time, however, the raid was carried out by No. 2 Army Commando under Lieutenant Colonel Charles Newman. During the Second World War the Army Commandos shared the sea raiding role with the Royal Marines and, for a while, might have taken over the Marines' role entirely. However, for a number of reasons, this was not to be.

The first Royal Marine Commando units were formed in 1942. Eventually there were two Brigades of Marine Commandos to match the two Brigades of Army Commandos. There were also several other marine units in the Special Forces organisation, paralleling army units of a similar nature. A not altogether healthy rivalry developed between the Marine and Army Special Forces units and it would not have been altogether surprising if the army had absorbed the Royal Marines, at least in their commando role. However, the Marines had expanded to a force of over 120,000 men during the war. That force included the equivalent of an infantry division which fought in Holland and Germany in the closing months of the war, two complete Naval Base Defence Organisations, six commandos and many small specialised Marine units. By the end of the war, the Marines had developed a power base, to some extent independent of their paymasters the Royal Navy, in the Combined Operations Executive. As we have said,[9] after the war, the Army and the regiments in particular, wanted to have no more to do with Special forces. Understandably they wanted to recover their best officers and NCOs for the difficult reorganisation which was bound to follow the ending of the war. The Marines managed to hang on to their commando role with the help of their friends and colleagues in Combined Operations and ended up as the sole proprietors of the commando forces. Many regular Marine officers had spent most of their war serving with the capital ships of the Fleet, whilst many of the officers with the Royal Marine Commandos, especially the more junior ones, were commissioned for 'Hostilities Only'. Towards the end of the war however, battle casualties in the marine commando units, which had been replaced since September 1944 with Army Commando Officer reinforcements, were replaced once more by Royal Marine Officers. The reserve of commando trained Marine Officers held at the Commando Depot was smaller than the reserve of Army Commando Officers. Nevertheless, from the Autumn of 1944, officers were taken from sea duties to keep up the number of Marine Officers in the commando units. So, by the end of the war, the Royal Marine Commandos were officered by a reasonably high proportion of regular Marine Officers. If this policy seems Machiavellian, it probably only demonstrates some forethought and forward planning for the ultimate resumption of a role which had always been exclusively that of the Royal Marines and which it seemed that in 1944 nobody else wanted. The fact remains, however, that if Army commandos had been retained, it is possible, in one of those cost cutting exercises where commandos might be surrendered for frigates, that the Marines might have found themselves as part of an unsympathetic Army and have gone the way of all amalgamations. A similar fate has overcome the French Marines, who are now counted along with the residual parachute units of the French Foreign Legion and the French Parachute Corps proper, as equal components of the *Force d'Intervention*.

An infantry force, paid for by the Royal Navy is increasingly vulnerable to rationalising pressures and economising Chancellors but, despite the disparaging comments of a recent Minister of Defence[10] the Marines have strengthened their position. The Commando Brigade is the centre piece of reinforcement plans for the Northern Flank of NATO and is the only British force trained in mountain and snow and ice warfare, which is an essential specialisation for this region. The Marines were also able to demonstrate in the Falklands Campaign how their equipment, organisation and training prepares them uniquely to maintain, even on a reduced scale, a worldwide intervention capability. The parachute troops have also demonstrated their ability to operate effectively in a global context but they rarely operate now as a Brigade Group and it would perhaps be fair to say that they tend to rely on élan, a very high morale and a certain reputation, rather than on a trained specialisation other than the very demanding one of parachuting itself.

We have said that none of the Corps has relied strictly on the regimental system either in organisation, numbers or mystique.[11] The Gunners and the Sappers have been organised in large administrative structures which have provided a central focus for loyalty, a repository for history and heroic legends and most important, the facilities for the specialised training which is the very *raison d'être* of their separate existence. Both Corps have managed without difficulty to instil and maintain a loyalty which does not suffer by comparison with that of the regiments. At the same time they operate 'in the field' in a wide variety of working groups from the gun crew or the forward observation team of the sapper section up to the field regiments, into which both Corps are organised. This organisation into field regiments has great historical significance for both Corps, and although, as we have said, the tactical unit may be quite remote from the Regiment in its size and method of operation, to gain command of a Regiment is still considered to be the acme of every Gunner and Sapper officer's ambition along with that of his colleagues in the infantry and armoured corps. In reality the 'Regiment' may be an administrative convenience in that it allows Gunner and Sapper units to operate effectively in the divisional and army corps context. There is an additional purpose, of course, where the regimental commander has an advisory role at the formation headquarters.

The Royal Marines, on the other hand, from the time in 1775 when the original 5,000 officers and men of the 'Marine Corps' were distributed between Chatham, Portsmouth and Plymouth in three 'Grand Divisions', have served in small detachments in the larger ships of the Fleet and, whilst embarked, have owed loyalty only to their ship. The Marines have never been subjected to a 'regimental' discipline and even the Commandos were structured on quite different lines. During the Second World War and for a few years afterwards, a 'Commando', whilst it was commanded by a Lieutenant Colonel, was about half the strength of an army battalion. Instead of companies it was composed of five fighting troops of sixty-five men and a support troop of about forty. It never numbered more than about four hundred all ranks. After the war, the disadvantage of counting on only half the number of bayonets found in a normal infantry battalion was recognised in what had become 'defence minded' services and the complement was made up to battalion strength. From then on, a Commando in the normal infantry role could take over the frontage and tasks of a battalion. This, of course, led to a dilution of the ratio of officers and NCOs to men, a high ratio of leaders being one of the original 'commando' ideas.

From the beginning, the strength of the Royal Marines rarely exceeded the original 5,000 of the Corps of 1775. Before the Second World War it numbered only about 7,000 men. During the war it did expand to a remarkable 120,000 but, as we have said, this included an infantry division, two brigades of commandos, several other major marine units and the manning of the vast fleet of minor landing craft that the peculiar circumstances of the war demanded. Unlike the United States Marine Corps, the British Marines, partly because of their dependence upon the Royal Navy for funding, have had a comparatively limited role. By contrast, the United States Marines are an independent service which, until recently, bore major responsibility for all external military interventions of the United States. The United States Army, until the Spanish American War in the early twentieth century, was a very small force whose main responsibility was in policing the Western frontier area of the United States, supported by a strong National Guard which was a volunteer force controlled by the individual States of the Union. Because of its major external role, the United States Marine Corps has developed as a separate force able to compete with the Army for funds and equipment and for national prestige where it has been particularly successful. The United States Marines stand in roughly the same position in America's national mythology as the Brigade of Guards do in ours. They have their own artillery, armour, engineers and logistic support. More important, they have their own air force. During the last war, the Royal Marines began to develop their own integral services but, with a post war reduction from 120,000 to a 1986 strength of 6,900 all ranks, it has been impossible to build up supporting arms and services from marine personnel. The Commando Brigade does include a Logistics Regiment Royal Marines and a Commando Artillery Regiment and an Independent Commando Engineer Squadron but both of the latter, whilst they are commando trained and permanently dedicated to the Commando Brigade are army units. In the Falklands, the Brigade was initially strengthened by the attachment of a parachute battalion, a Rapier anti-aircraft missile battery and other small supporting units. The Navy provided medical services, close support from naval guns and missiles and the crucially important air support from its carriers. However, by the end of the Falklands fighting, there were considerably more soldiers than Marines ashore.

Aberration—A Pattern For The Future?

The future of the 'Aberrant Corps' can be studied very profitably in the light of the Falklands Campaign. It must first be noted that only so-called élite troops were employed by the British in the land fighting. The land battle was almost, and could entirely, have been won by the 'new élites', the Royal Marine Commandos and two battalions of the Parachute Regiment. Members of the 'old élites', two battalions of the Guards and a battalion of Gurkhas took part in the final battle and advance on Port Stanley. Not a single line regiment took part in the campaign, although two troops of The Blues and Royals (RHG/D) played a part, but they would almost certainly call themselves élite troops on at least two counts.[12] There seems to have been some concern on the part of the 'Special Forces' involved in the early fighting over the time taken to settle in by the later arrivals and, in the case of the Gurkhas, by an unexpected lack of acclimatisation. 'D-Day' men are always a little disparaging of units which arrive even a few days after the stirring events of a landing but the newspaper reports and the hasty correspondents' 'books of the war', and even some of the books written at their leisure by military participants, appear to be a little uneasy at what could be seen as a degree of misunderstanding and some lack of co-operation between new and old élites.

The lack of sympathy, sometimes amounting to outright hostility between the representatives of the media and the representatives of the forces in the Falklands should surprise no one. Since the time of the Crimea, journalists and, more recently, radio and television commentators, as we have said elsewhere, have found it difficult to settle quickly into a comfortable relationship with the officers who must inevitably control access to information. In the Falklands the problem was further complicated by the distances involved and by the bottleneck in communications facilities between the South Atlantic and London. What is clear is that at the personal level, in the fighting units there were very few problems. Those that did arise could be sorted out, sometimes by a few sharp words but, as far as it is possible to see from the dispatches and memoirs, without lasting resentment. Nick Vaux, commander of 42 Commando, in his book on the campaign,[13] referring to the BBC World Service Broadcast of the formal surrender of the Argentine forces, says, 'for once the BBC had been neither premature nor indiscreet'. This does sound a little bitter but Vaux's own book contains a rather fulsome foreword by Max Hastings who was the doyen of the correspondents in the Falklands. The foreword also gives at least one instance of close co-operation and understanding between the media men and the military. Nick Vaux was asked by Kim Sabido of Independent Radio News if he might accompany 'L' Company of 42 Commando in its assault on Mount Harriet. Hastings reports Vaux as saying: 'Well Kim, if you're sure you want to, go ahead'. Sabido apparently went further forward than any other correspondent and in Hastings' words 'got the marvellous radio despatch that he deserved'. It would be nice to think that the brave and the good always got the help and assistance they needed whilst the others were not so fortunate but sadly, life is seldom like that.

Robert Fox in his book '*Eyewitness Falklands*', which was hurried out towards the end of 1982, appears to have got on quite well with his host units and makes some interesting points in his conclusions.[14] In the immediacy of his comments, whilst not saying anything wildly different from Hastings' more considered report, Fox does strongly stress the vulnerability of the surface fleet and casts considerable doubts on the possibility of any future 'blue water' role for the Royal Navy. Defence Minister John Nott had also come down against a worldwide role for the Navy and Marines in his projected defence cuts in the year before the Falklands Campaign. Nott repeated his comments in his two articles in *The Times* quite recently[15] but, even in such exalted company, if Fox had made such remarks whilst in the Falklands it is not surprising that he found the Navy to be 'anti-press'. More interestingly, he says that the Marines and Paratroops, after the campaign, were arguing openly for the setting up of a permanent Special Forces Division. They understandably deplored the run-down of amphibious warfare training and capability and believed that a specialist division would ensure the availability of ultra-rapid intervention forces. All this is very much as one would expect and smacks a little of being wise after the event. Fox seems to find it surprising that Special Forces are 'unpredictable' and that they have an ability to get what they want. This really should not cause surprise since private armies and mini military élites have always attracted strong and plausible, not to say eccentric personalities, with friends who have influence, and ideas for their employment. Fox says that the late H Jones, the hero of the attack on Goose Green, persuaded someone at the last moment to allow '2 Para' to join the task force. If this sounds a little too much like Evelyn Waugh, one has only to remember that Waugh served in the Royal Marines and at Combined Operations Headquarters and he certainly saw quite a lot of the to-ing and fro-ing that goes on.

This chapter started as an account of the 'Aberrant Corps' and an explanation of the differences between them and the traditionally organised regiments. In the Falklands, several centuries later, the 'Corps' almost inextricably mixed together, fought a successful and efficient campaign against the Argentine forces. Even what we have called the 'old élites', The Guards and the Gurkhas, could not be called 'traditional' regiments in the normal sense of the word, since both illustrious brigades have always consisted of several regiments or battalions owing allegiance to a larger organisation. The five Guards battalions are now incorporated into the Guards Division. The four remaining Gurkha Regiments transferred to the British Army when India gained her independence in 1947, together with Gurkha Engineer, Signals and Transport Regiments, constitute the Brigade of Gurkhas.

The 'regimental system' can obviously mean all things to all men and the former Chief of the General Staff's description of it as the 'bedrock of the Army but with traditions that had to be adjusted', expresses this pragmatic approach.[16] With the coming of the Administrative Divisions the advocates of change could be said to be pushing at an unlocked door. What is now necessary is to identify what has been essential in the past; good discipline, a high spirit and outstanding leadership and to ensure that these virtues are translated into the military organisation of the future.

The final three chapters of this book carry the narrative forward in time from the Boer War, through the two World Wars to the war which we have just glimpsed in the Falklands. The Falklands War, with its overtones of the nineteenth century punitive expeditions, has already been called the last of the Colonial Wars, and it was mainly for these that the British Army was designed and trained, however it may have been used in the event. History, nevertheless, warns us to expect and be prepared for the unexpected as well as the unthinkable. It is difficult, therefore, to accept the suggestion that a British Army of the near future can confine itself to a 'home defence and European Alliance' role alone. The Empire may have gone and the power to intervene worldwide has certainly become less as Britain has become economically weaker but a force that could intervene outside Europe, even in a comparatively restricted degree could combine the role with others that are becoming more pressing and more conspicuously in demand. Meanwhile, along with its other virtues, self-respect is as important to a nation as its balance of trade and even if they go together, the ability to defend ones legitimate interests must be an essential part of that self-respect.

8

Action, Reaction and Intervention

The Boer War came as a sad blow to many British ambitions and aspirations. The outcome of the war was never in doubt, once the expense had been accepted and once public opinion had been mobilised but it did represent a set-back in the rush to imperial expansion which had become headlong before the end of the nineteenth century. It also meant the end of some military reputations and the end of some military methods which had been artificially maintained, and in some cases revived, to meet the continuing demands of a barbaric and outdated colonial form of warfare. The forming of a defensive square and the taking of hostages were typical survivals used in this primitive kind of fighting.

The most outstanding British military reputation to be eclipsed in the Boer war was that of General Sir Redvers Buller. When Buller took over from Evelyn Wood as General Officer Commanding at Aldershot in October 1897, he was probably the most popular soldier in the Army and, indeed, in the country. Like Wood, Buller had been selected and 'brought on' by Wolseley and both had done well in the many minor wars in which they had been involved. Buller's reputation was based on his dashing performance in the Ashanti and Zulu wars but also on his genuine concern for the well-being of his men. Unfortunately, his reputation as a strategist, planner and military thinker, never his greatest qualities, had become unduly inflated over the years. Well aware of his own modest abilities, he was reluctant to take over the command in South Africa in 1899 but he allowed himself to be persuaded. By then he was very much overweight and given to eating and drinking in a manner that might have anticipated the bucolic Devonshire squire that he eventually became. After a series of costly defeats and some equally costly victories, he was superseded in

South Africa by Lord Roberts who was made Commander-in-Chief, with Kitchener as his Chief-of-Staff.

Buller returned to England to take up his appointment again at Aldershot whilst Roberts returned to become Commander-in-Chief of the British Army. Roberts took over from Wolseley whilst Buller, who as Wolseley's protégé had on past performance expected to succeed him, became more and more embittered and, after a series of acrimonious confrontations with the press and a tactless interview with the Secretary for War, was retired on half pay. Like Wood, and indeed like Wolseley himself, Buller was a man of the nineteenth century and had never had to lead an army against a European foe. As with Roberts, South Africa was Buller's first and last chance to lead a British army against a courageous, well-armed white enemy. Buller failed but Roberts had time to adjust and he had Kitchener, in his prime, as his chief assistant. Even so, Britain was taught a lesson that has had to be re-learned elsewhere most recently by the Americans in Vietnam and by the Russians in Afghanistan. The cost of victory, even against a poor and backward country, provided that it has modern weapons, courage and sanctuaries may be very high indeed and, in the end, may not be worth the candle. The British victory over the Boers appeared to be decisive but it left Britain isolated in an unfriendly world and it raised many questions about the leadership, training and general efficiency of the Army. The Army's attempts to reform itself or at least to go along with the reforms put forward by the Liberal Governments of the later decades of the nineteenth century were shown to be insufficient. If the Boers were so difficult to beat, what hope was there against the mass armies of the continental powers?

Haldane in his autobiography,[1] writing of the state of the Army immediately before and just after the South African War, said:

> Not only was there no General staff to do the thinking but the organisation in time of peace was different from that required for war, so different that there was hardly a unit that was capable of taking the field as it stood. After the Report of the Commission that followed on the South African War some things had been done but . . . nothing very illuminating from a military point of view had been brought to light . . . The public was profoundly dissatisfied with the state of our military forces, and a very large section of the Liberals, disgusted alike with the War Office and with war, had pledged itself to proceed to a tremendous reduction of War Office Estimates.

Although there was nothing new in this, it was not surprising that the Army for its part was utterly disillusioned by its political masters and, for the first and perhaps only time, began to consider, in however small, indirect and unconscious a way, actions which might directly affect the intellectual environment within which the Armed Forces operated in Great Britain. For their part, the politicians began to look for friends abroad and, by 1904, the *Entente* with France was an accomplished fact, with all its fateful consequences for a decade later. Whilst the Army was soon involved in the ramifications of the *Entente* across the Channel, its most obvious impact was nearer home.

In almost every sense the *Entente Cordiale* took on the form of a self-fulfilling prophesy. Before the end of the first decade of the twentieth century, most army officers and many civilians in Britain were convinced that war with Germany was inevitable. By 1911, a school history book,[2] after describing the growing trade rivalry in Europe was able to say, 'But I don't think there can be any doubt that the only safe thing for all of us who love our country is to learn soldiering at once, and to be prepared to fight at any moment.' The National Service League had been inaugurated as early as 1901, appropriately at Apsley House under the chairmanship of the Duke of Wellington. We do not know what his distinguished ancestor would have made of a conscript army but amongst senior officers opinion was fairly divided. Many officers were prepared to rely on the volunteer spirit to provide the men when they were required but others, including Lord Roberts, who spoke at the first meeting of the League, believed that only a conscripted army could be trained in time to meet the menace from the continent.

After the National Service League, other movements followed quickly. The 'Duty and Discipline Movement' was formed by Lord Meath. The ' League of Empire' and the 'Empire Day Movement' had their first meetings in 1904 but received no Government support until well into the First World War because of a fear of 'anti-jingoism'. A 'Lad's Drill Association' was formed and a 'Campaign for the Military Training of Schoolboys' was started. In 1905 Lord Roberts resigned his seat on the Committee of Imperial Defence so that he could devote all his time to warning his fellow countrymen against the coming troubles. Not only was he a tireless advocate of compulsory military service but he spent much time talking to the Officers' Training Corps of the Public Schools which, as the war approached, became more and more dedicated to the task of producing a seemingly inexhaustible supply of suitably inspired young officers. Although the Services were not always directly involved in raising the war spirit there was often a military figure, sometimes retired, lurking in the background when the more obvious attempts at sabre rattling were made. Thus when the notorious Northcliffe's *Daily Mail* published in 1906 Le Quex's 'The Invasion of 1910' (yet another version of a fictional and sensational German invasion of a helpless Britain, intended to stir an apathetic public into some awareness of the nature of the growing German threat) in serial form, Lord Roberts and the paper's naval correspondent collaborated in order to lend some authenticity to the lurid tale. Unfortunately, Roberts' carefully planned invasion of England was almost defeated by Northcliffe alone, who insisted that the invading armies should march through every town in the South of England where the *Daily Mail* needed to boost its circulation.[3]

The search for friends and allies, as we have seen, eventually brought together the British and French military staffs in talks, approved of and even set up by their political masters but the consequences of which were deliberately and with their own connivance kept from them. Thus the speed with which mobilisation was made effective and the despatch with which the first divisions of the Expeditionary Force were got across the Channel and into their pre-arranged positions, has something of a nightmare quality. However, the German plan for the invasion of France through Belgium, which could not be halted or reversed because of the pre-planned railway schedules appears with highsight to be even more horrific. Despite the German invasion of Belgium, which was the *casus belli* as far as the British public were concerned, it is likely that the insistence of the British staff that Britain was committed immediately to co-operating with the French, won over the waverers in the Government. The fact that Haldane, who was Lord Chancellor at the time, was able and willing to stand-in for an absent Secretary for War, remembered his War Plans of eight years previously and in modern parlance, 'knew which buttons to press' was probably the decisive factor.[4] According to Haldane the naval position in the crisis was one of pure farce. The dominant influence in British naval matters in the late nineteenth and early twentieth centuries was that of Admiral Sir John Fisher, later Lord Fisher of Kilverstone, Admiral of the Fleet and First Sea Lord from 1904 to 1910. Jacky Fisher's 'Blue Water' policy was opposed to a large British military commitment on the continent, but without plans or a planning staff or as the Chief of the Imperial General Staff (CIGS), Sir William Nicholson, pointed out, without even a German railway timetable, the Navy was in no position to criticise seriously the Anglo-French military plans. Only three years previously, the Admiralty had discovered, dusted off and put forward a plan which Fisher had derived 'by analogy' from the Seven Years War of more than one hundred and fifty years before. The plan was to land detachments of the Expeditionary Force on the Prussian Baltic shores in order to seize a bridgehead which could be exploited by a massive Russian force. A study of the railway timetable, presumably lent by the General Staff, was enough to show the Admiralty that any force we could land would be quickly surrounded by five times the number of enemy troops.[5]

But Admiral Fisher had by far the largest navy in the world behind him and he was well aware of the very small land force that Britain could involve in the early stages of a continental war. Whilst he was every bit as convinced as his military opposite numbers of the inevitability of war against the Germans in the near future, and every bit as much an interventionist, his obsession with a maritime 'Blue Water' strategy as opposed to what he called a 'blue funk' policy, led him to make some extraordinary proposals. At the time of the 'Fashoda Scare', when France attempted to take over an area of Africa which Britain regarded as in her sphere of influence, Fisher proposed and prepared a plan to kidnap the unhappy Major Dreyfus from 'Devil's Island' and release him in the dark of night on the French coast.[6] The crisis blew over and, in any event, it is most unlikely that Fisher's plan would have had any practical effect on the situation—but at least it was bold in conception. His high regard for Nelson, who was as much his hero as was Wellington to his army colleagues after the same gap of a hundred years, prompted an even more audacious plot against the German navy. Convinced, as were many army officers, that Germany would attack as soon as the widening of the Kiel Canal was completed, by when she would be completely armed, he suggested that the German fleet should be attacked by surprise in its base and 'Copenhagened'.[7] When Fisher put this plan to Edward VII in the Spring of 1908, taking advantage of his position as principal ADC to the King, the King commented, 'Fisher, you're mad'. Fisher genuinely believed that the Army should be run as a department of the Royal Navy. Admiral Bacon, Fisher's biographer, was prepared to accept that he probably was mad but mad with the kind of near genius that seems to be an essential component of every great leader.

Two other issues, both of which cast a long shadow forward, engaged Fisher's attention whilst he was the dominant influence at the Admiralty. Leaving aside the whole question of naval re-armament and the advent of the 'Dreadnoughts', with which Fisher was intimately connected but which do not concern us here, he had some interesting ideas about the Royal Marines and naval engineers. We have dealt with Marines and Engineers in a separate chapter but Fisher's views are worth stating. In the early years of the twentieth century he was responsible for reorganising the whole of the training of young naval officers and for the building of the Naval College at Osborne. Believing that Marine officers looked too much towards the Army and tended to look down on their naval colleagues as socially inferior, he suggested that young officer entrants to the Royal Marines should follow the naval syllabus of training as naval cadets until their early twenties and only then specialise in the soldier's role. Fisher saw the élite corps of young Marine officers largely wasted when at sea with the Fleet and hoped to create a reserve of executive officers able to replace battle casualties at sea. It is likely also that Fisher, with many other senior naval officers, underestimated the specialist role of the

Marines and resented the expense of maintaining their own little army. Be that as it may, the Marine officers would not accept the new scheme and under pressure, probably from the King, the plan was shelved.[8]

Engineers, with their dirty hands, less than immaculate clothing and often advanced education, have always been something of an embarrassment to their colleagues in the other professions. In more recent years, with the spread downwards of complex equipment, all officers and soldiers need at least a basic knowledge of military technology. It is no longer possible to solve or even to shelve the problem by setting up special regiments or corps composed of officers and men who don't mind getting their hands dirty, however much this may also be necessary. The Navy has had the same problem. Steel hulls, steam propulsion, wireless telegraphy and a more scientific approach to gunnery, mines and torpedoes at the end of the nineteenth century, brought the requirement for a body of Engineer Officers, educated in the appropriate technology to manage them afloat. Fisher was afraid that this could lead to the 'democratisation' of the naval officer corps and an influx of unsuitable people. He believed that the distinction between Engineer Officers and the Executive Branch should be abandoned and that some of the general run of naval cadets should be encouraged to train as engineers and in other specialisms. Fisher had in mind the analogy of the amalgamation of the old navigating and executive branches before which gentlemen commanded the ship and fought the enemy whilst a less prestigious range of officers, lacking the Sovereign's commission, supervised the navigation and the sailing of the ship. But this scheme fell through also and was not revived until after the Second World War. Meanwhile Fisher fought a determined battle against a vociferous and snobbish minority of naval officers who insisted on calling their engineers 'greasers'.[9]

An important organisation which, whilst not being overtly militaristic and which indeed was regarded generally and with some justification as working towards international co-operation, but which nevertheless incorporated a strong flavour of jingoism and war preparation, was the Boy Scout Movement. Founded by Robert Baden-Powell, the hero of Mafeking, and based on his experiences in Africa and India, his ideas were first expounded in articles written for 'The Boy's Own Paper' in the 1890's at a time when the paper was accepting articles from a number of young army officers. The 'Boy Scouts' first appeared in Mafeking organised by Baden-Powell as a cadet corps. They were used for a number of sub-military duties such as manning look-out posts, running messages and as orderlies. After the Boer War, through his charismatic personality, organising powers and heroic reputation, the movement expanded rapidly, becoming a very popular and influential force in youth work and in education. Ostensibly classless, Scout Groups composed of the three age groups of Cubs aged eight to eleven, Scouts aged eleven to eighteen and Rover Scouts from eighteen to almost any age, tended to recruit from a particular local area or school, village or suburb. This meant that a Scout Group tended to come from one particular social stratum. The leaders were usually retired Service officers or were connected with the Church, usually the Church of England. Before the First World War, the Scout Movement was strongly supported by the regular forces and by retired servicemen's organisations. Between the wars, this link was maintained and the Scouts paraded with the Ex-Service groups, carrying their banners at Empire Day and Remembrance Day services all over Britain. The Scout Movement was put forward by 'Punch' in 1909, and only half in jest, as 'Our Youngest Line of Defence'. Saki, in a genre novel of German invasion, 'When William Came'[10] shows the Boy Scouts in a similar patriotic role, refusing to take part in a pro-German parade. But patriotic the Scouts certainly were and there is evidence of at least one troop of scouts being marched to the recruiting office to be enlisted *en bloc* at the outbreak of war.[11]

Preparing For Armageddon

Whilst retired officers, army and naval correspondents of the national newspapers, novelists, playwrights and plain straightforward publicity seekers stirred up the public and prepared them to accept and even look forward to the coming of Armageddon, the politicians worked to make the transition to war as efficient as possible. Cardwell's work had been completed by Childers, on paper at least, in 1881 when the Regiments really started to lose their individual identity and in some cases their very existence. But the Boer War, like the Crimean War fifty years before it, exposed so many weaknesses in British military organisation that it was almost as though the great reforms of the 1870's and 80's had never taken place. The creation of a staff organisation and the provision of adequate reserves and reinforcements was as urgent in 1902 as it was in the 1870's, and the threat seemed much more immediate. Salisbury's Conservative Government, through the Esher Committee on War Office Reconstitution, reported in 1904. Surprisingly, the Committee comprised Admiral Sir John Fisher, Lord Esher (a favourite and confidant of King Edward VII) and Sir George Sydenham Clarke, a retired officer, an expert on defensive works and Secretary of the Hartington Commission. As early as 1890, the Hartington Commission had recommended the establishment of a Committee of Imperial Defence and

that the duties of the Commander-in-Chief should be taken over by
an Army Council. The Secretary of the Esher Committee was Major
Gerald Ellison. The Army gained its revenge for the anomalous position of Fisher on the Committee a few years later when Winston Churchill as First Lord at the Admiralty invited Haldane to attend meetings
of the committee which was to bring about a new Naval Staff System.
Haldane was at that time Secretary for War and was advised on the
Naval Staff reorganisation by Haig.

By February 1904, the office of Commander-in-Chief and the old
War Office Council and Army Board were abolished. The United
Kingdom was divided into seven Districts each of which was given an
operations and an administrative staff. An Inspector-General of the
Forces was nominated. The Duke of Connaught, as first Inspector-
General, continued the Royal connection with the Army and guaranteed a sympathetic interest on the part of the King in the other recommendations of the Commission.[12] The three members of the
Commission, despite firm guidelines from Arnold-Forster, the Secretary for War, laying down that all communications with the King
should be made through him alone, used Esher's influence with the
King to take executive action on their own recommendations. They
were anxious to see as many of their recommendations in action as
possible before what seemed to be the imminent fall of Lord Salisbury's Ministry. A new 'Army Council' was created on 6 February
and the office of Commander-in-Chief was abolished at the same time.
The Commission, ostensibly on behalf of Salisbury's Government,
appointed senior officers to posts on the Army Council without
informing the military. Hamer[13] describes how Sir Henry Wilson,
later to be Field Marshal and CIGS, found matters to be getting 'worse
and worse'. In his diary on 10 February he recorded, 'The "Triumvir-
ate" are appointing officers to billets here, and there, and everywhere,
quite regardless of anyone.' The next day Wilson was discussing the
situation with General Sir William Nicholson, a member of the old
Council, when General Grierson arrived hot foot from Aldershot having been 'ordered' to take over Nicholson's post. The Reorganisation
Committee was convinced that their reforms could only take effect if
what Hamer called 'the entire ruling clique at the War Office' was
forced into retirement. Field Marshal Roberts ceased to be Commander-in-Chief when his office was abolished and left the War Office
very understandably 'in the devil of a temper'. The whole reorganisation had been incredibly badly handled, however necessary the
changes may have been, and when the Ministry finally resigned at the
end of 1905, much still remained to be implemented.

One of the more unfortunate aspects of the mishandling of army
reorganisation by the Salisbury government was the legacy of mistrust

left behind in the Army. The decade immediately before the First World War was a period when, despite the insensitive blunders of the Esher Commission, selected mainly on the recommendation of the King, the Army, and especially its senior officers, turned away, at least in spirit, from elected government and towards the authority and influence emanating from the King. As we shall see, this reversion to an earlier time, when the Army was controlled by its Royal Master and his Commander-in-Chief, could have had disastrous consequences in Ireland and during the Great War, if the advent of a new King in 1910 had not brought a rather more constitutionally minded Monarch to the throne.

Sir Henry Campbell-Bannerman's Liberal Government came to power in 1906 with an immense majority in the House of Commons. Haldane became the Secretary for War and, whilst completing the reorganisation of the War Office, he was in the happy position of not carrying the opprobrium which had been heaped on the Esher Commission. He was able at last, having confirmed in place the new Army Council and accepted the new Army Staff system, to begin to prepare the Army for its new tasks on the continent of Europe. Over the next few years, Haldane, with the help of French and Haig, set up the Expeditionary Force of six divisions, guaranteed adequate reserves for the first time by forming the Territorial Army out of the old militia and volunteers and ensured its proper deployment and utilisation in the war through detailed staff talks between senior members of the British and French armies. Haldane's influence was felt throughout the Army and not just in the rarified atmosphere of the War Office. Aldershot, being the largest of the new United Kingdom Military Districts, and being the most accessible from London felt the change of tempo more than most of the outlying military headquarters. When General Sir John French gave up the Command at Aldershot to become Inspector-General of the Forces in 1907, he had already seen the arrival of the motor car and the aeroplane for military use. It was this acceptance of change, even if somewhat reluctantly, which encouraged him to find room on Laffan's Plain for the experimental kite, powered balloon and aeroplane flights of the flamboyant but brilliant 'Colonel' Samuel F Cody. Ironically, it was Haldane who had to close down the military aviation experiments at Aldershot when the Liberal Government found that they had cost the tax-payer £2,500. Such senseless extravagance was quite unacceptable to a Government pledged to economy. At least Haldane travelled down to Aldershot to give Cody the bad news in person and had the vision to allow Cody to keep his flying machine and to continue with his experiments on Laffan's Plain on a private basis and, of course, at his own expense. French's successor at Aldershot, General Sir Horace

Smith-Dorrien, continued to encourage Cody in his experiments and in his co-operation with the Royal Engineers Balloon Unit, which had moved to Aldershot from Chatham some years previously. Colonel Capper, who commanded the Balloon Unit, flew with Cody in a powered balloon over Buckingham Palace in 1907 and flew as Cody's first passenger in a true heavier than air machine when he had built one powerful enough to lift them both off the ground. These were the first beginnings of Army Aviation just as the 1899 parachute descent of Monsieur Caudron into the camp at Aldershot could be regarded as the fore-runner of British Airborne Forces.

The first two divisions of the newly planned Expeditionary Force were based on Aldershot and were the first to go to France at the outbreak of the war. Significantly, General French had been earmarked as the commander of the Expeditionary Force soon after the staff talks with the French Army got under way. So, just as Haldane's early familiarity with the 'War Book' allowed him to set *en train* a smooth and efficient mobilisation in 1914, it was French's early awareness of his destined role and of the detailed plans for the co-ordination of the British and French armies that made their speedy conjunction and co-operation so remarkable. Meanwhile, whilst preparations for war were being pursued more and more seriously by the Armed Forces and chauvinistic scaremongering was the order of the day in the newspapers, an extraordinary fatalism and acceptance of the coming war seemed to grow stronger as the war approached. Despite the wave of industrial unrest which swept the country from 1910 to 1912 and which involved the Army on several occasions, sometimes with fatal consequences, the overall mood continued to be one of facile optimism.

The question of women's suffrage and the militancy with which the cause was to be pursued emerged as early as 1905 and became progressively more violent as the war fever grew. Asquith, who had become Prime Minister when Campbell-Bannerman became fatally ill in 1907, was opposed to women's suffrage whilst his Foreign Secretary Sir Edward Grey, supported it. The last formal debate on the subject was held in May 1912 when Asquith and his Foreign Secretary led off for opposite sides much to the diversion of the House of Commons. The motion in favour of women's suffrage was lost by 268 votes to 221 and that was the end of the matter, for the time being, as far as Parliament was concerned.[14] Of course the issue rumbled on and continued to erupt violently from time to time until it was swept up into the infinitely greater violence of the World War. Happily the Army had not been directly involved in the suffragette disturbances, the police being able to cope with the troubles as they had not been able to without army assistance during the pre-war industrial unrest.

Neither the industrial nor the suffrage campaigns were in themselves of sufficient gravity to shake the foundations of pre-1914 society but they added to the general climate of violence and excitement for which the war was seen by some as a kind of cathartic release. Even more important, the crises of industrialism and the divisive nature of the suffragette question were exactly the kind of issue which might be postponed or even transformed for the better in a grand patriotic war, or so thought some of the politicians and other participants.[15]

Mutiny or Incident? The Irish Question

But for Asquith and his Liberal Government, an even greater crisis was to engulf them before the war came. The Army and the constitution were involved and a crisis brought about which, whilst it was postponed in August 1914, has not been settled to this day. The Irish question was one made peculiarly their own by the Liberal Party. Gladstone had wrestled with it and admitted defeat but it would not go away. By 1912, when Asquith's Government, already committed to Home Rule, was drafting the third Home Rule Bill, it needed the votes of Redmond and his Irish Nationalist Members to remain in power. The Conservative Party, which had always seen the Irish situation as a cross to be borne rather than a question to be answered, seized upon the obvious discontent of the Ulster Protestants as a cause which could ultimately be made to unseat the Government. As negotiations continued over the Bill through 1913 and early 1914, rumours of a Government plot to coerce Ulster into an all-Ireland Union began to circulate. Opinion in Britain was divided roughly on party lines into those who supported the Government, most of whom did not believe that force would be used against Ulster, and those who, whether they believed it or not, encouraged the Ulster Protestants to prepare to defend themselves by any means against forcible incorporation into an Irish Republic.[16]

The Army had traditionally recruited from all parts of Ireland but many of its officers, for historical reasons, came from land-owning families in Northern Ireland. In addition, there were some senior officers, it is impossible to know how many, who had, from conviction or calculation of career interest, overtly pursued a party political line. It is likely also that some of the participants pursued an adventurist line which would have been strongly disavowed by all the political parties, despite a strongly charged emotional situation. However, it is certain that a volunteer force in Ulster started to drill and arm itself. Equally well documented is the fact that Henry Wilson, at that time Director of Military Operations at the War Office and himself an Ulsterman, was in close contact with the volunteers, visited Northern

Ireland frequently during the crisis and may have acted as a go-between or as a political adviser. Colonel Seely, Secretary for War and Winston Churchill, First Lord of the Admiralty, may have over-reacted to gunrunning into Northern Ireland by taking rather clumsy and provocative action in using the Royal Navy to intercept and search ships, and by using troops rather than police to guard stores and depots. These moves alarmed or were used to alarm officers in the Irish garrisons some of whom were soon hinting, to put it no more strongly, that they would not take part in the military coercion of Ulster. Once it became known that there was a whiff of mutiny in the air the Commander-in-Chief, Ireland, General Sir Arthur Paget, spoke to the Commander of the 5th Infantry division, Major General Fergusson and Brigadier General Hubert Gough of the 3rd Cavalry Brigade. Paget assured them that there was no intention to use force in the North and reminded them, but in an apparently half-hearted fashion, of their duty, adding deliberately that the King naturally supported the orders of his Government. He also said that if it was a matter of conscience for officers domiciled in Northern Ireland, they could go on leave until the crisis blew over.

Fergusson appears to have had no difficulty in persuading his officers to continue with their duty, aided perhaps by his garbled version of the King's position. Fergusson had implied that the King actually knew of their orders and was happy with them. At any rate, their was no further trouble from the infantry division. Gough was a very different kettle of fish. A fiery and excitable Ulsterman in the classic cavalry tradition, he appeared to have a paranoid hatred of all politicians and many of the senior army officers at the War Office as well. Whatever he said to them, it seems that as many as sixty officers from the 3rd Cavalry brigade were prepared to follow his example and resign rather than march against Ulster. Within twenty-four hours, Gough and his three regimental commanders were 'on the mat' at the War Office. Sir John French, by then CIGS, Sir Spencer Ewart the Adjutant General and eventually Seely, the War Minister, each tried to get Gough, and through him his officers, to withdraw their resignations and return to duty. Gough would have none of it. He was obviously aware of very strong support from the Conservative Party and from the majority of the national press although it is possible that he did not welcome it. More congenial was the support of his brother John, a Brigadier General at Aldershot and Haig, who was commanding the 1st Division, also at Aldershot and in reserve for Ireland. They had come to commiserate with him and met with him at his mother's house in London. This may have given rise to the belief, which we have mentioned earlier, that Haig had spoken to the King about the Curragh Crisis. Certainly Gough, in his own book, published in 1954, seems to be very confident about what the King knew of the matter.[17] Gough's position was certainly strengthened and his confidence increased by his membership of a famous military family. Gough's father had served with the Guides and with Hodson's Horse at the Siege of Delhi where he won the Victoria Cross as had his younger brother, Hubert Gough's uncle Hugh.

With enormous '*sang froid*' Gough insisted on a written guarantee that British troops would not be used to coerce Ulster, before he would return to face his officers in Ireland. Seely and the CIGS wrote out the guarantee without consulting the Government and Gough returned a hero to take up his appointment with the Cavalry Brigade. Seely, the CIGS and the Adjutant General were forced to resign. The King proposed a Buckingham Palace Conference to try to reach a solution to the imbroglio. The Conference was accepted and attended by representatives of the Government, The Conservative Party, the Ulster Unionists and Redmond's Irish Nationalists. The conference achieved nothing and broke up with attitudes hardened and with a widespread feeling that real violence was about to occur. Roy Jenkins[18] refers to Asquith's thoughts on the failure of the conference and the 'mysteries of the celtic mind'. In a letter to Miss Stanley, whom Jenkins refers to as Asquith's great epistolary friend, Asquith describes what could have been the final and fatal parting between Redmond and Dillon, the Nationalist Representatives, and Carson and Captain Craig, who represented the Ulster Unionists:

> Redmond assured us that when he said goodbye to Carson the latter was in tears, and that Captain Craig, who had never spoken to Dillon in his life, came up to him and said: 'Mr Dillon will you shake my hand? I should be glad to think that I have been able to give as many years to Ulster as you have to the service of Ireland'. Aren't they a remarkable people? And the folly of thinking we can ever understand, let alone govern them!

The Palace Conference broke up on 22 July 1914 and, by the following Tuesday, Nationalist Volunteers bringing in guns to Dublin, following the example of Ulster, were fired on by the military, killing three and wounding thirty-eight. It must have been with relief that all the parties to the Irish dispute suddenly realised on Thursday 28th that questions of Home Rule and Partition were irrelevant for the time being. The Curragh Mutiny or Incident, if it is wished to play down the seriousness of the events in Ireland in July of 1914, was certainly the most widely reported attempt by members of the military to influence government policy in recent times. The uniqueness of the events is confirmed by the frequency with which they are cited in books and articles on civil military relations, aid to the civil power and *coups d'état* in general. After almost seventy-five years, nothing more interesting nor more decisive appears to have happened in this field as far as the British are concerned. However, this is not to say that a serious breach of discipline did not occur although, legally, it probably did not amount to mutiny. The fact that Gough and his officers had probably misread the Government's intentions does not excuse them their hasty over-reaction. It is only the incompetent handling of the situation, first by Paget in Ireland then by Seely in London, which can possibly explain why no disciplinary action was taken by the Government against the recalcitrant officers. Perhaps Gough and his officers, like so many other participants in the events of July were saved, if only temporarily, by the coming of war.

There is a further gloss that can be put on events surrounding the Curragh troubles. Ryan in his book[19] says that if there was a mutiny it was not on the part of Gough and his friends but by Henry Wilson, The Director of Military Operations, and some other unidentified officers at the War Office. Wilson certain intrigued with Carson and the Ulster Volunteers but whether this was on his own misguided behalf or to further the ends of others is not known. Wilson succeeded Robertson as CIGS in February 1918, retired after the war, and was assassinated on the steps of his London house by Sinn Fein gunmen in 1922. Wilson was a political general who may have worked too closely with a Conservative opposition or possibly even with some undercover organisation which attracted the attention of Irish terrorists. It is unlikely that the truth will ever be known. Jenkins, in a footnote to his book on Asquith,[20] picks up an interesting remark of Margo Asquith's which also casts a little doubt on General French's impartiality. In a letter to Lady Islington, which Jenkins accepts as authentic, she refers to French's resignation; 'after endorsing the unauthorised letter given to Gough' she says, 'French put his name to what he thought was a Cabinet document so he said he had better go . . . he is a hot Liberal and of course comes back to a high place in a very short time'. Within a few months French was in France as Commander-in-Chief of the British Expeditionary Force. He had, of course, been selected by Haldane and the Liberal Government for this supreme post several years before. Perhaps, in the end, both French and Wilson were merely emulating the actions of their illustrious predecessors Marlborough and Wellington, neither of whom were without political interests.

Recruiting Armies for a New Kind of Warfare

As the World War approached, the regiments again took their place at the centre of the stage. Haldane had intended that reinforcements for the British Expeditionary Force in France would be raised through the medium of the County Territorial Associations on whom the recruiting, training and despatching of the volunteers would have automatically devolved. But Asquith, with the agreement of his Cabinet and the joyful support of the general public, persuaded Kitchener, with no difficulty, to become Minister for War. Kitchener, described by Haldane as a man with great power and personality but knowing nothing of the modern science of military organisation, refused to adopt or make any use of the Territorial Organisation set up by Haldane. At the same time he practically dispensed with the services of the General Staff. Philip Magnus, in his biography of Kitchener[21] says that Kitchener had nothing but contempt for the Esher Committee and since Haldane was very largely putting into effect the recommendations of that committee, they were anathema to him. The new Kitchener armies enjoyed his official favour and he was deaf to any protests about the unnecessary waste and duplication involved in having the two systems in operation at the same time. Magnus goes on to say that although Kitchener paid unqualified tribute to the record of the Territorials, for their eagerness to serve overseas and for their behaviour on the field of battle, his dislike of the organisation was 'instinctive and inveterate, so that argument was useless'. His failure to use the General Staff was the more surprising since he had always stressed the importance of staff work and it has been suggested that what lay behind his neglect was a strong instinctive desire to act as his own Chief of Staff, as he had done in South Africa. The Kitchener armies were raised through the Adjutant General's department and, in the early days, there was inevitable confusion when it was found that equipment, weapons and even food and accommodation were not always available for the mass of impatient young men who responded to Kitchener's famous recruiting poster.

Almost the last of his line, Kitchener was, like so many of his predecessors, a colonial soldier, having fought all his wars in or from the British Empire of the nineteenth century. As late as 1914, a bizarre sidelight is thrown on his military thinking by his apparent concern over a homegrown version of the 'martial races' theory. Perhaps, although it must surely be unlikely, Kitchener thought he was baiting an easy victim, but as Roy Jenkins reports, at an Asquith Cabinet meeting early in the war, a dispute broke out between Lloyd George and Kitchener. Kitchener gave as his view that no purely Welsh regiment could be trusted. Asquith thought his (Kitchener's) handling of the argument 'clumsy and noisy'. Jenkins, in a footnote says with some irony, 'even an unusual delicacy and quietness might have left the argument an unappealing one to Lloyd George.'[22]

The war, when it came, had been anticipated and prepared for for so long, and even provoked by some individuals and institutions, that it was greeted with relief by many sections of the British public.[23] The phenomenal summer of 1914, bringing to a close the halcyon years leading up to the war, seemed so idyllic to many members of the upper classes that they appeared to induce a sense almost of guilt. Peter Parker, writing of the almost 'excruciatingly perfect' life of the public school boys and young *literati* at the universities immediately before the war says:

> The cult of the public school reached its zenith between 1900 and 1914, an orgy of celebration to which the Great War provided an ironic climax. So glorious was the youthful life that there seemed a feeling that, like the mythic summer of 1914, it could not, perhaps 'should', not last.[24]

That the euphoria could not last was still hidden from the young men taking part in the glorious adventure of 1914. The public schools provided the officers, already partly trained by the Junior Officers' Training Corps, founded with admirable foresight by Haldane in his Army reforms of 1907. The ranks were filled with what seemed to be a limitless number of young men, few of whom needed the admonitions of Kitchener or the goad of a white feather to send them into the New Armies. Whatever system was to be used for the recruitment and training of the New Armies, whether it was to be Haldane's territorially based force which trained less than a third of the newcomers or Kitchener's more centrally directed formations, which received more than two-thirds of the 2,467,000 volunteers enlisted in the first eighteen months of the war, it was clear that the old regiments would still be very much involved. Even when the new recruits were trained away from the old Depots in the new, and in many cases tented, camps, the senior officers, non-commissioned officers and above all the instructors, would come, in the early days, from the old regiments. There was no where else. The grip of the regiments, and especially the Regimental Associations, was strong and so there was an immediate expansion of battalions owing a loose allegiance to the historic regiments. The localisation measures of the 1880s, had been reinforced by the new territorial system and so it was convenient, as well as inevitable, that men should join their local regiment through their nearest recruiting office. At the beginning of the war, a regiment would number two regular battalions and perhaps two, three or four territorial battalions. By 1916 or 1917, the system had expanded beyond recognition. Many regiments had as many as forty battalions and some had many more. The Middlesex Regiment, formed in the 1881 amalgamations, raised forty-six battalions during the war and the Manchester Regiment, also an 1881 amalgamation, raised forty-two. At one time during the Great War the Regimental Colonel of the Manchesters pointed out that he had fifty thousand men serving under him in his regiment. Many of the expanded regiments could have manned an infantry division with ease but it seems that this was never an acceptable arrangement. Before the First World War, it was not unheard of but nevertheless exceptional for two battalions of the same regiment to fight or even to live side by side.[25] This enforced separation was of course part of the linked battalion system where the second battalion of the regiment acted as training, reinforcement and home administrative unit for the other battalion of the regiment which would be serving overseas. There may also have been a reluctance to have too many soldiers from one locality fighting together because of the adverse morale effect on the home towns and villages of overlong casualty lists. Early in the American Civil War it is said, localisation of recruiting and the naming of regiments after their main recruiting area was dropped for this reason. However, casualty lists were often so long in the Great War, in any case, that it is questionable whether the effect of having truly localised divisions could have produced a worse effect.

Another consideration which might have applied was the desire to maintain a comparatively homogeneous mix in the Armed Forces. Regionalism has not been a particularly potent force in England, at least not in recent centuries, but there may have been a subconscious desire to avoid the setting up of military organisations of regimental intensity, but much larger and more powerful, which through their local connections could become the focus for a disaffected area or town. It is only necessary to recall the extraordinary powers and pressures which were brought to bear by the old County Associations, to resist amalgamations or disbandments, to realise the scope for intervention which a large formation might possess. The territorial formations brought together at the beginning of the First World War, reflected an area or region rather than a national cross section and, at the start of the Second World War, the territorial divisions were much the same. By 1917, or by 1941 in the Second World War, however, it is unlikely that the divisions, even where they boasted strong local connections, would still contain more than a bare majority of locally enlisted men. The situation in the regiments would not have been very different. Certainly in the cavalry there has always been an element who have enlisted for the glamorous cap badge rather than for territorial reasons and with the increasing appearance on the battlefield of the fighting corps, armour, gunners, sappers and all the other specialists in modern warfare, formations on the battlefield have become more and more a regional and even a national mix.

With the recent bringing together of the infantry into six large divisions for administrative and recruit training purposes, only two of the new divisions have any area connections. The Scottish Division does include all the extant Scottish Regiments, but The Prince of Wales's Division, whilst it does include the two remaining Welsh Regiments, shares the honour of the Principality with six other proud regiments which, according to their titles hale from as far away at Devon and the forest of Sherwood. Perhaps Kitchener's unease about Welsh Regiments lives on somewhere in Whitehall! As to the other four large administrative divisions in the British Army of 1988, two of them, The Guards Division and The Light Division, do have honourable historical predecessors. The remaining two divisions and perhaps also The Prince of Wales's Division could be said to have revived the Royal connection in order to obscure the obviously strange and in some cases very uncongenial bedfellows found within them.

Meanwhile it must be said for every recruit in 1914 who joined his local regiment because of his 'county' loyalty and his family or friendly connections with it, another four or five joined because it was the nearest and most convenient part of the Army. The overwhelming desire was to get into the war before it was over and, if you had friends, to join up with them. Through 1914, 1915 and 1916 the unique aspect of the British Army was that it had expanded to unheard of and almost unbelievable dimensions and all through voluntary enlistment. To the Army from which an Expeditionary Force of seven divisions could be fashioned at the outbreak of war was added a new force of two million men taken into that Army in batches of 100,000. Each of the batches provided roughly six divisions, and six divisions made up one of Kitchener's five New Armies. The equipping and training of these New Armies almost caused the breakdown of the War Office administrative system. Many divisions did not receive their rifles until just before going to France and even units which were to take part in the opening of the Somme offensive on 1 July 1916 arrived on the Western Front in a state of training which John Keegan describes restrainedly as 'quite deficient'.[26] By July 1916, only a few battalions surviving from the original Expeditionary Force, and not many more from the Territorial follow-up formations, were available to join the Kitchener battalions for the Somme battles.

It has been said that the Somme battles were planned to be very simple affairs in order to take account of the lack of training in the new formations. The infantry was expected to advance behind an artillery barrage through the German barbed wire destroyed by the barrage and take the enemy trenches before the occupants recovered from the British shelling. The British would then defend the captured trenches against counter-attack and eventually advance again, protected by the pre-arranged barrage, planned to move forward with each advance, to take the second and third German defence lines. If all went well for the attacking infantry, it would eventually find itself in open country and a breakthrough would have been achieved. This never happened in the battles which raged from July to November for a number of reasons, none of them to do with lack of valour or determination on the part of the attacking troops who, inexperienced and half trained as they were, kept up the attack until sheer exhaustion made further effort impossible. The German defences could not be overcome. On the first day of the battle, the attacking divisions lost 60,000 men and by the time the attacks were abandoned in early winter, the British had suffered 419,000 casualties. In 1811, the men of the old 57th, The Middlesex Regiment, were mishandled at Albuhera and lost 422 all ranks out of a total of 570 which is on the same scale as the losses of the battalions on the Somme. The Middlesex battalions, the Diehards, fighting on the Somme did not have the satisfaction of seeing their enemy flee the field as did their illustrious predecessors in the Peninsula but, given the difference in circumstances, their performance was just as creditable. The 57th won its first and possibly its greatest honour at Albuhera but for many of the battalions, and especially the 'high numbered' ones, the Somme might well have been their first and last honour. The Middlesex Regiment was awarded over eighty battle honours for its actions in the First World War, as were many other famous regiments. Many of those honours, as the war ran its bloody course, were won by battalions which were numbered amongst the thirties and even forties of their parent regiment. What was demonstrated time and again was that, despite their lack of training, the battalions of Kitchener's Army, and, after these had been shattered in the Somme battles, the conscript battalions that arrived in France from 1917 onwards, did not lack in spirit and kept a high morale. They maintained a cohesion that would have made them acceptable members of the Expeditionary Force of 1914 or even of Wellington's Army of the Peninsula. Morale was perhaps the most remarkable feature of the battalions which fought in the great battles of attrition in 1915 and 1916.[27]

John Baynes in his study of the Cameronians at the battle of Neuve Chappelle in 1915, published under the title of 'Morale', emphasises the importance of the small group in building and maintaining morale:

Trust in the group is an essential part of the soldier's development. At the lowest levels, the individual is dependent on his immediate fellows to an extraordinary degree. A private soldier in action finds that his section becomes the centre of his life. He finds his platoon and company important as well . . . but the small groups are the vital ones. In the First World War, especially in the early stages, men were rarely conscious of more than their own companies.

Baynes also quotes Alan Clark's *The Donkeys* where he describes the men of Kitchener's New Armies:

> Behind them stretched the ordered childhoods of Victorian Britain; decency, regularity, a Christian upbringing, a concept of chivalry; overriding faith in the inevitable triumph of right over wrong; such notions were imbued in them.

The solid background, belief in the rightness of the cause and trust and reliance on the immediate group of comrades emerge as the essence of good morale. Baynes' Cameronians were as jealous of their honour and their good report as were Mason's Indian Army soldiers fighting in the same war for:

> The good name in the world of their kith and clan and village, their own good name among those who knew them, and last of all, personal honour.[28]

An example and extension of this notion of personal honour is shown in the early history of the Royal Tank Regiment. Formed to break the deadlock on the Western Front and restore mobility to the battlefield it was at first composed of volunteers from the other regiments and corps, especially from those men who could claim some engineering or mechanical experience. In their new units they could no longer rely on the support and approbation of their parent regiments and corps, and in some cases in the face of their hostility and incomprehension were left to fight the good fight in the comparative isolation of the claustrophobic metal boxes in which they went into action. Nothing could be further from the classic view of the regimental system enhancing the fighting spirit of the soldier. The early tank crews had to look elsewhere for their courage and determination, and whilst the disparate individuals making up the crew would quickly settle down into a very small self-reliant group, compacted by their metal shell, it must have been to personal honour that they turned when leading those first and uncharted attacks.

It is a sad irony that tanks were first used in the hopeless moonscape terrain of the Somme battlefields. In September, with the battle still at its height, the first thirty-six tanks that could be got up to the front went into action leading nine British infantry divisions. With 1200 guns in support of the attack, many of the tanks were immobilised in the broken ground or lost their way in the maze of shell holes, but eleven of them fought their way into the enemy positions. There they caused sufficient havoc and consternation to confirm Haig in his view that, if the stalemate in the West was to be broken, the tank must be developed into a war-winning weapon. Whilst it is true to say that the tank and the innovating tank officers never had a sufficient chance to win the war through their new weapons and ideas alone, the much more successful Battle of Cambrai in 1917 and the great battle of 8 August 1918 when 604 British and 110 French tanks achieved a breakthrough, once more on the Somme, set the pattern for the future. Despite the disillusion and near despair of the tank pioneers in the inter-war years in Britain, it was the shape and promise of those battles at Cambrai and in the Somme salient in 1918 which led to the German development of 'blitzkrieg' tactics, the defeat of France in 1940 and the monumental tank battles on the Eastern front between Germany and the Soviet Union from 1942 until the end of the Second World War in Europe. We shall return to the subject of the tank regiments and their implications for the rest of the Army in a short while. Meanwhile it is necessary to note the emergence of another, predominantly mechanical branch of the Army which, whilst it appeared just before the outbreak of the 1914 war, owed its rapid development like the tank to the forcing conditions of the war itself.

As we have seen it was General French who first found room for 'Colonel' Bill Cody's aeronautical researches on Laffan's Plain, but it was significantly the Engineer Colonel Capper, Commandant of the Army Balloon School, who actually participated in the early flights. Having flown over Buckingham Palace with Cody, and despite the Campbell-Bannerman parsimony, he was able to demonstrate the military potential of the aeroplane. His flight as a passenger proved conclusively that the heavier than air machine could be used as an observation platform and as a fighting vehicle. Whilst the aeroplane started life as the child of the engineers and mechanics, it was soon taken up by the rich and sporty young men who had already graduated from fast motor cars. The development continued in makeshift workshops by the young men had already found in the early days of the war that the aeroplane provided them with a vehicle and a quest which restored to their role as officers something of the romance and knight-errantry which had been lost from their profession. It was this feeling of romantic, almost spiritual excitement, sensed as much by the onlookers as the young flyers themselves which was so aptly named 'The White Horse Syndrome'.[29] The growth of air power is interesting not only for the irresistible rise of the new force in all civilised countries or at least in all countries that could employ trained help, but also for the remarkable ease with which the new military phenomenon was absorbed by the existing Armed Forces. There were teething troubles, like those for example at Aldershot, where some reactionary officers joined the local press in deriding Cody's experiments, concerned that their horses might be frightened by the noisy new machines. They looked down on the 'mechanics' who flew the planes rather in the manner of Fisher's snobbish naval officers who insisted on calling their Engineer Officers 'greasers'. Despite this, most senior officers were able to appreciate the advantages of moving into the third dimension and accepted the new force without demur.

The new tank force did not have quite such an easy acceptance. Although the contending armies were locked in battle on the Western front by the time the tanks arrived on the scene and the weary soldiers were ready to welcome any new weapon which might break the deadlock of the trenches, it took time to work out suitable tactics. The Battle of Cambrai was not planned as a breakthrough attempt. The 378 tanks employed were intended to make a great demonstration against the German lines which would raise British morale and keep the Germans quiet for the remainder of the winter of 1917–18. The battle took place on 20 November 1917 and it was over by the evening of that day. The tanks performed well and successfully broke into parts of the enemy line but, in the centre of the attack, thanks to old-fashioned prejudice by one divisional commander, the supporting infantry were not allowed to co-operate closely with the tanks and so the opportunity to break out into open country was lost. At one stage it seemed that a genuine breakthrough was possible but the crucial moment passed and, although over 10,000 prisoners were taken, the ground captured was retaken by the Germans within a week. By the summer of 1918, however, once the last great German offensive had been halted, the British and French tank forces were able to spearhead the attack at Amiens which led on through the Somme to end the war.

A new corps, composed of men with mechanical aptitude and of above average intelligence, which rapidly became an élite in its own right, could have presented problems of integration to the pre-war army. Arriving in the middle of the Great War, the problems could be ignored for the time being. The machine gun, which had been with the Army from well before the Great War, was not fully accepted at first as the dominating weapon which it clearly was. But by October 1915, a separate Machine Gun Corps was set up recognising the importance of the new weapon. By November 1918 the new Corps numbered 6,432 officers and 124,920 men.[30] Some of the innovations introduced by the Machine Gun Corps were taken as the model for the new tank force. The tanks were first hidden behind a series of cover names linked to the Machine Gun Corps and it was only in June 1917 that they became the Tank Corps, and as we have seen, not until after the war, the Royal Tank Corps (in 1939, at the formation of the Royal Armoured Corps, the Royal Tank Regiment). Before the end of the war, the problems of recruiting an élite body of men and integrating it successfully into the main army were already apparent. In the Tank Museum at Bovington, home of the Royal Armoured Corps, is lovingly preserved a recruiting poster dating from the last year of the Great War. The poster depicts a tank in mortar board and gown and the caption reads 'Wanted—Smart Men for the Tank Corps. Let Professor Tank Teach You a Trade'. The cavalry had always been regarded as an élite section of the Army, but now a new élite had emerged and a new rivalry was added to the problems accompanying the reluctant and delayed mechanisation of the cavalry regiments.

Morale and the Regimental Spirit After the Somme

It is difficult to assign with any precision the importance of the 'Regiment' as such in the maintainance of morale and cohesion in the Army as a whole during the First World War. There can be no doubt that, even in those regiments which turned out fifty or more battalions during the course of the war, there was a sense of identity and belonging, at least under training. For how long it lasted and how quickly it was transformed into a more primitive and more atavistic state, must depend upon a number of factors. The officers and senior non-commissioned officers who really knew the regiment and had been socialised through knowledge of its history, through living in its messes and through taking part in its parades and ceremonies, would have acted as symbols of the parent body. For the time that these symbols were present and acting as exemplars, their influence, and thus the influence of the regiment, would be strong. By July 1916, however, the old regimental officers and NCOs must have become extremely scarce in the 'front line' battalions. By 1918, they would have been represented by only a few, returned to the front after convalescence from one or more wounds. The bulk of the officers and NCOs by 1917, for all their loyalty and determination to do their duty, could hardly have been sustained by any great feeling of belonging to a regimental family with whom they could at most have had only a few weeks acquaintance. That they were able to continue to carry out their duties after surviving the battles of the Somme, even if their compliance was somewhat mechanical, is remarkable and points to some other sustaining influence apart from regimental spirit. Philip Mason suggests[31] that for the Indian troops who fought bravely and loyally beside the British in the early part of this same Great War in France it was not the 'Regiment' for which they were fighting. He says that the Indian soldier who fought within a regimental framework every bit as strong if not stronger than that of the British soldier, fought to defend his personal honour and for the good report of his comrades in his home village. Janowitz and Shils, in their study of cohesion and disintegration in the *Wehrmacht* in World War Two, point to the sustaining power of the small, face to face military group;

the platoon or even the section.[32] Whilst a soldier has close friends within hailing distance, they report, he will fight on until his ammunition is exhausted or he is literally starving. They insist also that it was not the spiritual strength of National Socialism that made the German infantryman such a formidable opponent. German soldiers were likely to be as blasphemous, irreverent and sceptical as all soldiers everywhere. Janowitz and Shils' findings do seem to square with observations elsewhere. Soldiers become passionately attached to their immediate comrades. Private Waterfield in India, it will be recalled, had congenial companions in the 32nd Foot with whom he found it necessary to spend most of his spare time and with whom the common bond of home was very important. Most officers who have been with units in action can tell of casualties who, having recovered from their wounds, were exceptionally determined to get back to their companions. This was especially so before a renewed attack or before a move to another sector of the front. In front line units, tales about departed comrades reach epic dimensions and returning comrades are often greeted in embarrassingly emotional style. It seems that the small group is the receptacle of the honour of each of its members. It has been found necessary to make special arrangements for recovered wounded and stragglers to get back to their original units, rather than to some more convenient unit at the risk of a serious breakdown in morale.

It could be said that the regimental spirit, like some other aspects of military existence, is more important in a peace-time environment or in training than in war. Really tough training in itself, in so far as it is successfully completed, builds morale and pride in one's unit but it also establishes close bonds between the recipients or 'survivors' of the training ordeal. The 'esprit de corps' of parachute troops and commando soldiers is at least in part due to the special nature of their training. Other aspects of 'high morale' units are a jealously guarded uniqueness in dress and accoutrements,[33] special punishments, the most serious of which might be expulsion from the unit, special rations, rates of pay and out of action living conditions, and an apparent lowering, at least to the gaze of outsiders, of some rank barriers. It is worth noting in this context that neither commandos nor parachute troops could be regarded as belonging to classical regimental configurations.

The Rise and Possible Fall of the Royal Tank Regiment

After the First World War but before the commandos or paratroops arrived on the military scene, the Royal Tank Corps found itself in a somewhat similar situation to these special formations. The Royal

Flying Corps had been 'hived off', perhaps to the relief of at least part of the Army, to form the Royal Air Force, leaving the tank men as the only soldiers who actually drove machines into battle. Gunners had always been soldiers with rather more powerful weapons; sappers and signallers, for all their battlefield bravery, could never be quite accepted as part of the 'teeth' of the Army, whilst the transport and supply services, despite or perhaps in part because they were the first parts of the Army to be mechanised, found it difficult to throw off the 'tradesman' image. Gradually, and in spite of the evident ennui in the United Kingdom based Army in the twenties and early thirties, the horse was replaced by tractors, mechanised gun carriages, trucks, tanks and armoured cars. At first it was hoped that the 'cavalry spirit' could be preserved by keeping the armoured car and reconnaissance roles for the cavalry, but this was not to be. In the formation of the first British armoured divisions at the beginning of the Second World War, and increasingly during the war, the preponderance of tanks to armoured cars became more and more disproportionate. The cavalry armoured regiments outnumbered those of the Royal Tank Regiment and now, of the regular armoured regiments, only four out of nineteen are from the Royal Tank Regiment. It is ironical that the cavalry regiments which fought so hard to resist mechanisation should now dominate the Royal Armoured Corps. It was not until 1939 that the last of the horsed regiments, the 15/19th Hussars, were mechanised at York, twenty-three years after tanks were first in action on the Somme. Regularly through the twenties and thirties the cost of fodder for army horses exceeded the cost of fuel for mechanised vehicles.[34]

A visit to the Tank Museum at Bovington confirms a change of emphasis from the early pioneering, innovative role of the Royal Tank Regiment which dominated the Armoured Corps with its military intellectuals, scientists and engineers, to the present day, where a whiff of the stables now seems to confirm, at least to the outsider, a reactionary victory of the cavalry regiments over the progressive image of the Armoured Corps. The history of the tank is shown almost exclusively in terms of the Royal Tank Regiment whilst, in the main exhibition hall, the titles and badges of all the cavalry regiments make a brave if somewhat medieval show. In the corner is a small commemorative display dedicated to the Royal Tank Regiment. On the plan of the museum it is actually called 'RTR Corner'. Perhaps also significantly, the mess kit of officers in the Royal Tank Regiment was changed in the early 1970s from the rational, comfortable dress of the post-war era to the more glamorous but archaic model. Spurs have always been worn by RTR officers, just as they are by majors and more senior officers in some other corps without any apparent feelings of anachronism.[35] It is nevertheless a little odd that the backward looking, consciously archaic fashions of the élite regiments should seem to triumph over the rational, utilitarian preferences of what was once the trend setting, progressive spear point of the modern army. In any civilian business or organisation the signs surrounding the Royal Tank Regiment would indicate that it was ripe for disbandment, and given the apparently vulnerable state of current armoured philosophy and armoured vehicles, and the pressure on the establishment of armoured regiments, we may soon find an 'all cavalry' armoured corps.[36]

9

The Long Armistice and the Second World War

With hindsight it is clear that the period of twenty years between the two world wars was an extended armistice rather than a genuine peace. In the war of 1939, the early defeat of France; the German induced accretion of the Soviet Union to the Western Powers; the late intervention of Japan, bringing-in decisively the United States of America; and even Italy's change of sides after defeat, merely serve to confirm the renewal of an unfinished conflict. Thus the years after the Peace of Versailles were seen as a breathing space, in which to recuperate and eventually to re-arm, by those countries swept along by the new ideologies. In Britain, America and France, the victorious Allies of the war, people were more than willing to accept the Peace as permanent. Armies could be disbanded warlike equipment and experiment forgotten and the nations seemingly safe within their recently secured boundaries could return to business very much as usual. Russia too was more concerned with safeguarding the revolution of 1917 and was prepared to remain quiescent within the boundaries agreed with Germany at Brest-Litovsk whilst waiting for the liquidation of capitalism on a world scale through the inevitable triumph of the proletariat. Italy fell prey to a rabid ideology which, with its tawdry trappings, concealing for a while a neo-Roman expansionism, attracted a dubious European following for its corporate dictatorship.

Germany, clumsily, but inevitably, victimised by the *Dictat* of Versailles, accepted the constitution of Weimar and then proceeded to make it unworkable. Thus, by the early 1930s, the German people were conditioned to believe in Hitler as the longed for Messiah. The horrors of the Third Reich were the price to be paid, regrettably but of necessity in unequal shares, for the defeat and humiliation of the Great War. The mixture of industrial and geographical expansion, cloaked in Italy and Germany and to some extent Japan, in a pseudo-historical and bogus philosophical justification, proved to be a heady concoction. In Germany especially, with its powerful and re-invigorated industrial base and its recent tradition of militarism, the national revival under Hitler and the Nazi Party could only lead to the second round of World War.

In Britain, after the Great War, apart from the natural reduction of a large war-time army, the traditional attitude of distrust and parsimony towards standing forces, especially when they are based in the United Kingdom, quickly reasserted itself. The problems of a much reduced Army, which now had to accommodate a tank arm however much attenuated, and machine guns and a new Royal Corps of Signals and a degree of mechanisation, were made worse by the hiving off and setting up of an independent air force. Whilst the Royal Navy retained its share of the Royal Flying Corps, the remainder was formed into a separate third force, the Royal Air Force. Thus whilst it developed its own philosophy, *modus operandi* and contacts with Parliament and the public, it competed with the Royal Navy and more particularly with the Army for the decreasing funds made available for the forces between the wars.

In the general revulsion at the idea of war, caused by the enormous casualties on the European battlefields, the Army reverted to a pre-war, even a pre-twentieth century, mentality. It became again, in spirit and almost in fact, a colonial police force. This, in itself, favoured the reassertion of a 'Regimental Ethos' as opposed to one favouring the Corps and the advocates of new and more effective military formations and structures. In 1928, Churchill, as Chancellor of the Exchequer, put the 'Ten Year Rule', which laid down that no war could be expected for at least ten years, onto a rolling basis. The intention was that the Government could carry forward the condition from year to year so that no re-armament and only a minimum of army maintenance need be considered[1]. By 1931, the provision was obviously invalid and the Chiefs of Staff persuaded a reluctant Cabinet to withdraw the rule. But, as Brian Bond points out, in cancelling the rule, the Cabinet warned that this was not to justify any expansion of expenditure by the defence services. As late as 1937, when Germany's first great re-armament programme, inaugurated by Hitler, was well under way, the British Minister of Co-ordination of Defence, on the advice of his experts, placed any continental commitment for the Army fourth in a list of its priorities[2]. Defence of imperial commitments remained at the top of the list. Training for the Army in the United Kingdom still consisted of drill, musketry, marching and digging. Manoeuvres occupied two weeks of the year at most. Posters advertising 'The Finest Job In The World' emphasised sport and travel and job satisfaction but hid the dull lethargy of barrack life.

The creation of the Royal Air Force and a new belief that 'The bomber will always get through' diverted funds from the Army and downgraded it in public esteem. A most important priority for army equipment and manning in the 1930s was the air defence of Great Britain. In 1934, it came second only to the defence of the Empire. The 'Searchlight Tattoos' of the 1930s emphasised with increasing shrillness the importance of air defence and the manning gaps in the Territorial Army units dedicated to the air defence of London[3]. Despite the rising concern over air defence, Parliament and public were as determined to avoid the imposition of conscription as they had been before the First World War. In the face of massive German re-armament, successive British Governments refused to take the necessary steps to provide a deterrent to the Dictators. No doubt this was partly from a desire for financial retrenchment in a period of acute economic depression but it was also from a craven fear of provoking Hitler. Correlli Barnet says[4] that a trained conscript army, ready to go to the assistance of France in 1914, would have prevented the First World War and perhaps the Second World War also, or at least have delayed the defeat of France in that war. Again, it is easy to make judgements with the benefit of hindsight but, with the writing so clearly on the wall, it is extraordinary that even a moderate provision for National Service was delayed until a few months before the war in 1939, By the time that compulsory military service was reluctantly introduced in 1939 it was clear that the French would require substantial military support from Britain. Not only would they expect to be supported by many squadrons of the Royal Air Force, based in France, but that any projected British Expeditionary Force would be expanded beyond the few divisions which British Goverments traditionally regarded as an adequate contribution to mutual defence.

In 1934, whilst debating the proper role for Britain's defence forces, The Defence Requirements Sub-Committee of the Committee of Imperial Defence suggested that an expeditionary force of five divisions, supported by appropriate air forces, would act as a deterrent to an aggressor and exercise a force for peace out of all proportion to its size[5]. It seems that the lessons of the First World War had been quickly forgotten. The proposed force in 1934 would not have been superior to that of 1914; the air force contingent being matched presumably by the air forces of the potential aggressors, but by 1917 it had proved necessary to introduce general conscription and to field an army in France of fifty-six divisions. The belief that 'the bomber will always get through' seems to have occupied a place in British strategic thinking similar to the modern doctrine of the deterrence inherent in the threat of mutual nuclear destruction. But in the 1930s the evidence already showed that even if the bomber got through unacceptable destruction did not necessarily follow. Any destruction, especially in the cities, may have seemed unacceptable in the early thirties but a more objective analysis might have been expected from the defence experts. In Abyssinia, in Spain and in the cities of Britain and Germany, it became clear that an army's and a nation's determination to resist could not be crushed by conventional aerial bombardment alone[6].

Advocates Of a New Model, Liddell Hart and Boney Fuller

Despite the financial drain imposed by the new air force, with its seductive theories of holding land areas by air power alone, and the continuing industrial depression through the 1920s and early 1930s, it was not easy for the Governments of the day to ignore pressure from the advocates of the tank, armoured warfare and mechanisation in general. The Great War, raising as it did the scale and intensity of warfare in Europe to an unprecedented level, encouraged the emergence of a new school of 'scientific' military thinkers. The new machines and the growth of military science and technology suggested whole new concepts which were as far from 'regimental' thinking as it was possible to get. The chief of these critical new thinkers was Captain Basil Liddell Hart who left Cambridge without graduating in May 1914 and joined The King's Own Yorkshire Light Infantry. Although he wished to become a regular officer and had shown some interest in aviation and military history, he believed, like many others, that the war would be short and he was not prepared to spend even the minimum of three months required for training at Sandhurst. He joined Kitchener's army as a volunteer. After two short spells of front line service in the autumn and winter of 1915, he was invalided home after being concussed by the blast from a shell exploding close by. He returned to his battalion, 9th King's Own Yorkshire Light Infantry, in time for the Somme offensive of July 1916. Although left out of battle on the first day, when his division, the 21st, and his battalion, were almost completely wiped out, he was badly gassed going out of the line with his company on 18 July. He eventually made a recovery from the effects of the poison gas but he was never completely fit again. Whilst still on a temporary commission, he served after the war as adjutant to various volunteer units and in the training organisation. He applied for an appointment to the Historical Section of the Committee of Imperial Defence but was turned down. He also applied for regular commissions in the newly formed Army Education Corps and the Tank Corps, but was rejected for both on medical grounds and by 1924, he was invalided out of the Army. Meanwhile he had begun to write about military matters and had become closely acquainted with the other outstanding British military thinker of the inter-war years, Colonel J F C Fuller[7].

Fuller was seventeen years Liddell Hart's senior and had joined the Army in 1898 when he was commissioned in The Oxfordshire Light Infantry. Unlike Liddell Hart, he appears to have been a severe critic of the Army and of his military superiors from the beginning but as Anthony Trythall points out[8] in his biography of Fuller, the Army can be surprisingly tolerant of 'loners' and of dissenting voices as long as orders are obeyed and social scandal is avoided. Trythall also makes the point that all regiments are equal but some are more equal than others and in the cavalry and the light infantry there may be more tolerance of ambiguity. Both Liddell Hart and Fuller joined prestigious regiments although Hart, being a temporary officer, found himself in the comparatively highly numbered 9th Battalion in a Kitchener division; even so, by the end of the war, his regiment had raised a further seventeen battalions. Fuller had served with his 1st Battalion in the South African War from where, although he does not seem to have taken part in any stirring actions, he was invalided home to recover from a serious appendicitis operation. He returned to South Africa in time to lead a group of irregular and unreliable Kaffir scouts which he seemed to manage after the style of his famous contemporary, Robert Baden-Powell. Typical of Fuller's attitude towards his fellow officers and the way in which the war was being fought were the sentiments expressed in a letter to his mother before he was invalided home. Amongst other opinions given was that 'the country is quite impossible' and 'I begin to wonder what we are fighting for. I have been in the Army long enough to see that nine officers out of every ten. . . know no more of military affairs than the man in the moon'. Trythall, who quotes this letter in his biography, describes it as 'strong, thoughtful and critical language for a young infantry subaltern of twenty-one in the middle of an uncomfortable war'. Sadly it also gives some evidence of the hyper-critical and self-opinionated young man who would later develop into the suspicious, ungenerous, almost paranoid man that he became. Although Fuller did not start to write books or pamphlets on military training until 1913, the first book noted in the list of books published by Major General Fuller given in Trythall's biography is one on Aleister Crowley, which appeared in 1907[9]. Fuller's interest in magic and the occult and esoteric religions foreshadowed his later conversion, after meeting Sir Oswald Moseley, to the irrational anti-semitic and cult-like British

Union of Fascists. Again, as Trythall says, 'joining the British Union of Fascists was in many ways a natural development of his previous political thinking and beliefs.'[10]

In 1913, at his second attempt, Fuller passed into the Staff College but with the outbreak of war, his two year course at Camberley was cut short and he found himself, with many other Staff College graduates, on the 'Movements Staff' at Southampton. After a third grade staff post in England, he eventually arrived, in July 1915 on the staff of HQ VII Corps some ten miles behind the front. By Boxing Day 1916 he had arrived at Bermicourt to occupy a new GSO 2 post at the Headquarters of the embryo Tank Corps and his real life's work had begun. As his biographer points out, Fuller was not involved in the design of the early tanks and there were already many sound ideas about their proper employment before he appeared on the scene but his knowledge of military science and his breadth of vision gave him a unique position with regard to the future development and employment of armoured forces. It is extremely difficult to disentangle the various claims to be the originator of the ideas that emerged towards the end of the Great War concerning the employment of tank forces. It is likely that many of them emerged simultaneously and, certainly, the plans and schemes had many overlapping features. There can be no doubt that the failure of the Somme offensive brought a change in intellectual climate for the military planners. By the end of 1917 Foch had been appointed Allied Commander-in-Chief and early in 1918 Henry Wilson replaced Robertson as CIGS. These, as well as other important army leaders were already converted to the idea of the tank as a war winning weapon.

Meanwhile, Major General Sir John Capper had taken over as Administrative Commandant of the Heavy Branch Machine Gun Corps in May 1917. Capper, it will be recalled, had commanded the Balloon School at Aldershot before the war where he had been responsible for encouraging and taking part in William Cody's aeronautical experiments. To have taken such a vital part in the early development of the two weapons that would be of such decisive importance until the arrival of the atom bomb is quite remarkable but appears to have gone almost unnoticed except within a small circle. He eventually became Colonel Commandant of the Tank Corps and adds one more name to that extraordinary list of engineer soldiers who have emerged from their Corps to play a part on a wider stage.

Fuller was never in action on the Western Front but he did observe many of the battles of the last years of the war. His main contribution to military thinking was in his attempt to apply scientific method, as he understood it, to the study of war and in his advocacy of the tank and especially large armoured formations as the irresistible weapons of the future. His planning at Bermicourt, and the writings which soon began to pour from him in a constant stream, made him known throughout the Army and to a wider public and, in 1923, he was selected as an instructor for the Staff College. Fuller and Liddell Hart met and corresponded frequently whilst Fuller was at the Staff College. After his retirement from the Army in 1924, Liddell Hart became a military correspondent. Having successfully reported on the Territorial Army manoeuvres of 1924, he was chosen to succeed Colonel Repington as military correspondent of *The Daily Telegraph*. Liddell Hart had arrived and, as though to make the point, he was able to repay Fuller's previous and ill-fated sponsorship when he attempted to join the Royal Tank Corps. The boot was now clearly on the other foot and, in the course of a conversation with General Sir George Milne in an Arundel pub, Liddell Hart was able to suggest Fuller as a suitable 'ostensible' Military Assistant to the General, who had been selected to be the next CIGS. It was ostensible only because Milne had accepted Liddell Hart's idea of using Fuller as a 'thinking ahead organ'.[11] At the end of 1925, Fuller left the Staff College and by February 1926 he was installed as Military Assistant to the new CIGS. It is more than likely, as Trythall says, that General Milne did not know what Liddell Hart had let him in for but he was soon to find out. The idea of establishing an experimental mechanised force had been talked about for some time but by early 1926 the pressure from Liddell Hart and other critics of military policy had become so strong that action had to be taken. In March, the Secretary of State announced the formation of the Experimental Mechanised Force. The force was to be composed of tanks, mechanised artillery, armoured cars, sappers and signallers and rather 'over egged', as Fuller and some others thought, by having three 'mechanical infantry' battalions.

Interestingly, Colonel Lindsay, the then Inspector, Royal Tank Corps, opposed the perpetuation of the Regimental system in the Experimental Force. He believed that the 'experiment' should be kept firmly under the hand of the Royal Tank Corps and opposed the distribution of mechanised fighting vehicles outside the RTC, at least for the time being. The CIGS however was a realist and, whilst he had offered the command of the Experimental Force to Fuller, his response to Lindsay was 'I do not propose that the Tank Corps should swallow the Army, but as this corps is the only one which possesses trained personnel at present, we must draw on it to initiate the Experimental Unit'.[12] Lindsay also, for what were probably thoroughly Machiavellian reasons, proposed that the conversion of cavalry regiments should be postponed. But it was not Lindsay who put the most important restrictions on the experiment but Fuller himself. For a number of reasons, some of them personal and even petty, admirably explained by Tony Trythall, Fuller refused command of the Experimental Force and left the War Office, one imagines much to the CIGS's relief. He continued with his writing and was promoted to Major-General in 1930. His writings were influential, certainly outside the Army but it seems that he had missed his big chance in 1926 and nothing could ever be the same again. He was never happy in an army posting after leaving the War Office and after a series of posts and offers of posts, some of which he regarded as deliberately insulting, retired finally in 1933 after three years on the unemployed list.

The place of Fuller and Liddell Hart in the history of military theory is assured and their influence amongst military intellectuals, especially outside their native land, is profound. Practically, however, they could have achieved much more if they had not both been such appallingly difficult people to deal with. Fuller's brief but acrimonious connection with the Experimental Force and his later obsession with fascism, anti-semitism and the consolations of the occult and irrational speak for themselves. From the beginning, Fuller seemed to despise the Army and most of his fellow officers. He seems to have had no affection for his regiment and in the end, no doubt, he was just an embarrassment to it. Liddell Hart, on the other hand, entered the Army full of hope and with high regard for his regiment and the military system and an almost sycophantic respect for his senior officers. Brian Bond describes him in those early days as a typical English public school boy filled with enthusiasm for the war and sustained by a high patriotic spirit. As with so many soldiers, those high endeavours and regard for the generals responsible for the higher direction of the war did not survive his battle experiences and his gassing.

Like Fuller, he continued to think and write about war. Both applied a deductive method to their study of war and both prided themselves on their scientific approach to their chosen subject. But neither of them used what would be accepted today as scientific method and Fuller, tragically, rejected the one chance to try out his theories on a reasonably experimental basis that he was ever to receive. Liddell Hart's views remained curiously old-fashioned in some respects, right up to his death, and Correlli Barnet insists on his partial responsibility for Britain's unpreparedness for war by arguing against any form of conscription almost until the outbreak of war in September 1939[13]. The CIGS had to tell Fuller not to be silly over some of his more egocentric demands in connection with the Experimental Force and T E Lawrence whose biography was being written by Liddell Hart, said much the same thing to him but in a more elegant language. In the Strand with Liddell Hart, Lawrence pointing to a match seller, remarked, 'If you let your passion for truth grow upon you like this, you'll finish by selling matches in the Strand'[14].

Unlike Fuller however, Liddell Hart was not attracted by totalitarian philosophies, although his demonstration of this fact seemed sometimes to stand accepted beliefs on their head. One of his arguments against conscription was that it drew into the Army all kinds of unwarlike and unsuitable, not to mention unwilling, recruits in contradistinction to our successful policy in India where we had constituted our forces from the good 'fighting animals' of the martial races. It is difficult to conceive how Liddell Hart imagined it might be possible to recruit from the British 'martial races'. Perhaps we are back yet again to Kitchener's unfortunate remark to Lloyd George. The whole argument could be dismissed as grotesque but for its frequent recurrence. The most recent example appeared in *The Times* published on 5th April 1988 where a leading article purporting to support the end of a colour bar in recruiting suggested that one of the advantages of a wider ethnic entry was that we could obtain good recruits from those immigrants in Britain who came originally from the martial races of the old Indian Army[15].

Contrary to popular belief, there is evidence that Fuller and the Experimental Force were supported by more senior officers than is generally supposed. Apart from the CIGS, who had, after all, set up the Force and offered Fuller the command, General David Campbell, who had been Military Secretary when the offer was made and then went to the very senior appointment of GOC-in-C Aldershot, begged Fuller to withdraw his resignation. Similarly, Major General Burnett-Stuart, who was GOC of the 3rd Division at Tidworth had declined to take the Experimental Force under his wing and had asked for a 'visionary commander' for the new organisation. This could only have meant Fuller. There must also have been many, more junior officers only waiting for a lead. As we have said, it seems likely that the CIGS was glad to accept Fuller's resignation and to see the back of a 'difficult' officer. The Experimental Force went to an infantry officer 'with no experience of mechanised troops'[16] and in 1928 the talk was still of tanks supporting cavalry in the attack. Even after the First World War, the limitations of the horse were still not grasped and Colonel Lindsay, in his desire to postpone the mechanisation of the cavalry, would have received overwhelming support from every horsed unit in the British Army. One is sadly reminded of a quotation reported by Jan Morris in her review of The Marquess of Anglesey's *History of the British Cavalry, Volume 4*. The 12th Lancers own historian recorded the observation of Queen Victoria's Army, but it clearly applied equally well to a later age; British cavalry officers 'talked more and knew less about horses then anyone else on earth'.

Re-Armament and The German 'New Model'

Between the wars, Italy, followed by Germany, rearmed, paying particular attention to the air arm and to mechanised forces. Germany especially, having learned a hard lesson in the Great War, was quick to take up the ideas of Fuller and Liddell Hart. Although restricted by the Treaty of Versailles to an army of 100,000 men, Germany was able to enter into secret arrangements with the Soviet Union which allowed for the training of mechanised formations even where the formations were, of necessity, sometimes made up of token armoured vehicles. Fascist and Nazi ideology introduced a militaristic note into their respective societies which, at the very least, encouraged a warlike attitude in the civil population and facilitated the move towards a war economy. Hitler came to power in 1933, pledged to avenge the alleged wrongs and injustices of the Versailles *Dictat* and immediately embarked on a programme of rearmament which was able to capitalise on the training and experimentation carried on in the 100,000 man army. Both Italy and Germany used the Spanish Civil War to try out weapons and equipment and both countries 'blooded' their growing air forces in that conflict. The German Army had managed to steer clear of serious involvement with the Nazis although there had been an unfortunate incident at the Munich Officers' School during the 'Hitler Putsch' of 1923. General Von Seekt, as head of the Army, castigated the young cadets involved as mutineers and moved the Academy to Leipzig, away from the pro-Nazi atmosphere of Munich, but no other action was taken[17]. Again, some young officers succumbed to the wave of agitation in support of the National Movement of 1929/30. Nazi cells were set up by a small number of officers of whom three were arrested, tried and found guilty of High Treason. As the power of the National Socialist Party grew, the German Army and its commanders tried to secure its position vis-à-vis the Nazis. In 1932, General Schleicher, acting as Army Minister, warned Hitler, 'If you come to power legally that will be all right with me: If not, I shall shoot'. After his success in the German election of 1933, President von Hindenburg appointed Hitler as Chancellor who thus came legitimately to power. After the election, Hitler paid homage to Hindenburg and, by implication, to the German Army, in the Guards' Chapel at Potsdam. This was meant to seal an agreement that the German Army should be the sole bearer of arms in the new Germany. In 1934, when Hitler was under strong pressure from the SA, the left wing of the Nazi movement under Röhm, he used the excuse of his pledge to the Army, to murder Röhm and several other SA leaders and disband the radical element in his movement. The elimination of the SA in the 'Night of the Long Knives' was carried out by the SS *Leibstandarte*,

Hitler's personal bodyguard commanded by Sepp Dietrich. Suitable weapons were provided by the Army through the Chief of Staff, von Reichenau. One of the victims of the SS murder squads was General Schleicher who, for a few weeks, had been Chancellor before Hitler came to power. General Schleicher and his wife were murdered at the door of their house in Berlin.[18]

The failure of the German Army to react to the SS terror, and especially to the murder of General Schleicher, marked the beginning of the moral degradation of the Army under Hitler. From that time on, even if it was able to avoid involvement in the worst acts carried out by the SS, the German Army could not avoid its share of the responsibility. In 1935, Hitler's Government abrogated the Treaty of Versailles and re-introduced Universal National Service. The German General Staff, had they been asked, would have proposed, in that rather näive way which seemed to characterise all their dealings with Hitler and the Nazis, a strength of twenty-one divisions. Like it or not, the German Government gave them thirty-six. It is likely that some opposition within the Army was bought-off by the massive expansion and modernisation programme put in train in 1935. Expansion was good for promotion at every level. Hitler interested himself in technical matters and encouraged General Guderian to continue with his practical application of Liddell Hart's ideas on large scale armoured penetration. The first three Panzer divisions created in 1935 clearly owed something to Liddell Hart's pioneering work but, as Brian Bond explains[19], the balance within the divisions between an infantry brigade and a tank brigade was not in accordance with either Liddell Hart's or Fuller's ideas. The creation of a new type of infantryman, the *panzer grenadier*, followed early Royal Tank Corps ideas of getting away from the traditional infantry regiment but it was never followed up in the British Army although the motor battalions introduced into the British armoured divisions soon after the outbreak of the Second World War, which were traditionally, but not exclusively, found by the Green Jackets, performed a similar function and with great effect. Germany had been banned from having an air force under the provisions of the Treaty of Versailles but, in March 1935, the German Government announced that a German air force was already in existence. In the absence of anything more than solemn protests from Britain and France, the arms build-up went ahead, much to the delight of the young German aviators who had been restricted to gliders in their aeronautical training.

In August 1934, on the death of President von Hindenburg, Hitler, with the agreement of all concerned, including the German Commander-in-Chief General von Blomberg, assumed the combined office of President and Chancellor as well as that of Supreme Commander-in-Chief of the Armed Forces of the Reich.[20] All officers and men in the Armed Forces took an oath of loyalty directly to Hitler and this, as we have said in an earlier chapter, was used by many senior officers to justify their acquiescence to the horrors perpetuated by Hitler and his criminal henchmen. Despite a strong guarantee of the Army's loyalty, Hitler maintained and built up the Waffen (armed) SS as a counter balance to the Army. By the last years of the war, the Waffen SS had expanded to a force of many divisions. The Panzer SS divisions were the most powerfully armed in the German forces, receiving as they did priority in reinforcements of personnel and material. The SS elite formations were amongst the best fighting units of the Second World War but the SS also provided the concentration camp guards, the executioners and torturers, and many SS units were composed of the sweepings of Europe. Despite their protests to the contrary, they could not choose between their roles; and the SS badge can only be regarded as the mark of infamy.

By the beginning of the Second World War, the German Army had expanded to one hundred and five divisions of which six were panzer divisions and ten were mechanised and included some armour. Britain could oppose three armoured divisions, one of them in Egypt whilst the other two were not much better than in embryo, one of them being completely without tanks. The mobilisation of the British forces, overlapped and confused to some extent by the beginnings of militia training, had nothing like the planned completeness of the mobilisation of 1914. In 1914, four infantry divisions and a cavalry division were across the channel in the first two weeks of the war. In 1939 the French were warned that it would be thirty-three days after mobilisation before four infantry divisions and one armoured division could be deployed in France. By some blessed misfortune, the armoured division never got to France and so it was available for the defence of Britain in the crisis days after the retreat through Dunkirk. In March 1939, the Territorial Army had been doubled to twenty-six divisions, bringing the strength of the British Army to thirty-two divisions. In May, three months before the outbreak of war, the Compulsory Training Act, calling for six months training was passed. To add to the tale of unpreparedness, despite the tank being a British innovation giving us at least ten years in development lead over our enemies, there were no satisfactory British tanks with fighting units until 1943. Except for the short period at the beginning of the Desert War in Egypt and Libya against the Italians, British tanks were almost always inferior to those of the enemy.

Special Forces, Another 'New Model'

As in the First World War, the Regiments tended to get lost in large formations fighting the battles of the Second World War. Even in the Desert War, which most closely resembled, in scale at least, earlier British campaigns, it was and still is the famous divisions which are remembered rather than the regiments, the Desert Rats (7th Armoured Division) and the Highland Division are remembered and their insignia still recognised whilst the identities of the many famous regiments which composed them were hardly known. Another phenomenon which moved the media glare away from the regiments was the emergence of the private armies and special forces. In the desert which was good country for the creation of small irregular forces one found the Special Air Service, the Long Range Desert Group, Popski's Group, the Special Boat Service, several different Commando organisations and several other small groups operating under the umbrella of Combined Operations. None of these were the really secret organisations, of which there must have been many. However much they wanted to avoid publicity, and not all of them did, they were inevitably magnets for the media, diverting the newspaper reports and news-reel coverage from the less glamorous and less excitingly employed regiments. Lack of publicity and the consequent lowering of morale which occasionally brought forth guilty stories about 'The Forgotten Army' but not much about forgotten regiments was not the only unfortunate result of the setting up of private armies and Special Forces. A constant seeping away into special organisations of the best of their officers and men, was an ever present fact of life for most commanding officers. Outstanding officers volunteered for the Commando Forces from 1940 onwards and ambitious and adventurous soldiers and NCOs went with them. Apart from the attraction of the parachute regiments and the other special forces, new organisations were set up as the war went on which seemed to offer better prospects of a commission or promotion such as the Glider Pilot Regiment and the regiments of the Reconnaissance Corps. All drained the ordinary regiments of the Army of their natural leaders. Whether the military gains resulting from the setting up of special organisations and 'super élites'; compensated for the weakening of the Army as a whole and, indeed, whether the very severe casualties which almost always accompanied special operations were worth the candle, has been hotly debated and we will return to the question. The scale of the problem can be seen however from the fact that by 1944 there were two complete British Airborne Divisions, four brigades of Commandos made up of six Army Commandos and six Royal Marine

Commandos, several independent commando units, a Special Air Service Brigade and many smaller irregular units.

There have always been élite troops in the British Army, and in the early days they were the household troops of the King. They would have been specially recruited for their size, strength and bearing, and of course for their absolute loyalty. The special loyalty of Household troops would have been ensured through an oath sworn to the King just as Hitler insisted on officers and men making their oath directly to him when he took over as combined President, Chancellor and Supreme Commander-in-Chief. After the Civil War, when the Guards regiments were first formed, in addition to better pay, brighter uniforms and better weapons, the special status of the Guards was marked by special distinctions of rank, precedence and prestige.[21] Even so, the Guards regiments recruited and trained their own men, and officers were not normally tempted to transfer to Guards regiments, even where they would have been acceptable, because of the additional expense of serving in a Household regiment, incurring in addition the heavy outgoings which came from being permanently based in the capital city.[22] The Guards did have their own 'seepage' problems early in the war when many officers and men volunteered for the newly formed Commandos. But the Guards were quite used to the problem since a disproportionate number of drill instructors in the Army training organisation, Garrison Sergeant Majors and senior administrative posts were supplied by the Brigade of Guards. On a more exalted plane, the Guards have, at least until recently, filled a disproportionate number of General Officer appointments in the Army as one of the obvious perquisites of belonging to the Brigade. Until comparatively recently also, seniority as a Guards officer was enhanced automatically by one step in the ordinary Army List. The élitism and the attraction of the Special Forces was of a different kind.

After the war almost all the special units were disbanded. There had always been suspicion and some resentment of the prestige and influence of the new élites and, if only for the need to regain strength, the regiments claimed back their own. Many officers and NCOs were in any case regular soldiers who could only progress in the Army in the environment of their original regiments. Only the Special Air Service was retained by the Army or rather re-instituted after two years of non-existence and only then as a Territorial Army Unit. In 1947 the SAS reappeared as the 21st SAS (Artists) Regiment. The Artists Rifles had an honourable history, first as a volunteer and later as a Territorial battalion. The Army was quick to give up its commando forces but the Royal Marines through some inspired aberration which has served them well ever since, took over the

Commando role. The Marine Commando forces were reduced to one brigade but they have managed to remain in being, despite some very serious threats to the existence of the Royal Marines as a whole which have already been mentioned. At one stage in the early seventies it was rumoured, and believed by many Royal Marines, that there was a choice to be made between retaining the Royal Marines or the Gurkha Brigade. It was also assumed in the Marines that if the Royal Navy had to choose between them and another ship the Marines would have to go. They were even more cynical about their chances during a later financial crisis when the Minister for War happened to be an ex-Gurkha officer.[23] It is possible that the Falklands campaign saved the Royal Marines, as it is said to have saved some other institutions. Over thirty years of specialised training in snow and mountain warfare, and a genuine amphibious operation, which had always been the justification for the Marines existence, came together, but only in the nick of time. Whilst they may not have operated with the panache of the parachute troops, their performance was utterly reliable and completely professional so that where mistakes were made in the Falklands it was sometimes because the expert advice of the Marines had been ignored. The Royal Navy may also have discovered, to its surprise, that the only justification for maintaining its larger surface ships was in being able to support similar operations by its amphibious forces. Without one the other would be pointless.

Conscription was retained in Britain until 1962 but whilst this did produce the largest pool of military manpower ever available in Britain in peacetime, it also brought its own problems. First of all, in the name of social justice, the system produced too many recruits, so that too large a proportion of the regular forces were employed in training conscripts. Many of the enforced recruits were unhappy with their role and tended to blame the Army for their predicament. Some National Servicemen were able to enjoy their time in the Forces and took advantage of the opportunity to travel abroad and to become leaders for the first time, but for others the period of their service was at best boring and time wasting and at worst was regarded as very near to a prison sentence. In retrospect it was probably a mistake to recall regular reservists rather than use National Servicemen during some of the emergencies which arose during the fifties and sixties. There is evidence that where they were employed with regular troops in action they behaved in exactly the same way as the regular soldiers. For many reservists it seemed unfair, in many cases having served through the Second World War, to be recalled for duty in Korea or elsewhere, whilst sufficient conscript soldiers were available. A comparison of the French experience in the post-war period with that of the British is instructive.

Decolonisation and the French Army

After the Armistice of the 8th May 1945, the French Army was faced with two tasks. One was similar to the British task of reducing the inflated wartime forces to a peacetime and affordable establishment. The second resulted from the French defeat in 1940 and the subsequent rebuilding of the Army from the disparate elements which survived or arose after the collapse. The 2nd Armoured Division of General Leclerc, formed from the Free French Forces of General de Gaulle, landed in Normandy with the Allies in 1944. The 1st Army of General de Lattre de Tassigny had rallied to the Allies in North Africa and had landed in Provence a little after the Normandy landings. In addition, there were the French Forces of the Interior (FFI) who came together from the various resistance organisations operating against the occupying German Army before the liberation. General de Lattre tried to absorb the FFI into his force along with the other elements from Britain and North Africa and, eventually, the returning officers and soldiers who had been transported as prisoners of war to Germany. It was obviously a very uneasy mix but an even more urgent problem was the perennial postwar necessity to reduce the military budget, which was running at 25 per cent of the total French budget in 1946. Under the 'Law of Disengagement' 40 per cent of officers and 45 per cent of NCOs were discharged and, as is usual in these circumstances, it was the best qualified who chose to leave. Over 50 per cent of St. Cyriens, who were the regular 'tooth arm' officers, and an even higher percentage of *Polytechniciens*, who provided the officers for the Engineers, Artillery and other specialist services, left the Army. Thus although conscription was reintroduced and fixed at one year, it was an army deficient in modern equipment and trained leaders which had to face the difficulties of de-colonisation and the trauma of the ten years war in Indochina[24]. As we have said, the French sent only their regular troops (including elements of the Foreign Legion) or those on short contracts, to fight in the East. The conflict grew in scale until it became literally insupportable. For the last seven years of the war in Indochina, one French officer died every day, 800 St. Cyr graduates were killed in the war. Over 100,000 soldiers were killed, wounded or captured in Vietnam, Laos and Cambodia and 129,000 had been sent as reinforcements. By 1954 only 879 regular soldiers remained in France available to be sent to the East[25].

When the French finally withdrew from Indochina, there were only 117,000 men containing the troubles then spreading throughout the whole of North Africa. At the end of 1955, Tunisia and Morocco were given complete independence but the French would not accept that Algeria, which had a large French colonial population and was regarded as a province of Metropolitan France, really wanted independence. Before long, 400,000 French troops were engaged there in a bitter war. But North Africa, being near home and containing a large French population, was considered a suitable theatre for conscript soldiers. For the first time since the war, the numbers of conscripts killed exceeded the other categories of servicemen. (Professionals, Gendarmes, *Légionaires*, North Africans and Africans). 9,349 conscripts out of a total of 18,207 and 32,003 wounded out of 55,549[26]. The French regular officers and men in North Africa, most of whom had served in Indochina and many whom had been captured by the Vietminh, at Dien Bien Phu were determined not to allow themselves to be defeated again. The French Army, especially the two parachute divisions, the Foreign Legion and the Marine parachute battalions, threw themselves into a struggle which took on the nature of a crusade. The French version of what was known in Britain and America as the 'Hearts and Minds' programme was a system which they had seen being operated by the Vietminh with some success. The setting up of 'parallel hierarchies' was intended to deny to the enemy the financial and moral support of the civilian population. The guerrilla was no longer to be allowed to swim in a warm friendly sea, collecting contributions for the rebels and organising civil disobedience. The 'hierarchies' set up by the Army were mainly in the large towns where the aim was to keep an eye on and limit if possible the activities of the *Front de Libération Nationale (FLN)*. The largest effort went into the recruiting of 'delegates' for every block, building and district. In some areas where retired native veterans could be recruited some success was achieved. Elsewhere, lack of protection for the delegates and lack of interest or hostility from the general population doomed the experiment to failure. Other methods adapted from the emergency in Malaya were tried out. The frontiers between Algeria and Tunisia and between Algeria and Libya were sealed off but not efficiently and the French Army and Air Force was not allowed to attack FLN bases in the sanctuaries across the border. For some years, up to 1959, some two million Muslims were forcibly relocated where they could be supervised and cut off from all contact with the enemy. But in many cases this proved to be counter productive. Conditions in some of the new locations were so bad that the civil population became even more disillusioned with the authorities, who became rapidly alarmed about the human and social consequences of the enforced movement[27].

It was also necessary for the Army to set up a massive progamme of indoctrination or justification, in order to convince the large numbers of conscripts that their role in Algeria was legitimate. The effect of the 'uncertain trumpet' was felt very strongly in Algeria where the

Army had to take over the police role and soon became entangled in a system of repression and torture. In Metropolitan France, there was strong opposition to the war in North Africa not only from the Trade Unions and the Communist party but also from the Catholic Church and from many liberal political and academic institutions. Because of the lack of commitment of the non-regular soldiers, the main thrust of the campaign was left to the élite regular units of the Paras , the Legion and the Marines. In some areas, garrison troops engaged on pacification or policing activities would actually draw back from their tasks and send for the Paras or the Legion to do what could be considered as their 'dirty work' for them. The strong opposition of the Catholic Church to the repression and the brutal methods employed infuriated many of the regular officers who were Catholics themselves. But without doubt, the Army was besmirched by taking on police methods in its necessary administration of justice. The actions of the Tenth Parachute Division under General Massu in the 'pacification' of the city of Algiers during the winter of 1956/7 led to general revulsion at their methods but also, for the first time, to an understanding of the basic contradictions of a system which led to the permanent alienation of the Muslim population. Many officers refused to torture captured guerrillas or to execute them out of hand, but Massu and some other officers admitted and took responsibility for their methods as being the only way in which the war could be won. In the end, after attempting to put pressure on the Metropolitan Government, and successful at first in bringing General de Gaulle to power, the group of Generals who wished to keep Algeria as part of France were isolated. Faithful to their officers, seven parachute battalions were prepared to back a last coup but the rest of the Army refused to co-operate and severed the communications with sympathisers in France and in North Africa, making it clear that they would resist any action against the legitimate government. This was by no means only the work of the conscript soldiers but their strong links with Metropolitan France, their easy access to radio broadcasts from home and their awareness of support from the overwhelming majority of the French population, helped them to resist the call to rebellion[28].

By April 1961 it was clear that the Army was not going to take any further part in attempts to maintain French power in Algeria. There were further incidents, some of them bloody, involving the French settlers and later the *'Organisation de L'Armée Secrète'* (OAS) but the Army operated clearly and unequivocally on the side of the Government in Paris and, by mid 1962, the North African war was over. For the French Army, what followed was a period of quiet reorganisation and reconsolidation. Some officers were tried for their part in the attempted coups or for their membership of the OAS. The sentences of most of those found guilty were suspended. The élite troops, especially the parachute battalions, went through a difficult period. They were convinced that in North Africa, as well as in Indochina, they had been defending Western civilisation. It was hard to feel that they had lost again and still the world went on. There were resignations and transfers and redesignations but the élites remained what they had become since the war, the toughest and best of French fighting troops. The parachute battalions carry the titles of the Army, the Marines and the Legion but they are more highly regarded in France now than ever before and their many operations in Chad and in support of the Governments of former French colonies elsewhere have re-established them in the eyes of their countrymen. Now the French *'Force d'Intervention'* is composed of almost equal numbers of regulars and conscripts but, significantly, the vast majority of officers and NCOs in the Force are regular soldiers.

There are some points to be made and some parallels to be drawn from the two great wars of decolonisation in which the French Army was involved in the decades immediately after the Second World War. The first concerns the scale of the conflicts. The figures we have given for the casualties in Indochina and the Army's involvement in Algeria, emphasise the fact that the French post-war conflicts were of an order far larger than those 'small wars', police actions and anti-insurgencies in which the British have been involved. The second point is that, in both conflicts, it was the regular soldiers who carried the weight of the war. In Indochina, conscripts were not sent to the war and in Algeria, although conscripts were involved and took a high share of casualties, especially early on in the fighting, it was the regulars and, in particular, the élite formations, which had the will and the commitment to carry on the struggle to the bitter end. This last point has an importance for the abolition of National Service in Britain in 1962, for the continuing confrontation in Northern Ireland and for the way in which the Falklands campaign was fought in 1982. It is extremely unlikely that conscript soldiers could have been used in Northern Ireland during the emergency and it is generally accepted that it is the discipline and control of the British regular troops there which had made the twenty years confrontation bearable. We shall return to the Falklands War but meanwhile it should be noted that on the British side the war was carried on entirely by élite formations.

In both Germany and France, conscription has caused problems in the acceptable employment of soldiers who serve through compulsion. The 'uncertain trumpet' is a very real phenomenon. In France, apart from the non-use of conscript soldiers in Indochina and their equivocal position in Algeria, laws of 1959 and 1965 substituted for the classical concept of military service the broader one of national service. The new concept took account of conscientious objection to military service, the needs of the services, the provision of technical aid for overseas territories and for underdeveloped countries[29]. In Germany, when the Army was re-established after the Second World War, an essential part of the training of all servicemen was concerned with the personal responsibility of all ranks for the consequences of their actions and an awareness of their own and others' civil rights. Because of the seemingly over-riding needs of re-armament and military expansion the requirements of the so-called '*Innere Führung*' programme have been much reduced. Even more significantly, more emphasis has been placed on creating a balance between regular, conscript and short service soldiers.

The war in Korea, which started in 1950, came at a particularly bad time for the French because of their heavy involvement in Indochina, even so they diverted a battalion from Indochina which fought gallantly alongside the American forces. Britain, whilst not committed to anything like the same extent as the French, was nevertheless in confrontation in Egypt and Eritrea and was deploying twelve battalions in Malaya. The Mau Mau rebellion was also shortly to break out in Kenya. By the 29th of August, two British battalions were in Korea; they could only raise three rifle companies each and nearly half their strength was in National Servicemen. The first of the British Regiments in Korea were The Middlesex Regiment, the descendants of the 'Die Hards' of Albuhera and The Argyll and Sutherland Highlanders, who could include in their ancestry the 'Thin Red Line' of Balaclava. They were followed by the Gloucesters and the Ulster Rifles both of which regiments fought in the bloody battle on the Imjin River, and by The King's Own Scottish Borderers, The Royal Leicesters and The King's Shropshire Light Infantry. All the regiments had strong contingents of National Servicemen who did their duty and fought well, indeed, the performance of The Duke of Wellington's Regiment and the Black Watch, both battalions being almost entirely National Service in content, with excellent regular officers and NCOs, fought battles in defence of a feature known as 'the Hook' which will go down to history. It was the recalled reservists who, in some cases complained of having to serve for a further period of duty. There was no uncertain trumpet in Korea but there was some resentment of the heavy handedness of manning branches who, according to Max Hastings,[30] sent former prisoners of war of the Japanese back to Korea to be captured again and imprisoned in areas near where they had been held in the Second World War. The action in Korea was the first and probably the only war to be fought, theoretically at least, under the authority of the United Nations. The good luck and Russian miscalculation which allowed the United Nations to condemn and then take action against the North Korean invasion of South Korea is unlikely to be repeated. The United States was able to reinforce its skeleton forces from Japan and to hold on to a bridgehead until it was in a position to build an army, mainly American but containing contingents from twenty-three nations. By the end of the fighting there was a Commonwealth Division incorporating units from Britain, Canada, South Africa, New Zealand, Australia and elsewhere. One lesson that seems to have been learned in the conflict is that small contingents of troops in an allied force run the risk of exploitation. It has been said that until the Commonwealth forces had a General of their own to represent them in Allied councils, they were likely to be left for too long in exposed positions, like those on the Imjin River. However, once properly established, the Commonwealth Division quickly proved itself to be a model upon which incoming American generals were advised by their own Army Commander to train their own formations, in terms of operational efficiency and effectiveness. The common background of the Commonwealth contingents, dating from the Second World War, and a common military tradition, created a fighting formation which was the envy of all and probably only rivalled by the 1st United States Marine Division.

Apart from the war in Korea, most of the operations involving British forces in the years after the Second World War were a reversion to the pre-war colonial policing role, but there were two major differences from the pre-war situation. First, from the end of the European war, even before the acceptance of the Cold War as a fact of life, the centre of gravity of the British Army has remained in Germany. The three and sometimes four, British armoured divisions stationed permanently in the British Army of the Rhine represent the largest concentration of British military force in peacetime we are likely to see. Inevitably, this concentration of army units exercises an influence on the equipment design, training, ethos and morale of British forces everywhere. The Army in Germany attracts to itself most of the best equipment and most of the equipment trials and is the most important laboratory for testing Army doctrine in the course of development. It is also where the command ability of officers is tested from the regimental level through every formation up to Army Group. Ambitious army officers must rise through the levels of command in Germany.

Secondly, the colonial policing situation is different in that, since the war, British troops have, in most cases, been engaged in 'no win' situations. Not unlike the French in Indochina and Algeria, although on a smaller scale, the outcome of the conflict is clear to the outside observer but almost of necessity it must be hidden from the troops.

The limitation of damage and the screwing of the maximum advantage in terms of economic, political and strategic concessions in the post-conflict situation has led to some bizarre situations for the Army. In Palestine, Egypt, Kenya and Cyprus bitter conflict led only to withdrawal and the ultimate recognition of the hostile power and in Aden and South Arabia a similar process took place. Communist insurgency was defeated in Malaya after a protracted and expensive struggle and independence had then to be given to the Malays. The ambitions of the Indonesians were squashed very efficiently and very economically in the early sixties but this led to the abandonment of Singapore. Where the British Army has been able to impose its will and withdraw with some sense of satisfaction, it has been in situations paralleling more recent French experience where it has operated to protect a previous colony under some kind of treaty arrangement, in Chad, in the case of the French, and in Kenya, in the case of the British. Overseas wars since 1945 have tended to end in disillusion and withdrawal for all European powers. The withdrawals have been made easier by the gradual acceptance of the ideas that nationalism does not necessarily mean communism. In the climate of the Cold War, when the Russians appeared to be ready to exploit every power vacuum, the equation may have been a necessary guide to speedy reaction but events have falsified the too-easy assumption. Nationalist and even communist revolutionary parties, spurned and often opposed by the Western democracies, after gaining power through Russian military aid, have sometimes turned out to be at least neutral in the world struggle. China is perhaps the most important case in point.

The Post Colonial Army—the End of a World Role?

For the Army, and especially for the regiments, these changes have been little short of catastrophic. On the one hand, the many small and, in many cases, 'regimental size' postings or stations have gone, so that the Army rarely lives or indeed fights in regimental family units. On the other hand, the accumulation of military power in the Army in Germany produces a wide variety of anomalies and distortions which have changed the familiar pattern of British military life even further. The pool has been further muddied by the continuing emergency in Northern Ireland. Operations in Ulster are suitable for the employment of infantry regiments and for temporarily converted artillery and armoured units and, in the sense of getting the soldiers used to living under some stress and in providing excellent experience for junior commanders, they could be said to be good training for the Army. However, the Army's role in the Province is still more akin to policing than to fighting a war. Control and measured response , with a constant reference to the media and to the heterogeneous opposition to the Army's presence in Northern Ireland, may not produce ideal conditions in which the soldier can exercise his profession. For the soldier's family, the situation is even worse, living neither in peace nor war. The family separates or lives in a close garrison, remaining constantly alert and apprehensive and rarely able to enjoy the amenities and pleasures of serving as a family with a regiment at home or abroad. The final complicating factor has been the Falklands campaign. No families, no conscript soldiers and, by God, no uncertain trumpet! In the future, the Falklands campaign may be known as the 'War of the Élites'; Paratroops, Marine Commandos, the Guards and the Gurkhas. 'What war might we not have won', to plagiarise Fortescue's Horace.[31]

John Nott, who was Defence Minister at the time of the Falklands and who would have been responsible for the planned cuts which would have made any adequate response to the Argentine invasion impossible, believes that the campaign reinforces his view of Britain's military situation. In his two articles in *The Times* in October 1987, in the course of which he virtually eliminates the Sea Harriers and the Royal Marines, he complains of lack of conceptual thinking on the part of the Prime Minister and the Service Chiefs. Service experience has shown that if the carriers and the Sea Harriers and the Royal Marines had been got rid of in the name of what John Nott calls 'the fashionable political orgasm of the day, be it lower public expenditure, lower taxes or whatever' the expedition to recapture the Falklands would still have been mounted but with what consequences it is impossible to say. Despite all the evidence of continuing British involvement outside Europe, Nott comes down strongly against 'balanced forces'. The nuclear deterrent, he say's, is all that we can afford, and its defence in Europe and in the British base rules out any other line of action.[32] If Nott's view of the future is accurate, and it must have a certain attraction to the Treasury mandarins, it implies a very bleak outlook for the Army and particularly for its traditional institutions such as the regiment. It may be that Nott's vision only confirms the inevitable progress towards disintegration and reconstruction which we referred to in the introduction to this book. Clearly a restructuring or re-emphasis such as he suggests would mean an even closer contact with our NATO allies and an end perhaps to the opposition to a genuine European defence force. The formation of the Franco-German Air Mobile Brigade has recently raised the issue again but it is likely that the prejudices which prevented Britain from taking the lead in a similar but much larger European force in the early 1950s are still at work. Woodrow Wyatt in an article in *The Times* quotes Lord Slim, then CIGS, explaining why we did not co-operate in the formation of the combined force.[33] 'What would happen to the cap badges of The Royal Warwickshire Regiment?' Woodrow Wyatt adds ironically that the badges disappeared when the regiment was incorporated into The Royal Regiment of Fusiliers in 1968.

Persuasive as the vision of an army operating only in Europe as part of the NATO Force may be, it is only necessary to consider recent hijackings, terrorist outrages and threats, and the continuous role for British troops in Northern Ireland to realise that the vision is flawed. This is not to say that new structures are not necessary. More specialisation rather than less may be indicated. John Nott, speaking of balanced forces says 'to be ready to meet every possible contingency can lead only to a degradation of every capability'. This may not be true and it is certainly not self-evident but what is true is that if we have troops only available for action in Europe then our ability to protect our citizens and our interests in the rest of the world ceases absolutely. This may not matter but it does need to be argued.[34]

10

The End of the Family

A restructuring of the Army, whether it be of the John Nott variety or based on different premises, means a basic change in two aspects of army organisation and life. Any change now is almost bound to move in a certain direction, there can be no going back to an Army where the regiment was the dominant feature. The family life of the regiment is coming to an end as much for the young recruit who, in the past, was welcomed into the corporate family of the regiment, as for the young wife, officer's or soldier's, who was encouraged to feel that she had married into the regiment rather than into a family like the one she had just left.

For a while, the new recruit, who may not have come to the regiment or corps of his first choice,[1] will still wear the distinctive badges and embellishments of his uniform but they are fast disappearing. For reasons of economy alone, the old regiments, incorporated into the new administrative divisions, receive their basic training together with other regiments of the division. The recruits may not know which battalion they will serve with until after their early training and will look towards the division rather than the regiment. There will be an inevitable tendency for individual regimental matters of dress and of custom to be minimised. In the past, the history of the regiment, its honours, heroes, songs and trophies were an important part of the indoctrination of the recruit. Now, with the closure of regimental depots and the abandonment of so much of the trappings of the old regiments and the transformation of regimental museums into tourist attractions of doubtful purpose, the newcomer must find a new focus for his interest and loyalty.

The amalgamations of 1881 were, as we have said, the occasion of much regimental grief and for every winner, the new formations of linked battalions also produced a loser, or so it could be construed, in the second battalions. The determination to preserve a separate identity was stronger in some regiments than in others and the blatant

195

disregard of War Office intentions would be amusing if it were not evident of very deeply felt emotion. In 1881 The 26th (Cameronian) Regiment of Foot was amalgamated with The 90th Light Infantry Regiment, Perthshire Volunteers, to become The Cameronians (Scottish Rifles) (26th and 90th). The trouble was, as John Baynes points out,[2] The 26th (Cameronian) Regiment of Foot was more than 100 years older than the 90th but whilst it was of impeccable ancestry, it could be regarded by the young sprigs of a Light Infantry Regiment as a 'rather dull, heavy footed, "marching" regiment'. The 90th Light Infantry Regiment it will be recalled had been raised in 1794 by Lieutenant-Colonel Thomas Graham as the 90th Regiment of Foot in his ambition to become a regular officer. Graham of course had his good day at Barossa and became Wellington's Second-in-Command, having previously reached the rank of General. After the Waterloo campaign, when the distinction was finally conferred, the Perthshire Volunteers became the 90th Light Infantry Regiment, no doubt in part to honour its founder, the by now Lord Lynedoch. Both of the amalgamated regiments could feel embarrassed by the forced marriage of 1881. The Cameronians did retain the important part of their title but, more important, being the senior regiment, they became the 1st Battalion of the new regiment. The 90th became the 2nd Battalion but, from then on, called themselves the 2nd Scottish Rifles. Although there was some interchange of officers and soldiers between the battalions, especially during the First World War, the relationship seems to have been an uneasy one. Finally, in the 1968 defence cuts, The Cameronians, now reduced to a single regular battalion, were faced with the option of a further amalgamation or disbandment. Sadly, but perhaps not surprisingly, in the light of its experiences with the 1881 amalgamation, the regiment, or its decision makers, chose disbandment; but happily, through some sentimental quirk of War Office imagination, the regiment still lives on, ghost-like in the Army List, safe within The Scottish Division. That disbandments and amalgamations still cause disillusion and distress is shown by the biographical statement of a Warrant Officer who enlisted in The Royal Norfolk Regiment in 1943 and retired from the 1st Battalion The Royal Anglian Regiment in 1974. His statement is reproduced at Appendix IV.

Despite the brave words of the late CGS, Sir Nigel Bagnall, reported in our Introduction, the real message may be in his final statement, 'traditions had to be adjusted'. The traditions have been adjusted over a long period of time through amalgamations which have left very little of the old regiments in terms of their history, or individuality. The nomenclature of the new regiments has become so convoluted that it is seriously open to question whether attempting to retain a regimental title at all makes for more confusion and harm than doing away with them altogether. The new administrative divisions would seem to provide a new framework if an historical reference is still needed. In The Queen's Division and even more in The Light Division the move towards a new structure has been made, however reluctantly. The Queen's Division with three large regiments and The Light Division with two large regiments point the way towards a 'Divisional Regiment' divided into battalions and eventually a Corps of Infantry similarly divided. The problem of channelling reinforcements and returning casualties would remain, but it would not be a cross-regimental problem and, presumably, the time scale of any future major conflict is likely to rule out significant unit reinforcements on anything other than a first line level. Our Sergeant Major in the Royal Norfolks wouldn't like the new arrangements but it is almost thirty years since the Norfolks and Suffolks were amalgamated to their mutual dismay, and there can be few, if any, soldiers or officers serving in The Royal Anglian Regiment who remember the old County Regiments as their military spiritual homes.

The Regimental System and the Outside Observer

We tend to believe that all outside military observers view the British 'Regimental' system with unfeigned admiration. In so far as they were looking at a stereotype picture of a regiment which would incorporate a locally based and recruited unit with strong family links amongst the officers and soldiers, with well-trained and dedicated leaders at all levels, with picturesque and comfortable messes for officers, Warrant Officers and Sergeants and Corporals they would be looking at something worthy of admiration. If, in addition, the picture was of a unit steady on parade and in battle, dressed in well cut but not 'flashy' uniforms and above all had its own band, the stereotype would be complete. Of course this is a picture which probably never existed in life, not even in the golden age of the nineteenth century, although many regiments would have scored highly for at least some of the ideal characteristics. However, many admirers of the regimental system, as seen from a distance, would insist that many units of their own armies have fought well without the advantages of the British system. One would expect the foreign observer to add that his native troops fought well when they were well-led, well-trained and properly equipped, all factors which have an equal bearing on the performance of British troops. In the end, the foreign observer might have to admit that the things he most admired in the British regiment was the Officers' Mess, where he had been so splendidly entertained and, in that order, the extraordinary disciplinary system which would appear to be more rigid than the German, more lax than that of the United States Army and almost entirely self-imposed. It would be difficult to explain to an outsider that the paradox of British discipline lies in an accepted and understood hypocrisy so that it is true, for example, that British soldiers prefer to be led by gentlemen. However, it has been a part of the British class system that one can become a gentleman by first becoming an officer unlike the situation, at least until recently, in some Continental armies where one must first be a gentleman before becoming an officer. Equally, it is possible in British society to become 'no gentleman' by not behaving like a gentleman.

A more easily understood complication of the British military system lies in the fact that many different parts of the Army operate in peace and war with honour and reputation but without the support of a system which is recognisably that of the regiment in its accepted or 'ideal' form. What we have described as 'the Aberrant Corps', the Royal Artillery, Royal Engineers and Royal Marines operate from a structure quite different from that of a cavalry or infantry regiment. Whilst no one doubts their fighting ability, the Gunners, Sappers and Marines are able to function with an organisation not unlike the one which we have suggested could be based on the new administrative division. All three corps have developed alongside the other regiments of the Army and their traditions, dress and customs are not dissimilar. The only real point of difference, apart from that of function, lies in their ability to manage without the support of the comparatively small family group which, in theory at least, makes up the traditional regiment. In all three cases they have been able to base their allegiance and loyalty on a much larger group.

It would seem that for some observers the regimental system, at least in its normally accepted form, presents some distinct disadvantages which need to be set against its alleged indispensability. We have already mentioned the necessity, apparent in the last two World Wars, of ensuring that recovered battle casualties and men missing 'on line of march' are returned to the unit and even sub-unit in which they trained and ultimately fought. Even in the last war, this proved to be difficult at times; in any future war, it might become impossible. We have also said that, in any future war, fought on a large scale, the time scale may be so constricted and conditions so chaotic that the problem of reinforcements, reserves and returning casualties may not arise at all. In the organisation of the Experimental Mechanised Brigade in 1926, Colonel Lindsay,[3] wanted to avoid what he saw as the dead hand of the regimental system. Of course he was vitally interested in keeping the new developments and the new growth area firmly within the grasp of the Royal Tank Corps. His motives may have been altruistic and he might, at a very early state, have fostered the growth of a new kind of infantry but he played the regiments at their own game and lost out to influence and experience. Up to the present day, in British armoured divisions the infantry has been provided by the traditional regiments and, having lost another battle at the same time, most of the tank and armoured car regiments are manned by the traditional cavalry regiments.

A more important criticism from our NATO allies would seek to keep the British forces out of any multi-national formation because of the malign influence of the regimental system on international co-operation. In the Journal of the Royal United Services Institute for Defence Studies, March 1987, a report, put together by the staff of the Journal, gave the views of the late General Doctor von Senger und Etterlin on 'New Operational Dimensions'. The General was concerned about the formation of mobile, helicopter-borne reserve forces. After commenting on the lack of imaginative concepts for the future employment of helicopters in 'higher intensity conflict' in the British Army, he suggested that this in part might be due to traditional regimental thinking. The General goes on to criticise the division of responsibility between the Royal Air Force and the Army for the provision of helicopter support, even within 1st British Corps. This would seem to be the problem of regimental independence writ large. It may be that recent British attempts to pour cold water on the setting up of the Franco-German Air Mobile Brigade, outside NATO, has its origin in the same British unease over a lack of clear lines of responsibility and communication, and the independence assumed by British regimental commanders especially when they are co-operating with 'friendly forces'.[4] However, it should be noted that, despite the reservations expressed in the name of General Doctor von Senger und Etterlin, the British Government has announced its decision to convert one of the brigades of 2nd Armoured Division, based at Catterick, into a helicopter-borne specialised anti-tank brigade. The new force would act as a highly mobile reserve, available across the whole of the Northern Army Group front. However, the problem involved in divided responsibility between the Royal Air Force and the Army remains.[5]

Military Family Problems

Whether the future for British forces in Germany will see more involvement with other NATO forces up to the point of actual incorporation or whether they will remain as part of a strictly British army, the problem of the 'tail' will remain. There are ways in which the tail of services and families may be reduced but all the alleviations will cost money and will result in a lowering of amenity. Even more difficult, some suggested ways of giving the Army a 'leaner' look would have social consequences which might not be politically acceptable in a period of nominal peace. Perhaps the most obvious way of reducing the burden of social provision in Germany and the few other overseas stations remaining is to reduce or remove entirely the family element in a posting out of the United Kingdom. It would be possible to include Northern Ireland in this family ban but this would add to the political difficulties. There is already a question mark hanging over the heads of families in the British Army of the Rhine. Their future has recently been investigated by the National Audit Office and the Report by the Comptroller and Auditor General was issued on 11 January 1988. The report points out that 60,000 servicemen and staff serving with the British forces in Germany are accompanied, as of right, by 83,000 dependants of whom 44,000 are children. The report adds that the Ministry of Defence has not carried out a previously recommended review to ensure that costs of the present accompanied service policy are commensurate with its advantages. The Ministry of Defence replied that accompanied service was a long established and deeply-rooted policy for the Armed Forces and that where servicemen in all-regular forces were required to serve abroad for long periods, they regarded it as essential to unit efficiency, operational readiness and morale. It could be shown that to compensate for a 'no families' policy would be expensive. However, the Ministry of Defence reply, which is on traditional lines, like those used to defend the regimental system when it really no longer exists, begs a large number of pertinent questions.

We have already said that Germany no longer enjoys the popularity as a family posting it once had. Lack of jobs for wives and older children has recently been highlighted as a cause of discontent. The article in *The Times* of 7 July 1987, which had the headline 'Army Wives Set To Win Career Charter', reported that the Ministry of Defence was considering reorganisation of the Army's tours of duty to give units longer periods in one posting and to help wives to build a career. The same article mentions the CGS's concern that frequent moves of regimental units damaged family life. Under the new options, there would be more flexibility between the different regiments to ensure that individual officers received a well-rounded career. Some officers would be expected to leave their battalions and serve with another unit if necessary. As we said in our Introduction, the former CGS, General Sir Nigel Bagnall, in defending the regimental system accepted that traditions had to be adjusted and that important developments made it necessary to review the Army's tours of duty and career structure. This does look a little like putting the family cart in front of the war horse but there is an even more serious problem involved in trying to provide careers for army wives abroad. The

National Audit Office, in their examination of costs in the British Army and Royal Air Force in Germany, looked at the employment of more service dependants as a way of cutting overall support costs. Dependants were reported on average to cost £5,000 per year less than a non-dependant. However, there has been a long and disappointing history of trying to increase the number of employed Army and Royal Air Force family members. In 1987 the percentage of employed dependants in the directly employed labour force was 18.5 having risen from a low of 16.8 in 1985. The Civil Secretary at Headquarters, British Army of the Rhine had recently identified a further 5,000 posts which in theory could be filled by dependants but there are a large number of practical constraints which would certainly reduce this figure.[6] The Ministry of Defence has pointed out the mismatch between those seeking jobs, most of whom are stationed in the forward areas, and the jobs themselves, which are largely in the rear areas. There are other difficulties in particular jobs such as the necessity for fluency in German, the need for continuity, especially in the transition from peace to war and the requirement for specific qualifications in, for example, teaching and nursing posts. Altogether, the likelihood of increasing the percentage of employed dependants by more than a few points is not high. Of all careers, it is surely that of the serviceman which is least amenable to manipulation in the furtherance of social and family policies.

What has been achieved in terms of family support, despite all its shortcomings, is truly remarkable. The provision of housing and children's education overseas, despite some local variations and all the problems caused by military turbulence, is still above the average of that found amongst Local Authorities in Britain and in health provision is now considerably above it. What has caused the present outbreak of discontent is not the basic condition of service family life abroad but an upsurge of expectations about life in the United Kingdom and especially about civilian life there. The desire to own a house and to live in it, surrounded by all the conveniences of a consumer society, has brought about a disillusionment with life in an army quarter. In one sense the Army and army families are the victims of a widely propagated philosophy which implies that the values of the market place, competitiveness and piling-up of material possessions are the only criteria by which they should be judged. Young officers of today are as affected as much as their soldiers by 'the new realism' and it does not fit well for the military, and it fits even less well for the military family. As we have seen, many army wives are voting with their feet. The trend is for families not to accompany their husbands abroad and the measures suggested to increase the popularity of foreign postings may be too late to be effective. The very outcry about the lack of job opportunities in Germany is significant on two levels. It has been suggested that soldiers abroad are not paid enough to enjoy the standard of living which they are led to believe is the right of all people who actually have jobs. This may be true of soldiers in Britain also but recent changes in local allowances in Germany may have reinforced this impression. It may be true also that the apparently high standard of living enjoyed by those in employment in Britain is a result of wives and teenage members of the family working and bringing money into the household. Unfortunately, as we have seen, the work for families is not widely available in Germany. The options now seem fairly clear.

Ruth Jolly in her book *Military Man, Family Man,* concludes her excellent study of the problems of contemporary military families by suggesting three possible courses of action to counter what she sees as a serious situation in all three Services. Her first alternative is to encourage the tendency towards the 'Nine to Five and Home to Dinner' approach which we noted in our Introduction. Ruth Jolly dismisses this increased civilianisation as an answer to 'the ills of our time' mainly on the grounds of lowered combat-readiness which she feels would inevitably result. It is possible that this solution has been rejected too hurriedly. There are roles which could be undertaken by a more civilian orientated Army. Home defence is an obvious one, where the much admired but untested Swiss Army might provide a model. The Israeli Army could perhaps offer a better example of the combination of citizen and soldier but the Israeli forces are operating in what is virtually a Garrison State under semi-seige conditions which produce their own set of imperatives. Increased civilianism might work for parts of the Army, and before the notion is dismissed out of hand, for the Royal Navy and Royal Air Force the following points should be considered. The bulk of naval personnel does not now go to sea in ships and whereas, until recently, it was considered essential that Naval Dockyards should be firmly under Service control, it now seems that they can be civilianised when finance becomes more important than security. Similarly, a very small proportion of the Royal Air Force, in terms of personnel, actually takes to the air. Although the analogy is hardly exact, if the repair facilities of the Navy can be civilianised so confidently by Government there must be scope for increased use of non-service repair organisations by the Air Force. However, all this is at a price, not only to be reckoned in terms of reduced combat readiness but also in terms of morale which may be even more important.

Her second suggestion for reorganising the Armed Forces is based on what she describes as a Militia. Her militia would be built upon the existing reservist organisations, presumably with an enlarged voluntary sector, all or part of which could be recalled into regular service in an emergency. It is not entirely clear how this would remedy the social ills that she identifies amongst military families unless the regular forces could be reduced with the build up of her Militia or Reserve Force. She admits that a militia or voluntary reserve system would be subject to market forces or in other words, as with the regular forces, it would be necessary to pay the market rate for the number of reserves that would be required. In an increasingly technology based Army, this could prove to be very expensive indeed. Conscription, which could possibly be combined successfully with a Militia and reserve force, is dismissed as a 'highly unlikely development in Britain'. As we have seen, the experience of France in the employment of conscript soldiers in Algeria was not a happy one and there are many reasons why their employment in a British Army engaged in anything less than all out war would be no more successful. Sadly, the days of consensus over the use of our forces are gone. With the end of Empire a sizable part of the nation has concluded that there is nothing worth defending outside the British Isles and even response to clear Argentine aggression in the Falkland Islands met with less than one hundred per cent support. If conscript soldiers had been involved, some surely reluctantly, and all subject to intensive propaganda, the situation could have become ugly very quickly. Contrary to what Ruth Jolly seems to believe, conscription is not a cheap option which removes the necessity to consider market forces. Even if you can pay conscripts at a lower rate than regular forces, and this might become increasingly difficult, there are other costs which must be considered. The more technical the equipment of the Army becomes, the more complex becomes the training organisation and the longer the period of training required. If the trained conscripts cannot be used in small wars and confrontations for political reasons or because their training takes up too much of their time in the Service, the Regular Army would have to be increased quite considerably to cope with both the training commitment and the inevitably arising crises which call for military involvement. In recruiting there seems to be a curve which indicates that diminishing returns set in very quickly and to attract an increase of twenty or thirty per cent could be extremely expensive. Conscription appears to be a non-starter, unless we can return to a long-term period of consensus in defence matters and in the acceptable employment of our forces.

Her third possible development, and one which she personally favours, is for the Army and the Royal Air Force to evolve in their family policies in the direction which the Royal Navy has already taken. That is to say towards a situation in which unaccompanied tours are the normal thing. She draws the obvious inference that a great deal more would need to be done to make the necessary separation tolerable. She suggests that this would involve much more subsidised travel between home and base, much more effective house purchase schemes and a more highly trained and more extensive welfare service. There are problems for the Army at least, with which Ruth Jolly does not deal. Most of the armoured regiments of the British Army are more or less permanently based in Germany. Under present circumstances, her scheme would lead to soldiers in the armoured units spending most of their army career, assuming that they were married, separated from their families. There are obvious solutions to this situation but they would involve radical changes in the organisation and habits of the Army.

Recruiting the Army of the Future

Apart from the changes in army life which have become necessary for the social and family reasons set out in Ruth Jolly's book there are others which may force themselves upon the Army for demographic reasons. A recent report by Peter Evans in *The Times* says that a 'demographic time bomb', producing a 20 per cent drop in numbers of young people as Britain's population ages, is causing concern about future recruitment. He goes on to say that the Army could be up to 4,000 soldiers short in 1994, and that the Services are considering counter measures such as ending short service gratuities and employing more women in staff and other jobs and persuading older men to return to the Army. A more serious concern seems to be with quality, where, if the same mix of talents and ability is recruited in the future as in the past, the Army will be critically short of the 'quality in depth' which was such a feature of the Falklands campaign. Coupled with the problem of falling numbers is the decrease within the pool of available young males in the sub university and polytechnic categories from which the Army draws its recruits. Recent pronouncements of the Government that it is planning to increase the number of students in tertiary education by 200,000 by the end of the century can only add to the Services' predicament, if they maintain present recruiting policies.

Traditionally, when recruiting becomes particularly difficult, and, as we have seen, except in times of national crisis, recruiting is never easy, the Army lowers its standards in terms of physical, educational and age requirements. An increase in 'junior' or 'young' soldiers almost always follows a fall in recruiting. It certainly seems easier to 'catch'em young' but it is an extremely expensive process in terms of the extra facilities required and the high wastage rate which goes with the young entry. An alternative which has been advocated but never tried is to go 'up market' in recruiting terms. If there are to be more better educated potential recruits in the available pool and fewer less well educated young men, it might be sensible to set out to attract more from the upper reaches. This will in itself involve the Army in a number of significant changes in the military environment, both in living conditions and ethos. However, the Army may have no option but to accept the changes if the required extraction rate for recruits reaches an unattainable level using the old criteria.

Before discussing in more detail the effects of introducing a 'Constabulary' style into the Army, there are a number of other measures which could be taken, as alternatives or altogether, to ameliorate some of the difficulties appearing on the army horizon. Peter Evans in his article on the falling number of potential recruits says that the Army wants longer service from the same men. This, of course, runs counter to the suggestion for tours of duty overseas to be unaccompanied which is favoured by quite a number of service officers and soldiers in addition to Ruth Jolly. Short contracts to work unaccompanied in, for example, the Gulf States, have become a fact of life for many engineers and professional people in recent years. The comparative shortness of the contract makes the separation bearable but is also encourages unmarried people to try a role or a situation which would not have appealed necessarily on a long-term basis. Along with shorter service, it is suggested that a system of transferable pension rights could be instituted for periods of service as short as the minimum engagement. It has already been said that there is scope for a much improved house purchase scheme. At the moment the Army authorities, at least, are caught in the dilemma of attracting more recruits and encouraging the prolongation of service by offering a good house purchase scheme and of making it easy for dissatisfied soldiers to leave the Service early to live in their own houses. However, it is not impossible for the Services to negotiate a loan or mortgage scheme which is linked to contract of service and which could be transferred as or instead of a whole or part pension. The problem in the past has been the reluctance on the part of the Service Authorities to see servicemen living in their own houses whilst actually serving. This attitude must surely be outdated and one could well believe that a government of the 1990s would encourage the sale of army quarters to service buyers. However, there is a strong current running against living on a married quarters estate and this would be strengthened if the soldier served for most of his engagement away from the particular quarters area. Selling quarters to servicemen would have to be only a small adjunct to a house purchase scheme but it could have its place.

Another way of making the Army more attractive to recruits, especially under an enhanced short service programme or in a period of high unemployment, would be to guarantee civil employment after the completion of an agreed engagement. The government programme of denationalisation has rather reduced the scope of this possibility but it is still worth looking into. In nineteenth century Germany, positions were reserved in the Post Office and on the State Railways for retiring NCOs and men, and in Britain after the First World War the post delivery service of the GPO was almost entirely manned, although unofficially, by ex-servicemen. Again, the scope for the employment of ex-servicemen is reduced as far as the old service industries are concerned by the growth of tradesman and technician grades within the Services. Even so, the numbers involved would be small and the Government has sufficient leverage to guarantee civil posts in the police, security industry, Prison Service and defence industries if the will was in evidence. Guaranteed employment could be linked with an improved education and resettlement service aimed early in the soldier's career at an earmarked civilian job. Higher entry requirements through 'up-market' recruiting policies would lead, apart from the direct resettlement programme, to a requirement for better education facilities, perhaps linked with the Open College and the Open University.

Constabulary Soldiering and a 'Through' Promotion Structure

One of the consequences of attracting better educated recruits into the Army and moving the Army a little towards a 'Constabulary' model, so that advantage could be taken of the potential of the newcomers, is likely to be increasing pressure for a through structure in the present dual promotion system. There are increasing embarrassments in a system where Warrant Officers and Senior NCOs are often better educated than their officers and although under National Service it was commonplace to find soldiers more intelligent than their officers, it is not a very happy situation in an all-regular army where there is only a limited possibility of moving on to the commissioned officer's ladder from the ranks. In the Corps, in which specialist qualifications are more important, the chances of promotion to commissioned rank are good but in the Regiments, especially in peace time, the position is less happy. In both cases, the chances of promotion above field rank are very restricted. To some extent this re-inforces the 'us and them' attitude as between the Corps and the Regiments mentioned in the Introduction. Even though limited, there have always been opportunities for promotion from the ranks and Field Marshal Robertson, who is said to have held every rank in the British army from trooper to Field Marshal, and was Chief of the Imperial

General Staff in 1917, is the prime example. Usually, commissions have been given to soldiers in 'the field' to replace heavy battle casualties amongst the officers and they have often ended in disillusionment after the war. After the Napoleonic wars, most field commissioned officers were placed on half pay and never served again. Another very honourable route to a commission is to rise through the ranks of NCOs and Warrant Officers to become a Regimental Sergeant Major and then to be selected for a commission. RSM's are quite senior soldiers and if commissioned they usually have only a limited period to serve. They can serve on the special Quartermaster's list and if they get near the top of the list by seniority they have a chance to become a Lieutenant Colonel but this does not happen to many and in any event they are restricted to Quartermaster and administrative type work. During the last war for a fairly short period it was compulsory for all prospective officers to serve in the ranks for a few months before becoming a cadet. The system was liked by the popular press, if by no one else, presumably since it lent an air of spurious democracy to the officer selection process but it was abandoned even before the end of the war and has not been an absolute requirement since.

With the increasing requirement for technically trained troops and with the tendency for artificers and other Warrant Officers and NCOs to work for and gain qualifications in relevant technologies, there is now a quite discernible overlap in qualifications between officers and soldiers. Increasingly too, young men who, as NCOs, discover their own leadership potential, brought out in many cases by their practical leadership opportunities, are not prepared to climb the subordinate promotion ladder, where their officer qualities are often not recognised until after the decision has been made to leave the Army.

A through promotion structure does not solve all promotion problems in the Army and of course it is likely to bring in some problems of its own in the establishment of adequate 'pass over' criteria and in other ways. The time is surely right to look again at our dual promotion structure if only to encourage the many excellent young men who feel their talents are not recognised and that their prospects are better elsewhere. However, a further bar to a satisfactory selection and promotion system still exists, and this lies in the structure and assumptions of the Regular Commissions Board (RCB). Praise and acceptance of the RCB is so widespread and so obviously sincere that one hesitates to criticise such an obviously successful institution. One is reminded, in reverse, of the late Professor Laski's remark about The House of Lords. 'If you want to be cured of an excessive admiration for the peerage go and see the House of Lords in action'. The opposite seems to be true of the RCB. Many reporters, politicians and senior soldiers have arrived at Westbury ready to take the place apart, already prejudiced against what they see as an essential part of the Army's nepotistic, self-perpetuating, anachronistic and entirely infuriating nature. One of the criteria for selection for the staff at the RCB seems to be that they are without exception the nicest people you could ever meet. The staff are all experienced soldiers predominantly from the 'tooth' arms. They understand their selection system, which hasn't changed in essentials since it was first devised almost fifty years ago, and apply it with reasonable impartiality. They select from the limited sample of young men who present themselves, the best likeness of themselves as they were perhaps twenty-five years previously. They are doing the best they can. Dennis Barker in his book *Soldiering On*, in a 'Guardian Reporter's View' of the Army can only find one thing to criticise at the RCB; testing Officers know beforehand which schools individual candidates attended. This is a serious criticism, implying as it does that Testing Officers could be biased in favour of a particular school or schools, and since successful candidates tend to come from a comparatively narrow band of schools, the point may be worth making. What is apparent at the RCB is a devotion not so much to the *status quo* in the Army but to the *status quo ante*. What appears to be a devotion to the well-tried model of the regimental officer of the past is perhaps not even entirely appropriate for the 'tooth arms' of today; it is certainly inappropriate for the technical arms of the twenty-first century, by when some of the young men selected by today's RCBs will themselves be Testing Officers.

The great problem of the RCB is that it is expected to do too much. First, it must remove most of the burden of testing and rejecting from Sandhurst. A successful RCB candidate has a very high chance of being allowed to proceed to a commission in spite of a performance at the Cadet College which could cast doubts on his future role as an officer. We are no doubt talking of a comparatively small number of cases. Second, and much more important, the RCB has to assume that the candidates appearing before it are not only an acceptable cross section of young would-be officers, but that they are also the best available in Britain. It is not difficult to believe that the Testing Officers at the RCB do a very reasonable job selecting from their own experience and background for their own regiments and regiments like them. What is missing is any awareness that the young men they are testing are only a small and non-representative sample of what could be available. A vicious circle operates to limit the field of candidates to those whose parents and careers masters believe have a hope of passing. If the RCB is not prepared to take the risk of accepting more boys from non-conventional backgrounds, and backing their hunches at Sandhurst and in the regiments, however unpopular this makes them, then they will never be able to widen the intake so that it represents the best young men available. What is clearly needed is an intermediate finishing school, not a Potential Officer Development Course like the one run by The Army School of Education at Beaconsfield, which was successful enough in its way, but which was of too short a duration, and not a Rowallan Company at Sandhurst, which theoretically aimed at character development through 'outward bounding', in the main making stronger characters out of boys from the right background. What is suggested is making strong characters from the wrong background into potential officers. Welbeck College may be the most useful model on which to base an institution aimed at widening the officer intake for the tooth arms. Within its limitations, Welbeck does a good job with its sixth-form course preparing boys for commissions in the technical arms, mainly REME and the Royal Signals. It socialises them for the Army and the officers' mess and, in many cases, prepares them for a science degree course at The Royal Military College of Science. Only exceptionally do Welbeck boys go to a 'tooth' arm but there is no reason why this should not be changed. A different course would be necessary and a different location. Technical Arms Directors would not be pleased to lose an important officer recruiting source, so an additional facility would be necessary. However, if there is to be any genuine progress towards a wider recruiting policy for officers, it will only come about through a breaking of the inward looking RCB image. It may also be necessary to set up, in conjunction with a 'Tooth Arm Welbeck', a quota system so that some of the new entry find themselves in the élite as well as the line Divisions.

A finishing school on rather more serious lines than the makeshift courses that operate around the officer recruiting fluctuations would be a very valuable adjunct to the existing cadet selection and training facilities. Properly organised and presented, it could hope to persuade young men from a quite different background that the Army has something to offer them as officers. Without a genuine widening of the field for officer recruiting, the Army and the regiments will find themselves in an unenviable position by the end of the century.[10]

The Ministry of Defence has been at great pains to show that the RCB selects a representative group of young men for commissions and it is able to point to Grammar School boys and even the occasional Comprehensive School boy amongst its successful candidates. Colleges of Further Education also feature in the lists from time to time, although these have often been employed by exasperated parents to combat the deficiencies of some more prestigious fee-paying school. What is not made clear is the ultimate destination of these prodigies. Superficially, it is encouraging if a wider spread of schools features in the pass lists but if all the candidates from Eton go into the Guards and all the candidates from Winchester go into the Green Jackets and all the candidates from the Comprehensives and from the ranks go into the REME and the Ordnance Corps, we are not getting very far with our social mix. Of course many army officers, especially those from the more prestigious regiments, will say that this is the only way to do it. Boys from public schools, especially if they have some private means, will be happier amongst their fellows. Similarly, boys from the state schools would find it difficult and embarrassing to live and work with their more exalted fellow officers in the Guards, cavalry and more exclusive line regiments. These arguments are so thin as to be insulting to the Army, the Monarch and the public in general. Does anyone seriously think that our present Queen or our future King would feel anything but pleasure at a widening of the social base from which Guards officers are selected? Would they really feel less secure if they were guarded by troops officered by a more representative group of their loyal subjects? Similarly, we do not recruit doctors or engineers or paratroop officers or Marines or fighter pilots or indeed nuclear submarine commanders from a narrow and exclusive social class. In the past, it may have been necessary to recruit officers and sometimes whole regiments on a basis of social standing or religion or the ability to provide a horse and weapons. Even so, this kind of recruiting provided no guarantee of loyalty in a crisis and can hardly do so in the future. The comfortable and easy fit in the messes at their different levels may have been true up to the Second World War but there have always been many apparently suitable officers who have had little to do with mess life. A surprising number of British senior officers have come from this group of self designated 'outsiders' and they have been the last people to worry about being comfortable with their fellows in the mess. Young people, including young officers, no longer find it difficult to mix with their contemporaries from all backgrounds and in the Army would not find it difficult to accept colleagues on a basis of character and professional competence.

It is accepted that there might be a rather painful period of adjustment but we believe that the adjustment is not long off and the question is will the Army make its own arrangements or will they be forced upon it? One of the problems of the past has been trying to fit into the present structure a single newcomer from a different background but that is no longer the situation. It is not suggested that guinea pig subalterns, eating peas from a knife and reading the *Guardian* should be introduced into Guards and cavalry messes but that entry and promotion in all sections of the Army should be open to all young men of character and talents. The character and talents required should now be the subject of a new review so that selection and even more, placement, is not left to a good natured but blinkered group.[11]

From the standpoint of the soldier recruit, many circumstances are coming together which could make the Army a rather more attractive career than it has been in the past. It is suggested that, in many more cases in the future, there should be unaccompanied tours, at least officially. If soldiers and officers are paid a sufficient allowance to provide their own quarters some families may still prefer to follow the drum but they will have to accept that there will be no special facilities for them in terms of health, childrens' education or local employment opportunities, except what they can find for themselves. The only thing required from a family which chooses to go abroad might be an article of indemnity and an informed understanding of what they will find in the husband's overseas location. It is suggested also that soldiers are enlisted, in the first instance, on a strictly limited contract which could vary in length between corps, depending on the amount and expense of the training they require. Generous transferable pension contributions, possibly technical training but certainly resettlement training and the prestige which will come from having served in a revamped and newly designed, demonstrably exclusive organisation will compensate for the longer careers of the past. It is to be expected that there would be many more unmarried men in the Army. Allowances in lieu of quarters, travel concessions and exclusive health and welfare provision will encourage more wives to stay in a house or quarter of their choice where they will be free to build up or further their careers. They will, of course, be able to use all the local authority provision in terms of health and education and in need will be eligible for succour by the NHS 'safety net', which we are assured will remain for the foreseeable future.

If this picture looks a little bleak and even cynical, it may not be much out of line with contemporary views of the way our society should organise itself. However, what we are saying is that this picture of a leaner, less encumbered Army depends upon adequate payment and allowances and, again, this would seem to be in line with modern teaching. The introduction of the 'Military Salary' was a first attempt to introduce an appropriate structure of pay and allowances into the Army and, at the same time, it was intended to edge towards a more rational, leaner army where soldiers would pay the market rate for the facilities they received and, in their turn, be paid for the imponderables, the 'X' factor of military life. When it was first introduced, the military salary was thought to have been a success. A pay increase accompanied the new salary structure, designed to establish comparability with civilian pay rates for comparable (sic) work, but which, in practice, disguised the abolition of some allowances and perquisites without compensation. A more important issue has rendered the whole subject of a military salary, and especially the prerequisite of comparability, suspect. When the new salary was introduced in 1970, an intensive and much publicised study of the market and military employments established comparability. Already, by May 1974, The Review Body on Armed Forces Pay in its report (Cmnd 5631) estimated that between April 1970 and April 1973 civilian average earnings increased by about 8 per cent more than average service earnings.[12] This kind of faith-breaking with the soldier is unforgivable and, even if it is traditional to cheat him in quiet times, as Kipling says, 'Tommy ain't a blooming fool—you bet that Tommy sees!'. The peculation of soldiers pay is as old as armies but it is rarely attempted in the face of the enemy and increasingly the Army stands in the face of the enemy. The soldier is unforgiving and if we are to have another new structure for pay and allowances, it must retain its integrity for more than three years.

Under the new conditions outlined above and with the fall forecast in the pool of young men from which the Army recruits its soldiers, a new recruiting strategy will be necessary. We have suggested that the Army should go up market rather than down in its recruiting policy. To make this a more attractive development, the requirement in the future is almost certainly going to be for a more intelligent, better educated and more trainable and retrainable soldier than the Army has used in the past. This will mean that there will be far fewer places in the Army for those graded on enlistment as 3 minus, 4 and 5, of whom each corps had to take a proportion, although the majority ended up in the infantry. The prospect of a better educated Army leads on to the concept of a Constabulary type of force which is not divided abruptly into officers on one side and soldiers on the other, with only limited contact and movement between them. A 'through structure' or something very like it must have been what Wolesley had in mind when he wrote in 1869, in the first edition of his 'Soldier's Pocket Book', of the necessity to sink as far as possible the respective titles of officer, sergeant and private merge them into one cognomen of soldier.[13] The suggestion could hardly fail to shock in 1869 but over one hundred years later it still seems to attract the same unthinking and self-interested denunciation. Yet it can only be a matter of time when a distinction based on a feudal caste-like system, the utility of which is not understood by either side, is swept away. There are frequent examples of NCOs taking over the role of sometimes quite senior officers and performing far better than their lack of officer training would have led one to expect. At the margin between the accepted role for officers and for NCOs, there has always been some confusion. It is not clear at what level a junior commander should cease to be an NCO and become an officer. In the last war, at various times, platoons in the British Army were commanded by NCOs or

Warrant Officers Third Class, a rank now abolished, or by commissioned officers. In the German Army it was not unusual, especially in the First World War to find Infantry Companies permanently commanded by Sergeants. The question could hardly have been decided by function. To reverse the coin, and perhaps more in the past than now, it was not unusual to find men serving in the ranks who had come from the traditional officer producing classes in terms of birth, school and education, and some of them made good NCOs. The role of NCO is largely historical in origin and is not borne out by function except, perhaps, in some of the more bizarre duties that have fallen to the lot of the sergeants. It has been said that under early feudalism in Europe, when one tribe or race conquered another and took over its land and people, it was necessary to appoint a group of subordinate leaders from the conquered group, usually the surviving leaders of that group, who would act as hostages, go-betweens and interpreters of local custom and even language. It is said that this last function lives on in those British regiments where a wide gap still exists between officers and men.

Motivation and the Soldier's Job

Modern theories of motivation make much of good job design as playing an essential part in ensuring the satisfaction and commitment of workers in civil life. The theory applies just as much to the so-called service industries and equally to the Armed Services. The theory suggests that what motivates people is the ability to achieve their desired expectations and the job of management and leaders in all spheres is so to organise work, tasks, responsibilities and rewards that expectations can be achieved. The theory goes on to say that good performance and high satisfaction results when personnel are well-selected and well-trained; when the objectives are clear and obtainable and when adequate resources, in military terms troops and weapons, are available. These three conditions are quite familiar to the military. Selection and training, clear orders directed towards an attainable objective and sufficient troops adequately equipped and armed for the task in hand, are familiar elements in military planning but, from this point on, the theory becomes more complicated. Satisfaction or, in management jargon, desired outcomes, are of two kinds, intrinsic and extrinsic. The extrinsic satisfactions result from the actions which we have already described and which are part of every trained officer's bible, but the intrinsic satisfactions derive from the design of the job itself. It is suggested that there are five 'core dimensions' in good job design and for maximum satisfaction all five should be catered for. In military terms these are first, skill variety. For the soldier, NCO or officer this means that his job is designed so as to allow him to use all his trained skills, technical, professional and social in his work and the opportunity exists for him to develop and exercise new skills. The second dimension is the establishment of task identity. The job itself must be recognisable as a part of a tactical or even strategic plan and to that extent, part of the national purpose. It would rule out the old adage for recruits under training, 'If it moves, salute it; if it doesn't, whitewash it', which was always a bit too close to the mark for comfort but which did represent in caricature the cynical attitude of some NCOs to both their officers and their recruits under training. Third, the job should have task significance. Again, this is a concept which should be familiar to officers and NCOs. Explanation and an adequate understanding of group task and individual role is enjoined on every leader but for the soldier there is an additional complication. He has the moral right and some would say duty, to question the ethical purpose of his orders and it is the duty of the leader to ensure that the purpose of a proposed action falls within recently promulgated human rights guide lines and that these and the means to be employed are fully understood. The fourth principle of good job design is that of autonomy. In other words for work to be completely satisfactory it is necessary for individual responsibility to be as widespread as possible as often as possible. Soldiers can be given individual responsibility and this is perhaps one of the important differences between the paratrooper or commando soldier and the soldier of the line regiment, who may not be encouraged to think for himself. It may also account for the observed difference in motivation and commitment between the two types of soldier. The way ahead is clear and although this kind of individual involvement is partly a function of intelligence and education, imaginative training and adequate practical experience has an important part to play. Finally, the expectancy theory of motivation insists that feedback is an important part of designing work so as to ensure the maximum of intrinsic satisfaction. De-briefing, briefing, pep talks, victory parades, newspaper and television coverage, confidential reports and honours and awards are all part of the well-known feedback process in the Services. It is doubtful if the feedback goes as far down the line as it should and there is still a great reluctance on the part of some service officers to recognise the legitimate desire and right of their subordinates to publicity at home. Problems with the media during the Falklands campaign shows that this is still not fully understood.

The recognition and encouragement of intrinsic satisfaction is easier and more immediately rewarding in an army of intelligent soldiers where irrational barriers of rank and status no longer exist. So we are led at last towards a 'New Model' army. In our study of the British

Army and our brief look at some of the experiences of the French and German Armies, several possibilities for restructuring the Armed Forces have presented themselves. Whilst perhaps the moral conviction of Cromwell's Ironsides was missing from Wellington's veteran armies of the Peninsula and Waterloo, they could surely be regarded as the heirs of the New Model tradition. Even without the burning moral conviction, Wellington's armies possessed in full measure the qualities bequeathed to them from the past: Roman discipline and steadiness, Saxon spirit and a tendency to exuberance and what Scott called Norman chivalry, but what might be better described as an awareness of decency and what is right. The Army never lost these virtues through the nineteenth century but they were sometimes obscured by the muddle, incompetence and corruption of governments and their commanders. What could have been an opportunity to work out a new and exemplary Army, based on the scientific and increasingly humanitarian currents in civil life, was rejected in favour of withdrawal into an obsolescent and inward looking existence which condemned the Army to half a century of stagnation.

It was not until after the First World War that soldiers began to question the very fabric of the Armed Forces. Wolseley, for all his reforming zeal and celebrated 'modernity', had not questioned the basic structure of the Army. It took the horrors of the First World War and the arrival of the tank and aircraft to bring this about. The possibility of a New Model became dimly apparent for the first time in the experiments and research which went into the setting up of the first Experimental Armoured Force. All the clues were there. A new integrated army in miniature without regiments, to be organised and operated by the new Royal Tank Corps. The new corps dedicated to science, technology and enlightenment, demanded highly educated soldiers and the easy intimacy which comes from living and fighting within the confined quarters of the armoured vehicle. But the time was not right. A parvenu Corps like the Royal Armoured Corps was not, in the words of the CIGS 'going to swallow the army'. Fuller, who actually talked of new models, although he was usually referring to formations rather than men, lost his great chance and moved into the wings as we have seen.[14]

The disciples of Fuller and of Liddell Hart in Germany, in their development of the armoured division and the blitz-krieg tactics that went with it, and even more in its final evil manifestation, the SS Panzer Division, came perilously close to producing a 'New Model' that could have swept all before it. The monstrous ideology of Nazism, which gave the SS its allegedly spiritual dimension and which could mistakenly be equated with the religious fervour of Cromwell's Ironsides, provided the means for its own ultimate undoing. The beliefs and practices of the Nazis manifested in the behaviour of the SS were so clearly inhuman as to stir up a strength of opposition which in the end could not be denied. The war against the Nazis may well have been the last occasion when Britain was able to stand united against an unequivocally evil and threatening foe. The trumpets may never give such a clear sound again and our New Model will need to be exceptionally discerning.

The Army of the State of Israel has also been put forward as a model worthy of emulation. Born out of a struggle to survive, it was necessary for a small country, surrounded by potential enemies, to be perpetually vigilant. Able to mobilise all its forces rapidly and in accordance with pre-arranged plans, it has relied on the absolute commitment of its citizens and on the weight of its fire-power to compensate for the great numerical superiority and the encircling position of its foes. In its fervour and spirit, discipline and courage the Israeli Army has certain similarities to the Cromwellian New Model but it does not seem to be an army which could be successfully reproduced anywhere else. A strongly religious people, supported by massive aid from the United States of America and able to use the latest military technology because of the intelligence of its soldiers and its access to the most modern arms suppliers, can hardly be typical of Britain or of many other states. Without the economic aid that Israel receives from its Jewish supporters in America and Europe and even more from the American Government, it would be impossible to maintain the very high state of preparedness which is typical of that country and which it is not possible to reproduce elsewhere except under conditions of perpetual threat and near war.

If we are to have a New Model, and we may have one or be in the process of acquiring one whether we like it or not, there are features of both German Panzer formations and the Israeli citizen army which we might wish to incorporate. In the first place there is a feeling common to both that new weapons require new tactics and, above all, new men. In the case of the Germans, the explosive combination of new weapons, tactics and men was linked to a new ideology which aimed at world power and domination. For the Israelis the overriding necessity was to survive. In both cases there was an intellectual, emotional background to successful military innovation. The intellectual dimension of war and of armies has always been something of an embarrassment to British soldiers and it is only part of what must be considered if our forces are to be remodelled to meet the challenges of the twenty-first century. However, if we concentrate entirely on new weapons, new formations, selection and training and the conditions under which our military families live, it will not be sufficient. Like Cromwell's Army a British Army must be an army of conscience or it is nothing. In our concluding section we will try to put some of these disparate elements together and, informed by some of the lessons of the past, suggest how a British New Model Army might look by the year 2000 AD.

Conclusion

In Chapter 1 we suggested that the virtues which are regarded as the main characteristics of the good soldier and which became obvious in the British armies of the seventeenth and eighteenth centuries, found their origin, as far as Britain was concerned, in the peculiar overlaying of the habits, customs and character of the three main waves of invaders who arrived during the period of a little more than one thousand years from the Roman to the Norman settlements. These characteristics, of good discipline and steadfastness, high spirits and high morale and a sense of what is right and proper emerged when Britain had begun to play a part on the wider stages, first of Europe and later across the world. Whilst these characteristics were essential in the formative years of the Army, they are now taken almost for granted in any assessment of the strength and character of our Armed Forces. So much is this so that there is now a danger in any restructuring of the Army that it will be assumed that these military virtues are to a large degree inherent in the British soldier and that no special consideration need be given to their development and maintenance. In whatever way our forces may be remade, room must be provided for the continuance and encouragement of the virtues of 'The New Model', and this must include essentially, room for an easy conscience.

The structure of the Army from the 'New Model' onwards, and especially in what could be called its apotheosis, the Golden Age of the Peninsular Army, is seen as an unbreakable and irreplaceable mould which has inexorably fashioned the regimental pattern of the Army through the ages. The truth may be rather different. The 'Regiment', can mean and has meant all things to all men, but for much of the time over the centuries since The Restoration, it has hardly existed at all in the pure form in which it is so often visualised. Nevertheless, the benefits which seem to accrue to the regimental system, however defined, emerge regardless of shape, size or structure. What appears to be most important in the maintenance of morale and organised integration is the small face-to-face group. Self-pride and the desire for the approbation and admiration of one's fellows is born and finds its strongest expression in the group small enough for each member to know intimately and have regard for the good opinion of close companions. This easy intimacy is also the basis of good spirits, high humour, a private vocabulary and an in-group camaraderie. If, in addition, those close companions have other ties such as a shared home town or district or a common dialect, so much the better, although these latter may not be an essential part of the bond.

This is not to say that the larger groups do not have a part to play. If the small face-to-face group is the seat of honour as regards morale and steadfastness, the large grouping, whether it be the battery, battalion, regiment or corps has another purpose of equal importance, and this is where some confusion arises. The function of the large groupings, all of which would pay homage to the so-called regimental spirit, is to bind the small, self-centred groups to a higher purpose. The colours and parades, the regimental history and its recognition in terms of battle honours and individual awards integrate the groups into a wider loyalty where, like Cromwell's freeholders and freeholders' sons, soldiers can 'engage themselves in their country's affairs on matters of conscience'. In one sense the two groupings and two loyalties would seem to be in opposition and to be working against each other. In fact, no army can operate efficiently, and certainly not under adverse circumstances without both kinds of group loyalty. A small group provides steadiness, dourness and the graveyard humour we observed in Fortescue's description of the Guards at Fontenoy in 1745. Equally necessary is a regard for the higher virtues manifested in the advance in line with drums beating and colours unfurled, or in more modern terms, 42nd Royal Marine Commando marching off to the Falklands after their final parade before embarkation, on the inspired order of Nick Vaux, '42 Commando, to the South Atlantic – Quick March'.

The higher loyalties can be inculcated during training so that they can emerge almost regardless of the size and structure of the 'regimental' grouping, from a numbered Regiment of Foot in the late eighteenth century to the linked battalions of the Boer War or the five or more battalion regiment of the Haldane era. Leaving aside the extraordinary spectacle of the forty- and fifty-battalion regiments of the First World War and the mercifully smaller, but still large, regiments of the Second World War, the present trend through 'Large (amalgamated) Regiments' to even more amalgamated 'Administrative Divisions' does not by any means spell out the end of the regimental system. If the system were to be abandoned, something very similar would need to be created urgently in its place. What is not always understood is that such a system, similar in its essentials, is created every time an army is resurrected or put together for the first time. The necessity to seize upon the new recruit as he first enters the barracks, and to expose him to the rituals and rites of the enclosed and exclusive society which he has just joined is as important as mastering the new technology of his trade and infinitely more important than learning the esoteric mysteries of close order drill.

It is the extent to which the new loyalties can be introduced and at a later stage, successfully combined with small group regard and esteem, that makes an army a good army and a soldier a good soldier. Changes, amalgamations, disbandments and re-formings have gone on since the seventeenth century and have had remarkably few ill effects for the reasons which we have outlined. Now, however, the rate of social, economic and technical change is so speeded up that it must surely reach a climax in the near future. This rate of change, as we can see, is affecting the structure of the Army and only one change logically remains to be made. It seems that the advocates of a 'Corps of Infantry' have arrived at an open door. We have tried to show that in passing through the door, the regimental and fighting spirit of the Army need not suffer. What cannot be denied, however, is that the confusion, overlapping and weakening of loyalties, brought about by continuous and increasing change must add to that cacophony of sound coming from the trumpet of higher authority. It is this unclear sound of command which we have observed to be disastrous on some occasions in the past. The former Chief of the General Staff has said that traditions have to be adjusted and so they do. The Administrative Division has taken over so many functions of the Regiment, and it will inevitably take over more, that the Regiment has virtually ceased to exist for the infantry, except in some misty, historical way and this is almost the case also for the much amalgamated Regiments of the Royal Armoured Corps. Nothing will remain of the old Regiments except in the museums, which may continue to exist for a while like the derelict mine chimneys sticking up from a deserted Cornish industrial landscape.

Structure is nevertheless important and, to be of any utility, it must be determined by role. A Regimental structure was reasonably appropriate for small scale colonial wars but already, by the early nineteenth century, Continental and United States regiments were fighting units of three battalions. It can also be appreciated that 'localisation' was necessary in Britain in order to get support for the Army from a largely business dominated society. But by the time of the First World War, and perhaps of the Boer War, it was already inappropriate and largely irrelevant. The forty or fifty battalion regiment was a nonsensical monstrosity with many drawbacks. It was possible to maintain a broadly similar structure up to World War Two but by then the bulk of the Army was in the Corps rather than the Regiments, and the Corps proliferated even more during that war and immediately afterwards. Even more important, the 1939–45 War witnessed the arrival of the Special Forces, organised as Corps, and now with a permanent role.

Since the war, largely on grounds of economy, the 'Blue Water' naval role and world wide capability of the Army has been under attack. The importance of NATO and the crucial role of a permanently based British Army in North West Europe could only recently be challenged. We have noted that the Minister for Defence at the time of the Falklands War, John Nott, has recently declared that Britain could not afford even a small capability for intervention outside Europe and that to attempt more than a European role would fatally weaken our contribution to the NATO Alliance. The miscalculation and lack of balance which preceded the Falklands campaign can hardly be used as a justification for a massive global capability but the events of 1982 prove without the least doubt that the unexpected does happen. Even more, events in Northern Ireland and in seaports and airports around the world should be enough to convince us that British armoured divisions on the North German plain, however much they represent theoretical safety, are quite incapable of protecting British people and British interests from terrorism, political blackmail and large scale criminal activities. The British Army of the Rhine does have a limited capability to operate in Northern Ireland and a similar ability to act in support of the civil power in the United Kingdom and elsewhere, including assistance in disaster control and in situations of industrial unrest. But every time troops are taken from the 1st British Corps in Germany, it is at the expense of expertise in their primary role and may involve a period of re-training or the acceptance of a less than optimum performance in the secondary role. In any event, specialisation, which is such an important requirement in almost every contemporary military role, will be lost or weakened if a special reserve is not available to pick up and cope with the new tasks as they arise. Even if the new tasks are so large as to require the diversion of troops from their primary responsibilities, a readily available reserve, trained in at least some of the required techniques, would be of great benefit, especially since speed of re-action is one of the most important capabilities for such a reserve.

Even in the European theatre of potential operations there is a requirement for air-mobile reserves and although the new role for the United Kingdom based brigade of 2nd Armoured Division will go some way to meet this need, a super-mobile shock-troop force could provide a valuable re-inforcement over the whole of Northern

Europe. Current discussion of the possible obsolescence of heavy armoured forces may make the introduction of such a mobile, light but powerfully armed formation essential as an interim measure whilst new doctrines are being developed. The ideal form for such a force might be a Special Forces Division, made up from the existing Parachute and Commando Brigades, each doubled in size and including, as an integral part of the Division or Brigades, the supporting arms and services necessary to allow independent operations when necessary. In addition to its shock and mobile intervention role, a Special Forces Division, despite predictable opposition from some sections of the Forces, could provide an exemplary formation in terms of recruitment standards, specialised training and dedication to intelligent and sometimes independent action, not unlike what was expected from the riflemen and skirmishers of the Light Companies of the past.

There have no doubt always been élites in most armies and in the British Army no less than some others. Élites seem to be necessary for a variety of reasons, some of which we have explored. What is important is that the élite formations should be truly functional, meeting an obvious requirement and in so far as they are an élite, setting an example in bearing, discipline, training and courage which can act as a model for the rest of the Armed Services and to some extent for the youth of the nation. What we have called the 'old élites' may no longer be capable of meeting these requirements but the need is still obvious and a Special Forces Division would seem to be the ideal way of filling the gap. Under the terms of a strict analysis it is unlikely that the Guards or the Gurkhas have much of a long term future. When Britain withdraws from Hong Kong during the next decade, it is unlikely that the Gurkha Brigade will be stationed in the United Kingdom and even more unlikely that a convincing role will be found for them in the British order of battle in the twenty-first century. To keep two battalions of Gurkhas in Britain, as has recently been suggested, with all the support services they would require, would make the level of family support in Germany look very meagre. To keep two battalions in Britain to back up one in Brunei seems to be a new kind of military madness but, again, it has been the subject of a recent *Times* leak. Sooner or later this situation will have to be faced and, for the good of the Gurkhas themselves, it should be faced sooner rather than later. The Guards, on the other hand, who like the Gurkhas have always been acknowledged as first class fighting troops, have a ceremonial role which will increasingly inhibit their warlike function. It must be seen increasingly that special ceremonial uniforms, drills and perhaps even ceremonial weapons, can no longer fit into a modern army. Whilst there may be a role for the Guards, it is not one that will fit into an increasingly specialised and technologically orientated army. Sadly, that role may be more and more at odds with the values and beliefs of present day society. Whilst the ceremonial role is likely to restrict ever more seriously the ability of the Guards to be trained and kept up to date in military technology, the role is going to become more and more expensive. The fact that the Guards are one of the few sections of the Armed Forces that could probably show a notional financial profit on their activities, would appear to make them an attractive target for privatisation rather than that they should be retained as part of our conventional forces.

A more serious problem is the growing one of alienation within the Forces, especially the Army. As we have seen the problem here is threefold. First there is the problem of providing sufficiently wide career opportunities for senior officers from non-tooth arms. Gunners and sappers are able to progress their senior officers above the highest posts in their own Corps and frequently they can take a disproportionate number of the posts which require Lieutenant Generals and Generals. It is impossible to ignore the requirement for command experience in many of the higher posts but there are posts available at a high level within the capabilities of some of the best officers in the servicing corps. In the Royal Air Force, when it was decided to combine some of the minor services with the main administrative branch, it was feared that the smaller services would lose out to the main administrative stream. It was thought that the senior Royal Air Force staff posts would be monopolised by the main stream officers. In fact a recent Air Secretary, a member of the Air Force Board, came from the Instructor (Education) specialisation and so ended up in a post higher than anything available to him before the amalgamation. The problem is made more irritating in that the higher Command and Staff Posts in all three Services provide the entrée to a number of prestigious civilian posts on retirement which are usually not open to non-tooth arm officers, whatever their competence and specialisation.

The second factor producing a feeling of alienation in the Army is the 'chalk and cheese' syndrome. Some schools and social backgrounds produce cheese and some strangely, only produce chalk. The Army finds it very difficult to see through this analysis and is happy to perpetuate a situation where the young officers from one type of school and one social environment are gathered together in certain regiments whilst those from other schools and environments are put into regiments and corps where it is felt they might feel more at ease. The system is clearly a vicious circle which it will take courage and imagination to break out of but it really will not do to boast of the lowered social barriers and the career open to talents when the structure of the officer corps of the Army is warped in the way that it is.

The third cause of some disquiet is the comparatively narrow range, in terms of background, school and further education, from which the potential regular officers of the Army are drawn. It is seriously suggested that the Regular Commissions Board is no longer able to perform in an adequate way the task for which it was set up. This may be nobody's fault; it has presumably not been part of the function of the RCB to do more than test the young men that present themselves before it but so many questions have been begged in this process. Are officers born or made and is this an exclusive process or can some young men be made into officers regardless of their background and other young men remain unsuitable, again regardless of their background? Does the Ministry of Defence really want officers from a wider background and if so how much is it prepared to pay to get them? Could a sufficiently wide and potentially unlimited career be made available to this new type of entrant?

Taken together, the three causes for limited optimism about the open nature of the Army as it approaches the twenty-first century seem to present a fairly solid barrier to progress but more difficult barriers have been overcome in the past, and from within the Army itself. What is essential is for the Services to recognise the real problems of the day and to tackle them before unsatisfactory solutions are forced upon them by what Napier would have called 'incompetent persons, perniciously meddling with what they do not understand'.[1]

The structure of the Army and the seemingly permanent move of its centre of gravity to the North German Plain[2] has produced problems for the service family which, whilst they have almost certainly been present in one form or another since armies were first formed, have been accentuated by a growth of expectations about individual and family life in the United Kingdom. That Northern Ireland, which at present soaks up a large number of units in the infantry role, is also an unsatisfactory family posting makes matters that much worse. In a recent article in *The Times* on garrison life in the Province,[3] emphasis is placed yet again on the almost pathological nature of the way of life of some families in military settlements. The article points to excessive drinking, marital tensions and teenage vandalism as being typical. However, there is evidence that life in garrison towns is not markedly different from life in some Local Authority housing estates and, furthermore, the cancer of a racial undercurrent is happily rare. Although the availability of cheap liquor in Germany and the ever present military tension in Northern Ireland may raise the scale of the problem, it is not confined to the families of the Forces. This does not mean that every effort should not be made to reduce stress amongst military families if on no other grounds but those of military efficiency. Ruth Jolly's preferred solution is to reduce the number of accompanied postings in the Army in line with current practice in the Navy.[4] She does suggest that there would need to be financial incentives and improved welfare arrangements for the longer and possibly predominantly unaccompanied periods of married service life. Whilst the reduction of family postings may, in part, solve the problem it will produce other problems for particular sections of the Army like the Royal Armoured Corps, whose regiments, in the prevailing East–West political climate, spend most of their service life in North Germany. There is also a separate issue in Northern Ireland, made plain in *The Times* article, where it insists that it is politically necessary for service families to have as close a contact as possible with the local community. To the Army itself this last consideration may not seem to be particularly attractive and might well be one that army planners would do best to leave out of their calculations. It is not up to the Army and certainly not up to army families to make a political gesture by offering themselves up as hostages to fortune. Where the head of a family or his wife, under certain circumstances, are by birth or upbringing members of the local community, there is every reason why they should live within it if they so wish, but not without the support and agreement of their neighbours.

There are other problems for service wives and older children in British garrisons abroad and particularly in Germany. Lack of suitable jobs, as we have said, is unfortunate for two reasons. Not only does the service family tend to have a lower gross income than its civilian counterpart in the United Kingdom but the lack of a worthwhile occupation or the opportunity to further a professional career is now seen as a much more serious deprivation than it was in the past. It seems that the provision of jobs for dependants has gone almost as far as it can in Germany without reducing the efficiency of the forces there and the only way to make an impact on the situation is to restrict the number of families with the British Services.[5] For other reasons, living in service accommodation is a much less attractive proposition now than previously. This is mainly due to the very laudable desire of service families to buy and live in their own houses. The rental costs of a married quarter represent a considerable proportion of the mortgage repayments required for similar civilian accommodation. The number of quarters in the United Kingdom for all three Services fell from 87,500 in 1982 to an estimated 81,000 in 1988, whilst the total of married servicemen has reduced only marginally from 137,589 in 1981 to 137,140 in 1987.[6]

It is improbable that an acceptable solution will be forthcoming for the many different problems which beset the modern service family but a combination of restrictions, with some financial compensation, could make the perceived hardships more bearable. First, it is suggested, a decision should be taken at once to give up all service quarters in Germany from say 1992. There should be no ban on families accompanying servicemen but all British family support services would be withdrawn and those families which did choose to go to Germany with a serviceman, officer or soldier, would live entirely on the local economy for accommodation, supplies, health care and children's education where necessary. It might also be logical to abolish Boarding School Allowance but since this is, in practice, largely a middle and senior officers allowance, it would be bitterly fought for. In the long run, it might prove possible to give up most of the quarters in the United Kingdom and, in the short run, an attempt should be made to sell-off quarters to service occupants. If the Army is to encourage separation, two further consequences follow. Every effort should be made to bring about as far as possible an unmarried army, certainly as far as the junior ranks are concerned, and this leads on to the necessity for adequate financial compensation. Separation allowances would have to be very much increased as would free travel facilities. House purchase schemes would have to be improved and education, retraining and resettlement provision would have to be introduced much earlier in the serviceman's career.

Shorter tours, not the longer ones now being advocated, would then be in demand and at least from the career point of view this would probably be an advantage. The problem of the armoured exiles on the North German Plain would still be with us but even this difficulty could begin to solve itself if the hinted-at downgrading of armoured forces really materialises and even more if the political situation eased further. Even if the balance of arms and services remains roughly as it is, there is always the possibility of compensation in terms of an enhanced gratuity or pension, or in 'special to arm' pay. In industrial relations there is a well-known saying that disputes and dissatisfactions are very rarely over money but they are almost always settled by money. It is clear that any sort of reorganisation on the lines suggested will be expensive but a large amount of money could be saved and as long as this is not regarded, in the traditional way, as a money saving exercise, it could be self-financing. The real benefits should come from having a genuinely 'leaner' Army and from the removal of the current discontents and the mismatch between a perceived civilian life-style and what the Army can provide as a supporting service.

Finally, what about the Army itself? We have said that the Army appears to be ready for a broader functional organisation and we have tried to show that the best features of the traditional regimental system can be and indeed already are incorporated into a number of different sized and tasked Corps of the Army. We have supported the view also that fighting spirit and ésprit is nurtured in the small face to face group which is not an exclusive property of the regiment. However, that particular battle seems to have been won and the new Administrative Divisions may well prove to be an acceptable compromise between a Corps of Infantry and the famous regiments of the past. Since most of the technical training for the armoured regiments is now organised centrally it may now be opportune to absorb the much amalgamated cavalry regiments into a genuine Royal Armoured Corps. Perhaps the time has come for the former Royal Tank Corps to swallow at least part of the Army and for the pioneering and innovative spirit of the original tank men to re-assert itself.

It may be that a 'cooling off' period is urgently required after the hectic and not always well thought-out amalgamations of recent decades. It is to be hoped that another Sergeant Major X will not be left to cry 'Why does it have to be the Suffolks?'[7] It may yet be too early to persuade the authorities of the benefits that might accrue if a semi-constabulary model is used as a basis for army re-organisation and even more is it unlikely that the Army can be convinced, in the short run, of the advantages that might follow from a 'through' promotion system and the abolition of the dual promotion ladder. However, the twenty-first century is only a little over a decade away and already there are signs that two trends of the present decade are likely to be accentuated in the years immediatley to come. One trend is towards the belief that all privilege must be earned. Whilst in the past we have paid lip service to this principle in the name of democracy, a much more rigorous set of criteria is going to be applied in the future. Cost-effectiveness will be applied to the trappings of élitism in the Services as much as elsewhere, and to come quickly to the second point, this process will be used to investigate structures as much if not more than in the elimination of redundant bodies and practices. At the very least, the Services must generate alternative ideas, think about them and be in a position to reject, on rational grounds, the revolutionary proposals that are bound to come.

Fortescue has provided so much of the inspiration for this book that it is not inappropriate to return to him at the end. In the debate over the future role of the Armed Services and whether they should be confined to a 'NATO Alliance – Europe only' posture or be allowed to retain some kind of world-wide capability, there is a cost benefit which is sometimes forgotten. A successful Army, in peace and war is more than good leadership, organisation and weapons, it is spirit also and where the Army has shed its blood in the battles of the past is part of that spirit. At the beginning of each of his thirteen volumes Fortescue quotes the same line from one of Horace's odes:[8]

Quae caret ora nostro

Horace speaks with sadness and disapproval of the loss of Roman blood but Fortescue, taking for his translation 'What shore knows not our blood?', was doubtless thinking of the numberless battlefields around the world where British blood has been shed and where the British Army has earned its glory and built its unique spirit. In its day, the Regimental System was important in helping to build that spirit and translate it into military effectiveness. It is essential now that the trappings of an obsolete system are not retained at the expense of the vital spirit.

Appendix I

Senior Rank and 'Arm' Pyramids

The Generals Rank Pyramid, 1986

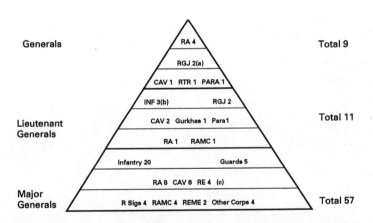

Generals   Total 9

Lieutenant Generals   Total 11

Major Generals   Total 57

RA 4
RGJ 2(a)
CAV 1   RTR 1   PARA 1
INF 3(b)   RGJ 2
CAV 2   Gurkhas 1   Para 1
RA 1   RAMC 1
Infantry 20   Guards 5
RA 8   CAV 6   RE 4   (c)
R Sigs 4   RAMC 4   REME 2   Other Corps 4

Notes: (a) The only Infantry generals in 1986 were from RGJ and Para.
(b) Infantry are broken down into RGJ, Gurkhas, Paras and others
(c) 'Other Corps' for Major Generals 1986 were RAOC, RCT, RAEC, ALC.

'Tooth Arm' Pyramid

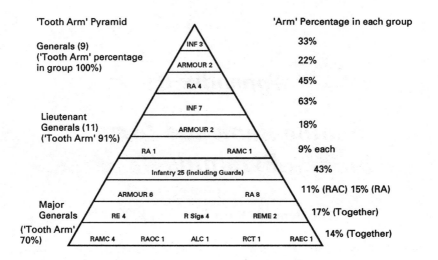

'Tooth Arm' Pyramid

Generals (9)
('Tooth Arm' percentage
in group 100%)

Lieutenant
Generals (11)
('Tooth Arm' 91%)

Major
Generals
('Tooth Arm'
70%)

INF 3

ARMOUR 2

RA 4

INF 7

ARMOUR 2

RA 1   RAMC 1

Infantry 25 (including Guards)

ARMOUR 6   RA 8

RE 4   R Sigs 4   REME 2

RAMC 4   RAOC 1   ALC 1   RCT 1   RAEC 1

'Arm' Percentage in each group

33%

22%

45%

63%

18%

9% each

43%

11% (RAC) 15% (RA)

17% (Together)

14% (Together)

Appendix II

Some Social and Biographical Details of the Army, 1986

Some Biographical Details for Major Generals in 1986 Army List (Total 57)

1.	**Schools attended**	Cat 1 20	Cat 2 21	Cat 3 16	No Data 5(a)	Cat 1 Top Public Schools Cat 2 Other Fee-Paying Schools Cat 3 State Schools
	Note: 5 for whom there is no data are 'best guessed' into other categories (Who's Who)					

2. **Sons of Service fathers:** 17 but could be 20 (No data on 3)

3. **Leisure pursuits** (Main one only) (Who's Who) Country pursuits 22 Cultural pursuits 23 Others or no data 12

4.	**University Degrees**	Arts	Engineering/Science	Medicine	None Shown
		7	4	4	42
	Note: Many will hold professional qualifications				

Distribution by Arm of Lieutenant Colonels and General Officers 1986

Arms	Lt Cols	Maj Gen	Lt Gens	Generals	Front Line Units*
RAC	126	6	2	2	24
RA	171	8	1	4	28
RE	147	4	0	0	20
INF	351	25	7	3	96
AAC	29	0	0	0	4
Others		14	1	0	

Note: In the 1986 Army List there were no officers above the rank of Major General in RE, AAC, REME, R Sigs, RCT, RAOC or in four other minor Corps
* Includes Territorial Army Units.

Army Family Accommodation, 1985
(Source: Statement on Army Estimates 1986)

1. Estimated House owners (in thousands)

Date	1970	1973	1977	1978	1980	1983
All Services	45.6	55.0	55.2	58.4	59.2	65.8
All Army	11.0	14.1	15.1	15.5	17.2	20.3
Officers	4.1	6.1	6.8	6.9	7.6	8.1
Servicemen	6.9	8.1	8.2	8.7	9.7	12.2

2. Percentage Owning Houses

Date	1970	1983
All Army	12%	24%
Officers	30%	70%
Men	9%	17%

3. Accommodation Occupied by Army Personnel 1983

	Own Home	Quarters	Other
Officers	32%	65%	4%
Men	10%	84%	5%

Note: Many Officers and soldiers, although they owned a house were living in quarters or elsewhere

Appendix III

Content Analysis and Comparison. United Services Journals 1840s and 1870s

Date	1840	1841	1842	1843	1844	1845	1846	1847	1848	1849	Subject of article
1	20	15	32	30	30	29	24	25	28	37	Professional studies
2	15	2	3	4	1	2	4	7	8	1	Military technology
3	24	40	37	41	49	35	45	40	36	37	Memoirs/Mil. Hist.
4					2	2				2	Faith & Religion
5	7	6	13	3	2	6	7	9	9	4	Literature/Poetry
6	7	55	7	12	12	24	30	15	19	31	Exploration/Travel
7	3	6		1	1	2	1		1	2	Adventure & Sport
8	1			1		1	3		10	7	Army & Society
9	5	5	7	2	9	4	9	7	5	3	Current Campaigns
10	2	1	4	2	9		3	1	2	14	Others
	84	80	103	95	115	123	126	104	118	138	Total for Year

Eighteen-forties

Eighteen-seventies

Date	1870	1871	1872	1873	1874	1875	1876	1877	1878	1879	Subject of article
1	56	80	80	59	47	37	52	51	54	37	Professional studies
2	14	6	13	6	6	6	4		1	1	Military technology
3	31	28	20	18	17	12	13	14	22	25	Memoirs/Mil. Hist.
4										2	Faith & Religion
5				2			2		2	3	Literature/Poetry
6	5	5	3	6	4	5	7	11	8	10	Exploration/Travel
7	2			1	1	1					Adventure & Sport
8	2	2	1	3	1		1	2	1	1	Army & Society
9				5	3			1		6	Current Campaigns
10	2	2	3	2	1	1	2	2	1	1	Others
	112	123	120	92	80	62	81	81	89	86	Total for Year

Comparison 1840s/1870s

Date	1840s		1870s		
	No. of articles	%	No. of articles	%	Subject of articles
1	240	23.50	553	59.00	Professional studies
2	47	4.50	57	6.00	Military technology
3	384	37.50	200	21.00	Memoirs/Mil. Hist.
4	6	0.50	2	0.25	Faith & Religion
5	66	5.50	9	1.00	Literature/Poetry
6	162	15.50	64	7.00	Exploration/Travel
7	17	1.50	5	0.50	Adventure & Sport
8	23	2.50	14	1.50	Army & Society
9	56	5.00	15	1.75	Current campaigns
10	38	4.00	17	2.00	Others
Total	1039	100.00	936	100.00	Total

Notes: 1. During the 1870s there were five articles on dress—usually pressing for modifications.
   2. In the 1870s unlike the 1840s there is almost nothing about the last great war (i.e. in the 1870s, the Crimean War).
   3. Exploration and Travel in the early 1870s was mainly concerned with Central Asia.
   4. 'Others' in the 1870s were largely an annual article on the Lifeboat Service

Appendix IV

Military Career Profile
Sergeant Major X

Sergeant Major X joined the Royal Norfolk Regiment in 1943. Because he was only seventeen years six months old, he was posted to the 70th Royal Norfolk (Boys) Battalion. Eventually he joined a battalion of the 'Beds and Herts' in India. He took part in riot control operations and came back to England for demobilisation in 1947. He returned to his native Norfolk and was married in the same year to a local girl.

He was not happy as a civilian and rejoined the Royal Norfolks in 1952. After a parachute course, he joined 1st Royal Norfolks in Hong Kong. After nine months unaccompanied service in Hong Kong, he returned with his battalion to Colchester where his family joined him in a quarter. He had been promoted Corporal in Hong Kong. He was corporal in the mortar platoon and then, after a course at the Support Weapons Wing of the School of Infantry at Netheravon he was promoted sergeant and became the battalion Provost Sergeant in 1954.

In 1956 the battalion moved to Cyprus. The 'emergency' was in full swing but, after about six months, things quietened down and he was joined by his family in January 1957. There were only four soldiers' families from the Royal Norfolks in Cyrpus at the time and they found their own accommodation. He had three children by now, the youngest born in Cyprus. In Cyprus, where he served as a platoon sergeant, the battalion was mainly composed of National Servicemen.

The battalion returned to the UK at the end of 1957 for leave and then reformed at Iserlohn, in Germany, where it remained for two and a half years. 'X' was now Provost sergeant again. When the battalion returned to the Depot at Bury St. Edmunds it was amalgamated with the 1st Suffolks to form the 1st Battalion the East Anglian Regiment (Royal Norfolk and Suffolk). There was some disbelief and consternation in the regiment at the amalgamation. 'They were our great rivals in everything, why did it have to be the Suffolks?' He became a drill instructor at Bury St. Edmunds and the family occupied a quarter at Harwich which they all enjoyed. Meanwhile, the battalion had been posted to Berlin and when they returned he rejoined them as reconaissance platoon sergeant.

The battalion next flew to British Guiana for a nine month unaccompanied tour. Their main duty was riot control. The 'recce' platoon was detached 60 miles from Headquarters. It was still very much a National Service battalion. There was still some 'us and them' feeling between the ex-Norfolks and the ex-Suffolks. The battalion returned to Felixstowe and his family was still in quarters at Harwich. The battalion then went to Aden whilst 'X' was posted to the Army Apprentices College, Carlisle as an instructor.

He rejoined his battalion in Aden in 1962. His Commanding Officer now, (an ex-Norfolks officer) had been Sergeant Major X's Adjutant when he was in Hong Kong as a corporal. He was once again the 'recce' platoon sergeant in Aden and he describes life there as 'a bit hairy'. There were more regular soldiers in the battalion by now.

The battalion then moved to Celle in Germany after leave in the United Kingdom. 'X' travelled independently, with his wife to a quarter in Celle. The battalion was mechanised by now and converted to Armoured Personnel Carriers. There were two children with them in Celle. One daughter worked in the NAAFI and one was at school. They took leaves in Germany including Berlin (using the leave Hotel there) and in Holland. He was promoted to Colour Sergeant in Germany and six months later to Sergeant Major. It was 1966 and he had been back in the Army for 14 years. He had some difficulty in getting the Army Certificate of Education 1st Class which was necessary for substantive promotion to Warrant rank. But he had been promised promotion to WO soon after reaching the rank of Colour Sergeant by his ex-Norfolks Adjutant now his CO. He eventually got his ACE 1st Class and got his substantive promotion to Company Sergeant Major after the battalion was posted to Catterick in 1967. Early in 1969, the battalion went to Northern Ireland but he went to The Queen's Divisional Headquarters at Bassingbourne as Company Sergeant Major. He then went to the 3rd Battalion, Royal Anglians (Beds and Herts). This battalion had a five month mechanisation conversion period and then moved to Paderborn at the end of 1969. He was accompanied by his family. They were two years in Paderborn and the battalion then went to Northern Ireland.

The Sergeant Major then went to the Territorial Army at Ipswich, as a Permanent Staff Instructor with the 6th Royal Anglians (TA). In 1973 he bought a house in Norfolk and retired in 1974. He had enjoyed being with the TA and was well regarded there.

Comments

1. There had clearly been some difficulty over the amalgamation with the Suffolks in 1959 and an ex-regimental clanniness obviously persisted for some time; cf. his relationship with his ex-Norfolks CO.
2. His daughter working in the NAAFI at Celle met a young sergeant from her father's company of 1st Anglians who had his potential son-in-law moved to another company to avoid any difficulties. Son-in-law eventually became Regimental Sergeant Major and was commissioned.
3. 'X' does not belong to the Regimental Association but does attend reunions.
4. He says resettlement procedure was a waste of time, but he was already resettled!
5. He had already got a good job as a radio operator with the police through a regimental acquaintance.
6. He enjoys the police work which is going well. Army discipline and smart dress and his service background have helped a lot.
7. He would recommend the police as a career but no longer the Army. He has no hard feelings or bitterness about the Army but the amalgamations still rankle.

Notes and References

Introduction

1. A recent popular calculation has it that there are more engineers alive and practising today than have ever existed before in the earth's history. Frank Kitson in his *Warfare As a Whole*, Faber & Faber, London, 1987, refers to the rate of technological change in his first paragraph and considers its effect on the Army. Donald Schon in the Reith Lectures of 1970 on *The Loss of the Stable State*, said that the accelerating pace of technological change was generating social problems at a rate greater than most social institutions were designed to cope with. Such institutions, like the American Federal Government, were in danger of becoming a series of memorials to old problems.
2. Of the twenty Generals and Lieutenant Generals in the 1986 Army List, only one is not from a 'tooth arm' and he is a Doctor. Of the fifty-seven Major Generals almost 90 per cent are from the 'tooth arms' if the Royal Engineers and Royal Signals are included in that category. In the past, the need for senior officers to have commanded large military formations has been a stumbling block in many, but not all promising careers. In the future, it may seem less important. However, an obituary in *The Times* of 29 March 1988 by Field-Marshal Lord Carver on Major General Sir Cecil Smith shows that even an experienced and competent staff officer could not advance very far in the Army if he came originally from the Royal Army Service Corps.
   See also Appendices I and II.
3. Although Frank Kitson, op cit page 12, does not draw an obvious conclusion from his argument, he does say that the use of nuclear weapons would produce total disaster for all those taking part [in a war] and probably for the rest of the world. I cannot believe that this view, if it is widely held, does not produce an unsettling effect on soldiers and planners alike. Major General J F C Fuller wrote in the *Daily Mail* of 8th August 1945, 'From August 5th 1945, onwards, armies, navies, and air forces as we know them, have metaphorically been sunk in the rubble and dust of Hiroshima'. See *Boney Fuller*, by Anthony John Trythall, Cassell, London, 1977. p232/233
4. Bond, Brian Ed. *Victorian Military Campaigns*, Hutchinson, London, 1967, lists 72 wars and punitive expeditions between 1837 and 1900 alone.
5. Dietz, P J and Stone, J F, The British All Volunteer Army, in *Armed Forces and Society*, Vol 1 No 2, 1975, analyses the factors affecting recruiting in Britain in the period following the end of conscription. Most of the conclusions drawn are still relevant.
6. All three Services provide information on house purchase but it has been mainly directed towards preparation for resettlement after retirement. Assistance in obtaining Local Authority housing is also available but again in a post–Service context. Until recently, many Commanding Officers have regarded private house ownership and occupancy as detrimental to the proper performance of military duties.
7. *The Times*, 7 July 1987 and *The Sunday Times*, 12 July 1987.
8. *The Times*, 9 January 1987, continued to stir a controversy which started with The Contagious Diseases Act of 1864; at that time the problem was syphilis not AIDS.

9. Scott, Sir S D, *The British Army, Its Origins, Progress and Equipment*. Cassell Petter and Galpin, London, 1867, Vol I Page 475 on Cromwell and the raising of Ironsides is worth quoting in full:

> The plan on which he proceeded to raise these invincibles was to secure a better class of men, most of them freeholders and freeholders' sons, and who upon matters of conscience engaged in their quarrel. He selected also none but religious men, whose hearts he sought to engage in the cause for which they fought, so that instead of a band of sordid mercenaries, each one regarded himself as a missionary going forth on a holy errand . . .

See also note (3) page 475.
10. Marshall, S L A, *Men Against Fire*. William Morrow, New York 1947, and an article by Shils, Edward A., and Janowitz, Morris, Cohesion and Disintegration in the Wehrmacht in World War II, published in *Public Opinion Quarterly* 1948, are still, despite their seeming antiquity, amongst the front runners in this field. It is interesting to compare this article of forty years ago with an article in the *RUSI Journal* of Summer 1988 on Social Structures in the Peninsular Army by Major C M St. G Kirke MA, RA. His conclusions are not dissimilar. See also a critical article in the *RUSI Journal*, Winter 1988 (Vol 113, No 4), by Professor Roger J Spiller with the title 'S. L. A. Marshall and the Ratio of Fire'.

Chapter I   The Origins of the British Army

1. Fortescue, J W, *A History of the British Army*. 13 vols Macmillan, London 1899–1930
2. Scott, S D, op. cit.
3. Holmes, Richard., in *Firing Line*, Penguin Books 1987, describes the dehumanising process in Chapter 9, pages 389–393 and discusses the My Lai affair as well as atrocities on the Eastern Front in the Second World War.
4. McEvedy, Colin, *The Penguin Atlas of Medieval History Vol 2*. Penguin Books, England, 1961, page 8.
5. Salway, Peter, *Roman Britain*, Oxford History of England, Clarendon Press, Oxford 1981, pages 262–263.
6. Ibid, page 118.
7. Ibid, page 142.
8. Ibid page 174.
9. John James, a psychologist working with the Royal Air Force in 1970, allowed the author to read the manuscript of a book which he had just completed on The Officer Concept. In his very learned and extremely amusing book, he coined the phrase 'White Horse Syndrome' to describe the idealistic, semi-mystical vision of leadership which he felt was inappropriate for today's Royal Air Force pilots, however well it suited the pilots of the First World War. As far as is known, his book has not been published.
10. Fortescue, J W, op cit. vol 1 pages 5–6.
11. The *Classis Britanica*, the Roman fleet based on Britain was withdrawn from British waters, perhaps only to the other side of the Channel, from the middle of the third century AD. Salway, op cit page 639, refers to the disappearance of the *Classis Britanica* from the records and says, page 445, by the fifth century there was no Roman Fleet in the North Sea.
12. Scott, S D, op. cit. vol I page 114.
13. At Truro in March 1987, Nick St. Aubyn, the Tory candidate, was so labelled by an opposing candidate.
14. McEvedy, Colin, op. cit, page 60.
15. Davis, R C H, *The Normans and Their Myths*. Book Club Associates, London 1976. See particularly chapter 2, but I have drawn on this work extensively in my section on the Normans.
16. Fortescue, J W, op. cit. Vol 1 page 129.
17. Ibid, vol 1.
18. Ibid, vol 1,
19. For discussion and comments on 'The Concept of Honour' as it affects the soldier see Spier, Hans, *Social Order and the Risks of War*, Stewart, New York, 1952, Janowitz, M,

The Professional Soldier, Macmillan, New York, 1960, esp. page 23 and Andreski, S, *Military Organisations and Society*. Kegan Paul, London, 1954.

Chapter 2   The Tempering of the Regiments

1. Fortescue, J W, op. cit. Vol I page 169.
2. Ibid, page 170.
3. Spier, Hans., op. cit.
4. Ibid, chapter 4.
5. See for example *The Story of the Royal Warwickshire Regiment*, in the County Life Series, Charles Lethgridge Kingsford, London 1921. The author of the history explains on page three that the recall to England of the Regiment from Holland by James II, in anticipation of the Monmouth Rebellion, was really only important in that it allowed the Regiment to take precedence over the Regiments raised by James, and ultimately in 1751 to be ranked as the 6th Foot.
6. Brereton, J M, *A Guide to the Regiments and Corps of the British Army*. Bodley Head, London, 1985. See the introduction to this most useful work of reference.
7. Fortescue, J W, op. cit. Vol 1. page 258.
8. Details are given in *Sir John Reresby's Diary* which can be consulted at York City Library.
9. Fortescue, J W, op. cit. Vol I page 237.
10. Relevant correspondence between The Horse Guards (Army Headquarters in Britain) and Army Headquarters, Ireland, is in PRO/WO/35/28
11. Gleichen, Major General Lord Edward, *A Guardsman's Memories*. Blackwood, London, 1932. page 250.
12. Ryan, A P, *Mutiny at the Curragh*., Macmillan, London, 1956, and Fergusson, Major General Sir James, *The Curragh Incident*, Faber, London, 1964, give intriguingly different versions of the same events. Even their titles indicate the different commitment with which they are written. A recent book published for The Army Records Society, edited by Ian F W Beckett, entitled *The Army and the Curragh Incident 1914*, Bodley Head, 1986, deals specifically with the King's involvement.
13. Fortescue, J W, op. cit. Vol 2. Page 102, footnote.
14. Wingfield-Stratford, Esme, *The Making of a Gentleman*, Williams and Northgate, London 1938. Page 247.
15. Woodham Smith, Cecil, *The Reason Why*, Constable for the Book Society, London, 1953, Gives a very readable account of Lord Cardigan's machinations.
16. Demeter, Karl, *The German Officer Corps in Society and State 1650–1945*. Weidenfeld & Nicolson, Trans. Angus Malcolm. London 1965.
17. Ibid, chapter 26 and see Alan Bullock, *Hitler, A Study in Tyranny*, Penguin, London 1952. Esp. Book III chapter 13.
18. Fortescue, J W, op. cit. Vol I, page 587
19. Ibid, Vol II, page 115.
20. Ibid, Vol II page 500. The stories of the German reaction to British musketry at the beginning of the First World War may be yet another myth. The British Expeditionary Force already had some machine guns, even in 1914, and these are reported to have been well handled, but the rapidity and accuracy of British rifle fire at Mons and during the retreat is noted by many contemporary writers. See also Jock Haswell, *The British Army, A Concise History*, Book Club Associates, London, 1975. Page 118, and Holmes and Keegan, *Soldiers*, page 70
21. Trevelyan, G M, *England Under Queen Anne*, Longmans, London, 1934. Page 123.
22. Mahan, A T, *The Influence of Sea Power Upon History*. Sampson, Lowe, London, 1889, 8th Ed. Chapter 6, page 241.
23. Fortescue, J W, op. cit. Vol III, page 8.
24. Ibid, Vol III page 11.
25. Ibid. Vol II. The whole of Chapter 12 gives a detailed description of the pay, conditions of service and organisation of the Army in the middle of the eighteenth century.
26. Ibid. Vol II, Chapter 12.
27. Ibid, Vol II, page 599.
28. There is an interesting discussion on the role of drink and drugs as preparation, and

anaesthetisation before and after combat in Richard Holmes, *Firing Line*. Jonathan Cape, London 1985. Chapter 6, 'The Real Enemy', deals with the problems of indoctrination and socialisation of the soldier and quotes from recent sources e.g. The Falklands War.

Chapter 3   The Golden Age of the Regiments

1. Fortescue, op. cit. Vol IV Chapter 13
2. Gill, Conrad, *The Naval Mutinies of 1797*. Manchester University Press, 1913.
3. Fortescue, J W, Vol VIII Chapter 2.
4. Brett-James, Anthony, *General Graham 1748–1844*. Macmillan, London, 1959. Page 206.
5. Ibid. Pages 209–210
6. Fortescue, J W, op. cit. Vol III Footnote to page 64. Brett-James op. cit., quotes two letters from General Graham about the dog. Pages 218–219.
7. The battle is described on the print as, *'exemple de bataille indécise où l'on fait de part et d'autres des prodiges de valeur dans l'estime réciproque'*. It is surprising that Barossa was included in the 'Great Napoleonic Battles' series. Napoleon was not present, it was not a 'great' battle, the French did not win it and it was hardly indicisive. It is nevertheless the only battle against the British depicted in the series.
8. Maxwell, William, *The Life of Wellington*. First published in three volumes, 1839. Newly edited with notes and abridged to one volume, Hutchinson, London, 1904.
9. Andreski, S, op. cit.
10. Otley, C B, Ph D Thesis, *The Origins and Recruitment of the British Army Élite*. A copy is held in the MOD Library. It gives details of this process. The one exception is Field Marshall W Robertson who entered the Army as a cavalry trooper, rose through all the non-commissioned ranks to RSM, was commissioned, rose through all the commissioned ranks to Field Marshal and was eventually Chief of the Imperial General Staff. Otley has some justification for regarding him as an exception but it could and did happen.
11. Wingfield-Stratford, Esme., op. cit. Pages 250–251.
12. Longford, Elizabeth., *Wellington, The Years of the Sword*. Weidenfeld & Nicolson. London, 1969. Page 309 and footnote. John Keegan, in his recent book *The Mask of Command*, attempts to show that every successful commander hides behind a constructed persona and that this is necessary to his function.
13. Maxwell, William, op. cit. Page 55.
14. Fortescue, J W, op. cit. Vol VIII, pages 213–215.
15. Keegan, John, *The Face of Battle*. Jonathan Cape, London, 1976. Chapter 3, Waterloo.
16. John Keegan and Richard Holmes in their individual books and in their joint work, *Soldiers*. Hamish Hamilton, London, 1985, do attempt a new approach to their material which draws heavily on sociology and psychology but they would no doubt wish to regard themselves still as Military Historians and subscribe to the 'broad church' principle. See also Note 28 to the previous chapter.
17. Keegan, John, op. cit. page 194.
18. Biddulph, Sir Robert, *Lord Cardwell at the War Office. 1868–1874*. London, 1904. Gives details of the various estimates of the number of troops required to meet the periodic scares over possible French attacks on Britain. The inability of the Home Forces to oppose an invasion is always emphasised.
19. Spiers, Edward M, *The Army and Society. 1815–1914*. Longmans, London 1980. Page 209.

Chapter 4   The British Army Between Waterloo and the Crimea

1. Tylden, Major G, *The Accoutrements of the British Infantryman 1640–1940*. The Journal of Army Historical Research, Vol 47, No 189, Spring 1969.
2. Ossowska, Maria, *Social Determinants of Moral Ideas*. Routledge & Kegan Paul, 1971, pages 169–170.

3. *Sergeant Pearmain's Memoirs*. Introduction by the Marquess of Anglesey FSA. Jonathan Cape, 1968, page 16.
4. Rundle, Edwin, George., *A Soldier's Life*. Toronto, 1909. He describes the wearing of the stock by regiments in Canada as late as 1858 and how eventually recruits got used to them. Wolseley, Sir Garnet, *The Story of a Soldier's Life*. 1903, Vol I, gives details of dress, drill and equipment at the time of the Gordon Relief Expedition. See also *The Times* 27 June 1988, 'On This Day'.
5. *Wolseley Papers*. PRO/W/Misc 18/lxxxi and 18/lxxxii.
6. Brereton, J M, op. cit. Page 109.
7. Marshall, Henry, *Military Miscellany*. London, 1846
8. Macpherson, Charles, Holland., *United Services Journal*, June 1846.
9. Cheltenham founded 1841, Marlborough 1845, Wellington 1853, Clifton 1862 and Haileybury in 1862 also.
10. Wingfield–Stratford, Esme., *The Squire and his Relations*. Cassell & Co. London, 1956. Pages 240–242 and 288–290.
11. Andreski, S., op. cit.
12. Otley, C B, op. cit.
13. Razzell, P E, See an article on *Social Origins of Officers in the Indian and British Home Army; 1758–1962*. Published in The Journal of Sociology, 1963.
14. Ward, S G P, *Wellington's Headquarters*. Oxford University Press, 1956. Many soldiers were commissioned 'in the field' in the Peninsula. See the *London Gazette* for the period. But by 1816/17 they were almost all on half pay. Compare the Gazettes with the relevant Army Lists. Commanders-in-Chief, 'in the field' had the right to give field commissions to replace battle casualties.
15. Lewis, M A, *England's Sea Officers: The Story of the Naval Profession*. Alan & Unwin, London, 1939, and *The Navy in Transition*. Hodder & Stoughton, 1965. In both these books Lewis uses W O Byrnes, *A Biographical Dictionary*, and Marshal's, *A Naval Biography*, as main source material.
16. Bond, B, op. cit.
17. Graham, Sir James, Home Secretary, *Secret memorandum 1844*. Earl Grey, *Paper on the Army, 1846*. Both papers are quoted in Biddulph, op. cit. See also a paper by Sir John Burgoyne, *Observations on Possible Results of a War with France*, later published in Burgoyne's *Military Opinions*.
18. The correspondence between Wellington and Burgoyne found its way into *The Morning Chronicle* (4 Jan 1848) where it was a source of considerable embarrassment to them both and was the occasion for Cobden saying 'The Duke of Wellington is now in his dotage'. See Bidulph op. cit. and Jay Luvaas, *The Education of an Army*. Cassell, London 1965, chapter 3 of part 1.
19. PRO/WO 32/111, Memorandum by Wellington of 17 June 1848.
20. *The Times*, 24 July 1843, and letter book of the Deputy Adjutant General of the Forces in Ireland. PRO/WO/35/28.
21. In England, where Chartism was not reinforced by nationalist sentiment, the troops were not at risk and only one reference appears to remain in official records concerning troops openly professing Chartist sympathies. PRO/WO/112 contains three letters from the police reporting on subversive talk by soldiers, including a party of twelve Scots Fusilier Guards who signed the Charter and said they would not fire on the people. The observations were made in a public house in London. There is no record of any action taken by 'The Horse Guards'.
22. *The Times*, 4 February 1840, reports the Duke of Wellington speaking on a motion in The House of Lords, introduced by the Bishop of Exeter on the spread of Socialist Societies saying: 'As Lord Lieutenant of Hampshire, I have told Magistrates to observe, watch and proceed against them if they are guilty of a breach of the law or peace'.
23. Wolseley, Sir Garnet, op. cit.
24. Sergeant Pearmain's Memoirs, op. cit. Page 24.
25. Woodham-Smith, Cecil, op. cit.
26. Bond, B, op. cit. Page 7.
27. Aron, Raymond, *Main Currents in Sociological Thought*. Vol I, Penguin Books, 1968. Pages 78–79.

28. Ibid.
29. Thomson, David, *Europe Since Napoleon*. Penguin Books, 1957, Page 187.
30. Hopkins, Harry, *The Strange Death of Private White*. Weidenfeld & Nicolson, London 1977.
31. *Hansard*, March 1841, Col U.
32. Private Letter Book, Commander-in-Chief, Ireland, 1840. PRO/WO/35/28.
33. Aydelotte, William O, The Business Interests of the Gentry in the Parliament of 1841–1847. Reprinted in *European Social Class, Stability and Change*. Ed. B Barber and E G Barber, Macmillan, NY. 1965.
34. Luvaas, Jay, op. cit. Pages 75–78.
35. Huntington, Samuel, *The Soldier and the State*. Harvard University Press, 1957, page 62.
36. An excellent history of the Purchase System in Britain is given in: Henry Bruce, *The Purchase System in the British Army, 1660–1871*, Published by The London Historical Society in 1980. Bruce points out that Purchase was a survival from medieval times and was not a result of Restoration corruption. Many state offices were sold apart from army commissions. Pepys was offered £500 for his Secretaryship of the Navy. Purchase emerged from a system where Scutage was introduced by Henry II in 1159, allowing Knights to escape their feudal service obligation by paying a money tax. The money was used by the King to hire mercenary soldiers, who organised themselves into a profit making company. By the time of Elizabeth I, the dangers of using troops who owed no national allegiance had long been clear. The Crown issued commissions to its subjects to raise companies only for its own service. The regimental system, which had just arrived, extended the purchase system into something like the arrangements which lasted until 1871. The Colonel and his officers were sub-proprietors and were able to supplement their pay, since the Crown paid for the total muster of men on the regimental roll, their weapons, equipment and sustenance. There were clearly many opportunities for corruption and fraud apart from the actual selling of commissions by 'agents' for more than the authorised price. Every commission was potentially valuable and its price was proportional to the profits likely to be made in the rank in question.
37. Editorial Article, A Requiem Upon Duelling, *United Services Journal*, Oct. 1848.
38. *The Annual Register* gives details of most of the duels fought in the early 1840s. Cecil Woodham-Smith, op. cit., chapters 4 and 5, gives a good account of the Cardigan, Tuckett duel. *The Duel, A History of Duelling*, by Robert Baldick, Chapman & Hall, London, 1965, gives a general picture of duelling in Britain in the first half of the nineteenth century. See also, *Gallant Gentlemen*, E S Turner, 1965.
39. de Tocqueville, Alexis, *The Ancient Regime and the French Revolution*. Part II Chapter 10. Collins, Fontana Library, 1966.
40. Ossowska, Maria, op. cit. Page 139.
41. Stearns, P N, *European Society in Upheaval.*, Collier, Macmillan, 1975. Pages 16–17.
42. *The Times*, 30 January 1840.
43. Woodham-Smith, Cecil., op. cit. Cardigan had banned the drinking of porter in the mess since he considered it the drink of 'factory hands and labourers'. At a mess dinner he humiliated one of his officers who had asked for Moselle for a guest, by choosing to regard the black Moselle bottle as a porter bottle. The provider of the Moselle and the guest were both officers who had served for some time in India and this was enough to damn them in Cardigan's eyes. The 'Black Bottle' affair became known to the public and reports were circulated of 'The Battle of the Moselle'. In the end Cardigan fought a duel with another of his 'Indian' officers, wounded him and was arrested. He asserted his privilege as a Peer to be tried by the House of Lords and was acquitted to the noisy indignation of the London public and the press.
44. Hobsbawm, E J, *The Age of Revolution 1789–1848*. Mentor Books, NY, 1962 Part II, Chapter 14, page 319.
45. Otley, C B, op. cit. and Razzell, P E, op. cit.
46. PRO/WO/30/118.
47. For a detailed account of attempts to abolish branding and flogging see: Blanco, Richard L, Attempts to Abolish Branding and Flogging in the Army of Victorian England Before 1881. Published in the *Journal of Army Historical Research*. Autumn 1968.

48. PRO/WO/71/309 reports the case of a major in New Zealand who was repeatedly found not guilty of drunkenness by a Court Martial, despite pressure from the authorities and at least one re-trial.
49. PRO/WO//35/28. 'Out Book' of the Deputy Adjutant General, Ireland.
50. Sergeant Pearmain's Memoirs. op. cit.
51. Marshall, Henry., op. cit.
52. Sergeant Pearmain's Memoirs. op. cit.
53. See an article by Lord Wolseley in, *The Reign of Queen Victoria—A Survey of 50 Years Progress*. Ed. Thomas Humphrey Ward, London, 1887
54. Bruce, H A, MP, Ed. *Life of General Sir William Napier*. John Murray, London, 1864.
55. George Eliot, a letter to J Sibree dated February 1848. Published *Pelican Book of English Prose*. Ed. Raymond Williams, Pelican Books 1969.

Chapter 5   The Regiments in India

1. Mason, Philip., *A Matter of Honour*. An account of the Indian Army, its officers and men. Macmillan. Papermac, 1986. First published 1974. An outstandingly useful history of the Indian Army.
2. Ibid. Chapter 5, page 75.
3. Fortescue, J W, op. cit. Vol II, page 174.
4. The most extreme example of annihilation by amalgamation is the formation of The Queen's Regiment on 31 December 1966. As one of the three 'large' Regiments in the Queen's Division it includes ten of the old Regiments of Foot from the 2nd to the 107th. Its honours, which must include almost every engagement in which honours were awarded, range from Tangier 1662–1680 to Korea 1950–1951. Its geographical catchment area is the whole of South East England.
5. Mason, P, op. cit. Chapter 6. Page 104.
6. Ibid. Chapter I. Page 22.
7. Kaye, M M, (Ed) *The Golden Calm*. An English Lady's Life in Moghul Delhi. Webb & Bower, Exeter, 1980.
8. Mason, P, op. cit. Chapter 10, pages 236–237.
9. Barr, Pat, *The Memsahibs*. The Women of Victorian India. Secker & Warburg, London, 1976.
10. Both Mason and Fortescue mention this dying cry of Nicholson's . He was a hero to both writers, as he appeared to be to everyone who met him.
11. Grierson, Edward, *The Imperial Dream*. Collins, 1972, page 83.
12. Waterfield, Robert., *The Memoirs of Private Waterfield*. Ed. Arthur Swinson & Donald Scott. Cassell & Co. 1968. Waterfield was born in Leicester and went to Portsmouth in 1842 with the intention of going to sea, possibly in the Royal Navy. However, he met old friends in Portsmouth and they persuaded him to join their regiment, the 32nd Foot, which was in garrison at Portsmouth at that time. The 32nd was a Cornish Regiment later to become The Duke of Cornwall's Light Infantry. He never really seems to have been at home in the regiment and this may be partly because of some Cornish 'clanniness' which he experienced.
13. PRO/WO/33/32/750 gives some details of the comparative costs.
14. Mason, P, op. cit. Chapter 13, 'The New Army'.
15. Wingfield-Stratford, Esme., op. cit. see note 14 Chapter II.
16. Tennyson and Kipling were by no means the only perpetrators of romantic myths about the exploits of the Army overseas. Sir Francis Doyle's poem about 'a drunken private of the Buffs' who refused to kowtow when captured by Manchu cavalry during the Arrow War of 1856-60 is typical of the misreading and misuse of facts to produce a poem which would appeal to the sentimental public of the moment. Some details are given in *The Arrow War* by Douglas Hurd, Collins 1967. Even Kipling's 'Gunga Din' raises some questions. It was supposed to be based on the recommendation, by a British cavalry regiment, of their native water carrier for a high honour. Soldiers had only just become eligible for what had previously been an 'officers only' decoration. It was certainly not available to native servants. Mason tells the story without comment but, sadly, the opening up of the award to all soldiers was strongly resisted by many senior

officers and the concession was regarded as an important radical victory. It seems possible that the recommendation by the Lancer regiment was made tongue in cheek.

17. Sergeant Pearmain. op. cit.
18. Parker, Peter, *The Old Lie*. Constable, London, 1987.
19. Parker seems to have picked a bad time to make his comparison. Officer recruits from the public schools before the mid 1860s would have been very different from the type he refers to. The reformed schools were hardly into their stride until the middle of the decade at the earliest, and some much later.
20. Mason, P, op. cit. Page 248.
21. Arthur, Sir G., *The Life of Lord Kitchener*. Macmillan, 1920. Vol II, Chapter LXVIII.
22. Mason, P, op. cit. gives the figures for Indian soldiers serving abroad. Norman F Dixon, *On the Psychology of Military Incompetence*, Jonathan Cape, 1976, has a short but interesting section on Kitchener and on Townsend and the disaster at Kut.
23. Mason, P, op. cit. Page 170.
24. Ibid. Pages 426–7 and RWE Harper and Harry Miller, *Singapore Mutiny*. Singapore, OUP., 1984.
25. Mason, P, op. cit. Page 418.
26. Ibid. Page 509. Mason quotes Field Marshal Slim here.
27. Ibid. Page 443.

Chapter 6   The Great Age of Army Reform

1. When General Sir William Napier, author of *The History of the Peninsula War*, was approached by The Army Reform Association he summed up the reaction of most senior officers by saying:

> If the persons composing the Society are military, their proceeding is an act of grave insubordination; if they are civilians, they are incompetent persons, perniciously meddling with what they do not understand.

Quoted in *The Life of Sir William Napier*, Writings edited by H A Bruce MP, John Murray, London, 1864.
2. On 'The Army Movement' see two articles in the *United Services Journal*, 1849.
3. See notes 16, 17 and 18 to chapter IV above, and see Spiers, op. cit. (Army & Soc) Chapter 3.
4. Libraries for officers probably date from the establishment of the Gibraltar Garrison Library in 1793. Certain Regiments and Corps, notably the Royal Engineers and the Rifle Corps, were providing books for NCOs and soldiers by the first decade of the nineteenth century but mainly in foreign stations. In 1838, the Commander-in-Chief asked for a library in each large barracks with an initial stock of 300 books. However, at the same time, a senior officer testified to a committee that 'the fewer men that read or write in a company or troop, the better behaved they are'. When Gleig visited the Royal Military Asylum at Chelsea in 1844, he found that, in forty years, all that had been accumulated in the way of text books were Bibles, catechisms, spelling books, Mrs. Markham's History of England and a volume entitled 'Manners of the Jews'. Details are given in *The Story of Army Education*, by Colonel A C T White VC, Harrap, London 1963.
5. White, A C T Colonel VC. op. cit. Page 34.
6. English law Reports, Vol 128, page 253 and Vol 105, page 882.
7. White, A C T Colonel VC. op. cit. Page 34.
8. Ibid.
9. Salt, Henry H, *Biography of George Thomson 1834-1882, Army Schoolmaster and Poet*. London, 1889.
10. An example of this kind of blinkered thinking occurred immediately after the 1945 election. A small but shrill group of people who it seems had learned nothing from the war just successfully concluded, were able to convince themselves if no one else that Mr Churchill had been defeated and dismissed by the electorate because of the subversive teaching of the then Army Education Corps. This fiction is repeated in an otherwise

excellent book by Henry Stanhope, *The Soldiers*, Hamish Hamilton, 1979, and resurrected by *The Times* as recently as 13 June 1987 in order to make a journalistic point.

11. PRO/WO/112.
12. United Services Journal, August 1842.
13. Details of the Bill, 10 Vict. 5 March 1847, and of the controversy and compromise between Grey and Wellington are in PRO/WO/112.
14. Lewis, M A, op. cit.
15. By 1856 another Royal Commission on Purchase found that the regulation price had been completely superseded by overpayments as follows:

	Regulation price	1856 price
Lt. Col. Cavalry	£6,175	£14,000
Lt. Col. Foot Guards	£9,000	£13,000
Company, Foot Guards	£4,800	£9,000
Lt. Col. Line Regt.	£4,500	£7,000
Company, Line Regt.	£1,300	£2,400

See Biddulph, Sir Robert, op. cit., and Spiers, Edward M, op. cit. (Army and Soc) Chapter 1.
16. The Report of the Commission on Naval and Military Promotion and Retirement, 1840.
17. Abrams, Philip, The Late Profession of Arms in *Archives Européenes de Sociologie*, 1965.
18. Purchase Defended. Editorial article in *The United Services Journal*, January 1842. The writer of the article conveniently forgets that the original Royal Military Cadet College was intended to provide an education for the sons of officers who wished to enter the Army and for whom no fees were to be paid. When the 'Junior Department' was moved from Marlowe to Sandhurst in 1812, there was still no charge but in the post-Napoleonic War re-organisation, with its inevitable economies, the 'free list' was reduced to 80 places. A second class of Cadet paid fees according to the rank of his serving father and the remaining one third of the Cadets, classified as nobility and gentry paid full fees. The 'free list' was eventually eroded away but a sliding scale of fees continued to favour Cadets with a service background throughout the nineteenth century.
19. Andreski S, op. cit. Shows how those soldiers who in the past provided their own weapons and especially their own horses and armour, were able to maintain their independence longer than their fellows. The nonchalant, relaxed manner of the stereotype of the cavalry officer, even of today, when in reality he may never have ridden a horse and goes to war in an armoured vehicle, must surely owe something to this privileged independence in the past.
20. PO/WO/35/28, The 'Out Book' of the Deputy Adjutant General in Ireland in 1949, gives details.
21. The effectiveness of the breech-loading 'needle gun' was demonstrated by the Prussians at Koniggratz in 1866. The Austrians with muzzle-loading muskets were completely overwhelmed by the Prussians with their breech-loading rifles. In 1870 the tables were turned at Saint-Privat outside Metz when the Prussian Guard Corps attacked the French position in company columns up a bare slope. The French were armed with the breech-loading '*chassepot*' and in less than half an hour had inflicted over nine thousand casualties on the attackers. The Prussians soon learned the lesson however and fought their subsequent battles in open order.
22. Luvaas, Jay, op. cit.
23. Biddulph, Sir Robert, op. cit.
24. Hansard, Vol. 203, Col. 398.
25. St. Aubyn, Giles, The Royal George. *The Life of HRH Prince George, Duke of Cambridge 1819–1904*. Constable, London, 1963.
26. Ibid.
27. Ibid.
28. Ibid.
29. Bond, Brian, MA Thesis (London) 1962. *The Introduction and Operation of Short Service and Localisation in the British Army, 1868–1892*. See also PRO/WO/33/46 and PRO/WO/33/41.
30. Ibid.

31. Hamer, W S, *The British Army*. Civil Military Relations 1885–1905. Clarendon, Oxford, 1970, Page 81–86.
32. Bond Thesis (Note 29 above).
33. Thomson, F M L, *English Landed Society in the 19th Century*. Routledge & Keegan Paul, London 1963. Page 74.
34. PRO/WO/33/26.
35. Spiers Edward M, (The Army and Society) op. cit. page 209.
36. Maurice, Major General Sir F, and Arthur, Sir G, *The Life of Lord Wolseley*. Doubleday, New York, 1924.
37. PRO/WO/33/32/490.
38. Huntington, Samuel, op. cit.
39. Luvaas, J, op. cit.
40. The Boer war may provide another example of the debilitating effect of the 'uncertain trumpet'. Although, in 1900, Britain may have been at the peak of her imperial expansion, and jingoism would have been widespread, The Boer Republic was not the new German Empire, even less the old enemy France. It is clearly difficult for a democracy to plan and fight a war against a small, seemingly democratic and seemingly civilised country, whatever the pretext. The fiasco of Suez may be another example of this, and there are others.

Chapter 7　The Aberrant Corps

1. See note 15 to Chapter VI, and see Bruce, Anthony, op. cit. page 42.
2. Graham, Brigadier C A L, DSO, *The Story of the Royal Regiment of Artillery*. 6th Ed. RA Institute, Woolwich, 1962.
3. *The Diary*, Miriam Green's Journal was reproduced in part from the *Royal Engineers Journal*, but it is not known in which volume of the RE Journal it was originally reproduced.
4. Fortescue, J W, op. cit. Vol III, Pages 412/3.
5. 'Britons, Strike Home!' Was written for Bonduca by Henry Purcell in 1695. Lewis Winstock in *Songs and Music of the Redcoats 1642–190*, Leo Cooper, London, 1970, says: 'although it appears dramatic by modern standards the soldiers liked it'. No doubt it was used as a suitable opening flourish to the bombardment.
6. *History of the Royal Corps of Sappers and Miners*, Connolly, 1855, gives excellent details of the Great Siege and of the early history of 'Sappers' on the Rock.
7. See Appendix II.
8. Bacon, Admiral Sir R H, *The Life of Lord Fisher of Kilverstone*, in 2 Vols. Hodder & Stoughton, London, 1929. Vol 1, page 194.
9. See Chapter 9.
10. See Chapter 9.
11. It must be said however, that the 'Corps' can be more regimental than the regiments. The author well remembers as a recruit to the Royal Marines in early 1943, sitting in a large hut with about three hundred other recruits to be drilled in the words of 'A Life on the Ocean Waves' by a very hard faced and tone deaf Sergeant Major. He also still cannot forget the appalling rhyme,

　　　'In 1802, the Royal Marine facings
　　　were changed from red to blue'.

12. Fox, Robert, *Eyewitness Falklands*. Methuen, London, 1982. It is reassuring to know that at least some traditions are maintained. Fox says of the two officers of the Blues and Royals, one a Lord and the other an Hon, one missed his polo rather badly whilst the other had entered a bronze for the Royal Academy Summer Exhibition and was only concerned about whether it had been accepted or not. Fox seemed quite scandalised that two such comparatively junior officers had been sent off on their own to look after the two troops of light tanks.
13. Vaux, Nick, *March to the South Atlantic*. Foreword by Max Hastings, Buchan & Enright, London, 1986.
14. Fox, Robert, op. cit.

15. See Chapter 9, notes 22 and 32 refer.
16. See the Introduction and note 7.

Chapter 8   Action, Re-action and Intervention

 1. Haldane, Richard Burdon, *An Autobiography*. Hodder & Stoughton, London, 1931.
 2. Fletcher, C R L and Kipling, Rudyard, *A School History of England*. London, 1911.
 3. Parker, Peter, op. cit.
 4. Haldane, R B, op. cit. But see also Spiers, Edward M, *Haldane: An Army Reformer*. Edinburgh University Press, 1980, for a less egocentric and more detailed view of Haldane as a Reformer and War Minister.
 5. Ibid.
 6. Bacon, Admiral Sir R H, op. cit.
 7. Ibid.
 8. Ibid.
 9. Ibid.
10. Saki, *When William Came*. John Lane, 1913.
11. Whether the Boy Scout Movement was founded with the conscious intention of increasing militarism and war preparation is extremely doubtful but the link between the Movement and the Army has always been strong. From the beginning, the Scouts were equipped, not with imitation army uniforms, but actual 'army surplus' from the Boer War. Even today, the Commander-in-Chief of the British Army of the Rhine is ex-officio Commissioner of all British Scouts living across the Channel in North West Europe. A recent British Chief Scout came to his appointment on retirement from his last military post as commander of a British Armoured Division in Germany. But whatever may have been Baden-Powell's motivation in founding the Scout Movement, there is nothing sinister in current military interest in its continuation. In Germany, it provides by far the largest, healthiest, most adventurous and educational set of activities for young people stationed there and it is surely a matter for congratulation that senior officers take an interest in it and support it. Together with amateur dramatics, and for the same reasons, scouting enjoys much more active support amongst the Army abroad than it does from the civilian population in Britain.
      See also, Turner E S, *Dear Old Blighty*, Michael Joseph, London, 1980 for Boy Scout activities in World War One.
12. Hamer, W S, op. cit.
13. Ibid.
14. Jenkins, Roy, *Asquith*. Collins, Fontana Books, London, 1964.
15. For the atmosphere of relief on the outbreak of war see Taylor, A J P, *Europe: Grandeur and Decline*. Pelican Books, 1967 and Turner E S, op. cit.
16. Ryan, A P, op. cit. and Fergusson, Major General Sir James, op. cit. and Jenkins, Roy, op. cit.
17. Gough, General Sir Hubert, *Soldiering On*. Arthur Barker, London, 1954. See note 12 to Chapter II.
18. Jenkins, Roy, op. cit.
19. Ryan, A P, op. cit.
20. Jenkins, Roy, op. cit.
21. Magnus, Philip, *Kitchener, Portrait of an Imperialist*. John Murray, London, 1958.
22. Jenkins, Roy, op. cit.
23. See note 15 above.
24. Parker, Peter, op. cit.. Pages 91–92.
25. Connell, John, *Wavell, Scholar and Soldier*. Collins, 1964. On page 43 he says for e.g. After the Boer War the two battalions of the Black Watch were together at Harrismith in June 1902 for the first time in their history.
26. Keegan, John, *The Face of Battle*, op. cit. Page 226.
27. Dunn J C, *The War the Infantry Knew*. Jane's, 1987. This recently republished classic confirms from eye witness accounts the lack of training of reinforcements arriving on the Somme. It says that large numbers had only been attested six weeks before they arrived, they had only fired five rounds in training and many could not load or unload

their rifles. The battalions had literally to train their reinforcements in the front line.

As early as July 1916, another problem which we refer to later had emerged. Drafts for the Royal Welch Fusiliers included Cheshires, Staffs and South Wales Borderers. There was a rumour that this was done deliberately to destroy the Regimental System. In any event, the Royal Welch Fusiliers managed to swap some Shropshires for some of their own men from a neighbouring division at a rate of one Welshman for two Englishmen.

28. Baynes, John, *Morale, A Study of Men and Courage.* Cassell, 1967. And see Mason, op. cit. Whilst Dunn, op. cit. in the preceding note, covers much the same ground as Baynes, he allows his participants to speak for themselves and leaves the reader to draw the obvious lessons from the detailed experiences described.

29. See Chapter 1, Note 9. James thought that the mystic, idealistic model of leadership was inappropriate for the pilots of today's Royal Air Force where he said, the pilot was more akin to a computer operator than to an officer with a classical leadership and exemplar role. However that does not make the model inappropriate for the young fighter pilots in the early days of combat flying.

30. Ellis, John, *The Social History of the Machine Gun.* Croom Helm, London, 1975. Chapter V.

31. Mason, P., op. cit.

32. See Introduction, Note 10.

33. The newly revived fashion for embellishment probably started with the Commando's green and the Paratroop's maroon berets of the Second World War although of course The Royal Tank Regiment has worn its distinctive black berets since 1922. Berets seem to have increased in distinctiveness and significance since the last War. The author remembers a rather disgraceful episode at the end of the war in Europe when a batch of commando soldiers, having left their virtually disbanded Commando, en route to reinforce a still active Commando in the Far East, came across a group of gunners wearing green berets. The encounter took place on the dockside at Ostend and the gunners ended up in the harbour. The gunners were part of a Forward Observation Team serving with the commandos and sharing their hardships and dangers for some months but they had not undergone the 'rites of passage' and their wearing of the beret was unofficial if understandable.

Peculiarities of dress always aroused strong emotions in the army in the pre-khaki era. The rows over dress for the Scottish Regiments, especially over bonnets and feathers, are legion and in this context it is easy to understand the trauma caused by the loss of the old numerals and the changes of facings in the 1881 amalgamations.

An interesting study could be made of the alternating waves of attraction and revulsion that military uniform has for the young and for dissident groups. The fashion for service greatcoats and 'bomber jackets', and especially for camouflaged battle suits, although it seems to be receding a little now, is only partly explained by easy availability and cheapness on the second-hand clothes market. Many clothing manufacturers actually produce new imitation military gear and camouflaged combat suits at high prices when military fashion is in season. Some of it is extremely elaborate with its straps, buckles, cartridge holding loops, map pockets and field dressing holders, and it can be extremely expensive.

34. Dixon, Norman, op. cit. Pages 116–117.

35. Since The Second World War the wearing of spurs and swords has occasioned considerable debate, mainly amongst civilians but also amongst officers in those Corps which have tried to establish rational standards in dress. Immediately after the last war, the United States Navy caused something of a furore by reintroducing swords as part of the full ceremonial dress of Naval Officers. But things have now clearly moved on. A short report in *The Times* of 12 November 1987, datelined Washington says:

'after twenty years of argument, the US Navy has decided that its men may carry umbrellas while in uniform. The ban has been enforced strictly by a succession of Navy Chiefs who believe that real men get wet (Christopher Thomas writes). Admiral Carlisle Trost, Chief of Navy Operations relented, after receiving a recommendation from the Navy's uniform board to make the change.

The Navy has issued rules saying that umbrellas must be black and must be carried only in the left hand.'

Presumably, the last point is emphasised so that the sword hand is left free.
36. See Keegan and Holmes, op. cit. page 140 and an article in *The Sunday Times* of 28 June 1987 reporting the alleged results of a six year secret study, codenamed 'Project Foresight'. The article says that the report casts some doubt on the suitability of the tank for today's battlefields and that future investment is likely to concentrate on the light attack helicopter and multiple launch rocket system (MLRS). The article quotes a Ministry of Defence source as saying, rather ominously but seemingly without conscious irony, 'What we are facing today are the kind of basic decisions that led to the replacement of the horse by the tank'.
 A more recent comment on the still (October 1988) unpublished report, 'leaked' in *The Sunday Times* of 21 August 1988, would have it that the 'horse lobby' has won again. Official reaction to the report is said to imply that whatever the report says, there is no acceptable alternative to the tank.

Chapter 9   *The Long Armistice and The Second World War*

1., Bond, Brian, *Liddell Hart, A Study of His Military Thought*. Cassell London, 1977. Page 65.
2. Correlli Barnett, *The Military Profession in the 1970s*. In *The Armed Services and Society*, Ed. Wolfe J N and Erickson, John, Edinburgh University Press, 1969.
3. Military Tattoos have been popular entertainment in Britain at least since Victoria's reign. Their purpose has never been altruistic but in the thirties the Aldershot tattoo, in particular, was used to publicise the Territorial Army and its air defence role. The appeal to emotion and fear was handled with professional skill to such an extent that it may have been counter-productive. Later in the thirties, the *Entente Cordiale* was publicised and popularised by the attendance at the Tattoo of prominent French Generals.
4. Correlli Barnett, op. cit.
5. Ibid.
6. Bond, Brian, op. cit. Page 42.
7. Ibid. Bond points out in his Appendix B. Page 279 that the only fully documented study of Liddell Hart is in *The Education of an Army* by Jay Luvaas, Cassell, 1965, which was emended in detail by Liddell Hart himself. Liddell Hart's *Memoirs* are published in 2 Vols. Cassell, London, 1965. Brian Bond's *Liddell Hart* cited above is highly recommended as a critical guide to Liddell Hart's military thought. Jay Luvaas, in his op. cit. also includes an interesting chapter on Colonel J F C Fuller.
8. Trythall, Anthony John., *Boney Fuller, The Intellectual General*, Cassell, London 1977.
9. Ibid.
10. Ibid.
11. Ibid page 118.
12. Ibid page 128.
13. Correlli Barnett, op cit, and Brian Bond op. cit.
14. Bond, Brian, op. cit. Page 85.
15. Ibid. Page 127. Another example of 'martial race mania' is in the recurring outbreaks of unthinking adulation for the Gurkha forces. This places a most unfair burden on them. Recent unfortunate publicity for the Brigade has been made worse by the uncritical attitude which preceded it. Some extraordinary thinking in high places would suggest that it is still better to employ foreign troops rather than maintain British regiments. However good and cheap they may be, the retaining of mercenary forces in the present climate of world opinion is unbelievably obtuse. For the Gurkhas themselves, one is reminded of Fortescue's comment that soldiers were after all men of flesh and blood, not puppets to be hugged or broken according to the caprice of the hour. (Fortescue vol 1, page 237).
16. Luvaas, Jay, op. cit. Page 358.
17. Demeter, Karl, op. cit.

18. Bullock, Alan, op. cit. Book II. A new book on Sepp Dietrich, *Hitler's Gladiator*, by Charles Messenger, published by Brassey's 1988, attempts a balanced view but inevitably spreads a good deal of whitewash. As early as the Polish Campaign, Messenger notes, (page 76) Army Commander Blaskowitz wanted to charge Dietrich with looting and murder but Dietrich's special relationship with Hitler prevented this. On page 210 Messenger says that Dietrich 'had nothing to do with the shooting of British prisoners at Wormhoudt'. This happened after a very gallant resistance well after the soldiers had surrendered and clearly in cold blood. Dietrich was in command of the SS troops involved. The fact that his men were an indisciplined and murderous rabble only makes his responsibility more obvious.

Messenger, after saying (page 209) that there is much evidence that Dietrich himself was not an ideologically committed Nazi, quotes Shirer in a short passage as saying Dietrich was 'one of the most brutal men of the Third Reich'. Shirer in *The Rise and Fall of The Third Reich*, page 277 is even more positive, 'Sepp Dietrich, whom this author recalls personally as one of the most brutal men of the Third Reich, commanded Hitler's SS Body guard in 1934 and directed the executions in Stadelheim Prison, etc. etc.'

19. Bond, Brian, op cit page 223.

20. Hitler enjoyed the doubtful honour of having assumed his senior military appointments in reverse order. He became Supreme Commander-in-Chief of the Armed Forces of the Reich on the death of President von Hindenburg in 1934, Commander-in-Chief of the Army in February 1938 when General von Blomberg was forced to resign after a trumped up scandal, (the same thing had happened to von Fritsch, Blomberg's predecessor), and he took over as Commander-in-Chief of the German Field Army when von Brauchitsch resigned in December 1942.

21. The precedence and seniority of Guards officers caused some comment towards the end of the nineteenth century when the final attempts to abolish 'purchase' were being made. Because of the blockage in promotion in the 'non-purchase' Corps it was necessary to advance captains in the Engineers, Gunners and Marines by one rank. There was a great outcry in the rest of the Army, led by the guards. But the public, guided by the newspapers, was outraged by this. The promotions went through and, in the end, Guards officers lost their special seniority. Spiers, Edward M op. cit. Chapter 1 gives an excellent account of the British Officer Corps as a profession in the nineteenth century and explains the nomination system, purchase and the social background of officer candidates. More details are given in Bruce, Anthony, op. cit. page 42.

22. See Note 15 to Chapter 6. The increase in the cost of promotion 'steps' would have been in proportion to the increase in 'purchase' price.

23. See two articles by John Nott in *The Times*, 5 and 6 October 1987. He virtually abolishes the Royal Marines in his second article.

24. Thomas, John-Pierre H, *The French Armed Forces Since the Second World War*. Originally prepared as Chapter 1 of *Armed Forces and Public Opinion*, for The University, Services Study Group, Scotland 1971/1972, and see de la Gorce, Paul-Marie, *The French Army, A Military-Political History*. Trans. Kenneth Douglas. Weidenfeld & Nicolson, London, 1963.

25. de la Gorce, Paul-Marie, op. cit.

26. Thomas, Jean-Pierre H, op. cit.

27. de la Gorce, Paul-Marie, op. cit.

28. Ibid.

29. Thomas, Jean-Pierre H, op. cit.

30. Hastings, Max, *The Korean War*. Michael Joseph, London, 1987.

31. See The Conclusion and its note 7.

32. See note 23 above.

33. *The Times*, 24 February 1988.

34. See Note 23 above.

Chapter 10   *The End of the Regimental Family*

1. An instruction issued to recruiting staff in 1975 but which obviously must still be a guideline, states with regard to 'selection', after testing the recruit is asked to choose or

confirm his previous choice of arm or service and is then allocated according to his ability, personal choice and vacancies.

2. Baynes, John, op. cit.

3. Trythall, Anthony John, op. cit. Page 128.

4. *The Times*, Second leader, 2 February 1988.

5. A BBC Reporter commenting on the 6 pm news on Wednesday 14 September 1988, reported the first exercise on Salisbury Plain of the newly organised Helicopter-Borne Anti-Tank Brigade. He stressed that problems remained to be solved and mentioned specifically the continuing RAF control of the heavy lift helicopters required to support the brigade.

6. National Audit Office, *Report by the Comptroller & Auditor General on the Ministry of Defence: Costs and Financial Control of British Forces Germany*. No. 236, Published 11 January 1988.

7. Jolly, Ruth, *Military Man, Family Man* Brassey's. London, 1987.

8. *The Times*, 2 March 1988. An article by Peter Evans on the falling population of the United Kingdom.

9. Barker, Dennis, *Soldiering On, An Unofficial Portrait of the British Army*. Andre Deutsch, London, 1981.

10. It seems that the Royal Military Academy Sandhurst (RMAS), like the RCB, is also in need of some urgent re-vitalisation before the arrival of the twenty-first century. Frequent changes in curriculum and even its aims and purpose, appear to have left it weakened and self-critical. In his recent Sandhurst book, *Sandhurst A Documentary*, published by Harrap in 1987, Michael Yardley writes of the changes occurring there, no less than to the rest of the Army. He calls them controversial and irreversible, and being made with alarming speed. He identifies, I believe correctly, the danger to an institution of being seen only as the symbol of a two-tiered class-based society. He notes the attraction to cadets and some staff at least of the Barbour Jacket clad, Sloane Ranger caricature, for which he takes some personal responsibility, as a substitute for the archaic Public Schoolboy image but he can suggest no acceptable alternative whilst he deplores both images. Yardley pays tribute to the store set by the old fashioned concepts of honour and duty but he feels that the RMAS, because of its concern with external appearances, and confused by the large intake of what he calls State sector secondary school students, has become unsure of its role. He says that over 50 per cent of all male students at the RMAS in 1987 had attended such schools. I believe this figure requires very considerable qualification but, even if it means what it appears to say, it does not solve the problem mentioned above of the ultimate destination of this new wave of entrants. The book provides an interesting and provocative analysis of contemporary problems at the RMA but it is sadly lacking in ideas to improve matters. Yardley himself says Sandhurst is 'sacred ground' and must be trodden lightly.

11. An extraordinary variation on pre-service training is now being provided by some Local Education Authorities, presumably with Manpower Services blessing and funding. Plymouth College of Further Education, for example, is now advertising Pre-Service Courses for would-be entrants to the Armed Forces, police, Fire Service and nursing. The courses are offered as suitable for potential entrants at officer or lower levels and are for a minimum of one year or a maximum of two years. The courses include fitness training, military studies including map reading and general education. The course for officer entrants could take up to two years we are told, which is twice as long as the present Sandhurst course. Whilst it is impossible to judge the utility of such courses at this stage it is truly remarkable what can be funded under the pressure of heavy unemployment and loss of employment prospects in areas like the dockyard town of Plymouth.

12. Dietz, P J, and Stone, J, op. cit., contains a detailed discussion of the impact of the Military Salary and forces' pay increases in general.

13. Wolseley's 'Pocket Book' is described in more detail in Chapter VI.

14. Trythall, Anthony J., op. cit.

Conclusion

1. See Note 1. Chapter 6.

2. For the first time since the last war, it is just possible to visualise a significant reduction in British Forces in Germany. The advent of Mr Gorbachov and the progress made with President Reagan over the reduction in nuclear weapons in Europe, has produced a significant mood of optimism in some quarters. If this is continued after the next Presidential election, redeployment of some of NATO's forces will be inevitable.

3. *The Times*, 17 June 1988. An article by Michael Yardley.

4. Jolly, Ruth, op. cit.

5. See Note 4, Chapter 10.

6. Statement on the Defence Estimates 1988. Part 2, Table 5.10.

7. See Appendix IV.

8. Horace: Odes, Book II, Lines 33-36. Writing on the Civil War which followed the death of Julius Caesar:

> *Qui gurges aut quae flumina lugubris*
> *ignara belli ? quod mare Dauniae*
> *non decoloravere caedes ?*
> *quae caret ora cruore nostro ?*

Bibliography

Andreski, S, *Military Organisation and Society*. Kegan Paul, London, 1954.
Aron, R, *Main Currents in Sociological Thought*. Penguin Books, 1968.
Arthur, G, *The Life of Lord Kitchener*. Macmillan, London, 1920.
Bacon, Admiral Sir R H, *The Life of Lord Fisher of Kilverstone*. 2 Vols. Hodder & Stoughton, London, 1929.
Baldick, R, *The Duel, A History of Duelling*. Chapman & Hall, London, 1965.
Baeker, Dennis, *Soldiering On, An Unofficial Portrait of the British Army*. Andre Deutsch, London, 1981.
Barr, Pat, *The Memsahibs*. Secker & Warburg, London, 1976.
Baynes, John, *Morale, A Study of Men and Courage*. Cassell, 1967.
Becket, Ian F W, *The Army and the Curragh Incident, 1914*. Bodley Head, 1986.
Biddulph, Sir Robert, *Lord Cardwell at the War Office, 1868–1874*. London, 1904.
Bond, Brian I (Ed), *Victorian Military Campaigns*. Hutchinson, London, 1967.
   II *Liddell Hart, A Study of His Military Thought*. Cassell, London, 1977.
   III *War and Society in Europe*. Fontana Press, 1984.
Brereton, J M, *A Guide to the Regiments and Corps of the British Army*. Bodley Head, London, 1985.
Brett-James, Anthony, *General Graham, 1748–1844*. Macmillan, London, 1959.
Bruce, A P C, *The Purchase System in the British Army, 1660–1871*. Royal Historical Society Studies. No 20 in the History Series. London, 1980.
Bruce, H A, (Ed). *The Life of Sir William Napier*. John Murray, London, 1964.
Bullock, Alan, *Hitler, A Study in Tyranny*. Penguin Books, London, 1952.
Connell, John, *Wavell, Scholar and Soldier*. Collins, London, 1964.
Connolly, *History of the Royal Corps of Sappers and Miners*. London, 1855.
Correlli-Barnett, *The Military Profession in the 1970s*. In, *The Armed Services and Society*. (Ed). Wolfe, J. N., & Erickson, John, Edinburgh University Press, 1969.
Creasy, Sir E, *Fifteen Decisive Battles of the World*. Everyman Paperbacks, 1960.
Cunliffe, Barry, *Greeks, Romans and Barbarians*. Guild Publishing, London, 1988.
Davis, R C H, *The Normans and Their Myths*. Book Club Associates, London, 1976.
Demeter, Karl, *The German Officer Corps in Society and State. 1650–1945*. Weidenfeld & Nicolson, Trans. Angus Malcolm, London, 1965.
de la Gorce, P M, *The French Army, A Military Political History*. Weidenfeld & Nicolson. Trans. Kenneth Douglas, London, 1963.
de Tocqueville, Alexis, I *The Ancient Regime and the French Revolution*. Collins, Fontana, 1966.
   II *Democracy in America*. 2 Vols. Collins, Fontana, 1966.
Dixon, Norman F, *On the Psychology of Military Incompetence*. Jonathan Cape, London, 1976.
Dunn, Captain J. C., *The War the Infantry Knew. 1914–1919*. Republished by Janes, 1987.
Ellis, John, *The Social History of the Machine Gun*. Croom Helm, London, 1975.
Fergusson, Sir James, *The Curragh Incident*. Faber, London, 1964.
Fletcher, C R L, & Kipling, R, *A School History of England*. London, 1911.
Fortescue, Sir John, *A History of the British Army*. 13 Vols. Macmillan, London, 1899–1912.

Fox, Robert, *Eyewitness Falklands*. Methuen, London, 1982.
Fuller, Major General J F C, *The Conduct of War, 1789–1961*. Eyre & Spottiswoode, 1961.
Gildea, Robert, *Barricades and Borders, Europe 1800–1914*. OUP, 1987.
Gill, Conrad, *The Naval Mutinies of 1797*. Manchester University Press, 1913.
Gleichen, Major General Lord Edward, *A Guardsman's Memories*. Blackwood, London, 1932.
Gough, General Sir Hubert, *Soldiering On*. Arthur Baker, London, 1954.
Graham, Brigadier C A L, DSO, *The Story of the Royal Regiment of Artillery*. (6th ed). R A
    Institute, Woolwich, 1962.
Grierson, Edward, *The Imperial Dream*. Collins, London, 1972.
Haldane, Richard Burdon, *An Autobiography*. Hodder & Stoughton, London, 1931.
Hamer, W S, *The British Army, Civil Military Relations, 1885–1905*. Clarendon, Oxford, 1970.
Harper, R W E, & Miller, Harry, *Singapore Mutiny*. Singapore OUP, 1984.
Hastings, Max, *The Korean War*. Michael Joseph, London, 1987.
Haswell, Jock, *The British Army, A Concise History*. Book Club Associates, London, 1975.
Hobsbaum, E J, *The Age of Revolution, 1789–1848*. Mentor Books, New York, 1962.
Holmes, Richard, *Firing Line*. Penguin Books, 1987.
Hopkins, Harry, *The Strange Death of Private White*. Weidenfeld & Nicolson, London, 1977.
Huntington, Samuel, *The Soldier and the State*. Harvard University Press, 1957.
Hurd, Douglas, *The Arrow War*. Collins, London, 1967.
Janowitz, M, I *The Professional Soldier*. Macmillan, New York, 1960.
    II *The New Military*. Russell Sage, New York, 1967.
    III *Military Conflict*. Sage, Beverley Hills, USA, 1975.
Jenkins, Roy, *Asquith*. Collins, Fontana Books, London, 1964.
Jolly, Ruth, *Military Man, Family Man*. Brassey's London, 1987.
Kaye, M. M., (Ed). *The Golden Calm*. Webb & Bower, Exeter, 1980.
Keegan, John, I. *The Face of Battle*. Jonathan Cape, London, 1976.
    II. *Soldiers*. (With Richard Holmes). Hamish Hamilton, London, 1985.
    III. *The Mask of Command*. Jonathan Cape, London, 1987.
Kennedy, Paul, *The Rise and Fall of the Great Powers*. Unwin Hyman, London, 1988.
Kingsford, C L, *The Story of the Royal Warwickshire Regiment*. County Life Series, London,
    1921.
Kitson, Frank, *Warfare as a Whole*. Faber & Faber, London, 1987.
Lewis, M A, I *England's Sea Officers: The Story of the Naval Profession*. Alan & Unwin, London,
    1939.
    II *The Navy in Transition*. Hodder & Stoughton, London, 1965.
Liddell Hart, Sir Basil, *Memoirs*. 2 Vols. Cassell, London, 1965.
Longford, Elizabeth, *Wellington, The Years of the Sword*. Weidenfeld & Nicolson, 1969.
Luvaas, Jay, *The Education of an Army*. Cassell, London, 1965.
Magnus, Philip, *Kitchener, Portrait of an Imperialist*. John Murray, London, 1958.
Mcevedy, Colin, *The Penguin Atlas of Medieval History*. Vol II. Penguin Books, 1961.
Mahan, A T, *The Influence of Sea Power Upon History*. Sampson Lowe, London, 1889.
Marshall, H, *Military Miscellany*. London, 1846.
Marshall, S L A, *Men Against Fire*. William Morrow, New York, 1947.
Marwick, A, *War and Social Change in the Twentieth Century*. Macmillan, London, 1974.
Mason, Philip, *A Matter of Honour*. Macmillan, Papermac, 1986.
Maurice, Major General Sir F & Arthur, Sir G, *The Life of Lord Wolseley*. Doubleday, New
    York, 1924.
Maxwell, William, *The Life of Wellington*. Hutchinson, London. Abridged to 1 Vol. 1904.
Messenger, Charles, *Hitler's Gladiator*, Brassey's, London, 1988.
Napier, Sir W F P, *History of the War in the Peninsula*. 7 Vols. London, 1851.
Ossowska, Maria, *Social Determinants of Moral Ideas*. Routledge & Kegan Paul, 1971.
Parker, Peter, *The Old Lie*. Constable, London, 1987.
Poole, A L, *Domesday Book to Magna Carta. 1087–1216*. Oxford History of England, Claren-
    don Press, Oxford, (2nd Ed.) 1986.
Robertson, Field Marshal Sir William, *From Private to Field Marshal*. Constable, London,
    1921.
Rundle, E G, *A Soldier's Life*. Toronto, 1909.
Ryan, A P, *Mutiny at the Curragh*. Macmillan, London, 1956.

St. Aubyn, G, *The Royal George, Life of HRH Prince George Duke of Cambridge, 1819–1904.* Constable, London, 1963.

Saki, *When William Came.* John Lane, 1913.

Salt, Henry H, *Biography of George Thomson 1834–1882, Army Schoolmaster and Poet.* London, 1889.

Salway, Peter, *Roman Britain.* Oxford History of England, Clarendon Press, Oxford, 1981.

Scott, Sir S D, *The British Army, Its Origins, Progress and Equipment.* Cassell, Petter & Galpin, London, 1867.

Seely, J E B, *Adventure.* Heinemann, London, 1930.

Sheppard, Edgar, CVO, DD, *HRH George, Duke of Cambridge.* 2 Vols. Longmans, London, 1906.

Shirer William L, *The Rise and Fall of the Third Reich.* Pan Books, London, 1964.

Simmons, Major G, *A British Rifleman.* Greenhill Books, Napoleonic Library, 1986.

Smith-Dorrien, General Sir H., *Memories of Forty-Eight Years Service.* Murray, London, 1925.

Smyth, Brigadier Sir J, VC, *Sandhurst.* Weidenfeld & Nicolson, London, 1961.

Spier, Hans, *Social Order and the Risks of War.* Stewart, New York, 1952.

Spiers, Edward M, I *The Army and Society, 1815–1914.* Longmans, 1980.

II *Haldane, An Army Reformer.* Edinburgh University Press, 1980.

Stanhope, H, *The Soldiers.* Hamish Hamilton, London, 1979.

Stearns, P N, *European Society In Upheaval.* Collier Macmillan, 1975.

Stenton, Sir Frank, *Anglo-Saxon England.* Oxford History of England, (3rd Ed), 1986.

Sweetman, John, (Ed). *Sword and Mace.* Brassey's London, 1986.

Taylor, A J P, *Europe: Grandeur and Decline.* Pelican Books, 1967.

Thompson, J, *No Picnic.* Leo Cooper, London, 1985.

Thomson, D, *Europe Since Napoleon.* Penguin Books, 1957.

Thomson, F M L, *English Landed Society in the Nineteenth Century.* Routledge & Kegan Paul, London, 1963.

Trevelyan, G M, *England Under Queen Anne.* Longmans, London, 1934.

Trythall, A J, *Boney Fuller, The Intellectual General.* Cassell, London, 1977.

Turner, E S, I *Gallant Gentlemen.* London, 1965.

Dear Old Blighty. Michael Joseph, London, 1980.

Vaux, Nick, *March to the South Atlantic.* Buchan & Enright, London, 1986.

Verner, Colonel Willoughby, *The Military Life of HRH The Duke of Cambridge.* 2 Vols. John Murray, London, 1905.

Ward, S G P, *Wellington's Headquarters.* Oxford University Press, 1956.

Waterfield, Robert, *The Memoirs of Private Waterfield.* (Ed). Arthur Swinson & Donald Scott. Cassell, London, 1968.

White, Colonel A C T, VC, *The Story of Army Education.* Harrap, London, 1963.

Wingfield-Stratford, Esme, I *The Making of a Gentleman.* Williams & Northgate, London, 1938.

II *The Squire and His Relations.* Cassell & Co. London, 1956.

Winstock, Lewis, *Songs and Music of the Redcoats 1642–1902.* Leo Cooper, London, 1970.

Wolseley, Sir Garnet, I *The Story of a Soldier's Life.* 2 Vols. 1903.

II *The British Army.* In *The Reign of Queen Victoria, A Survey of Fifty Years Progress.* (Ed). Thomas Humphrey Ward, London, 1897.

Wood, Field Marshal Sir Evelyn, *From Midshipman to Field Marshal.* 2 Vols. Methuen, London, 1906.

Woodham Smith, Cecil, *The Reason Why.* Constable. For The Book Society, London, 1953.

Yardley, Michael, *Sandhurst, A Documentary.* Harrap, London, 1987.

Articles, Reports, Papers, Diaries and Theses

Andreski, S, *Imperialism, Past and Future* in The Year Book of World Affairs, 1975, Vol 29. Stevens and Sons, 1975.

Abrams, Philip, *The Late Profession of Arms.* Archives Europeenes de Sociologie, 1965.

Aydelotte, William O, *The Business Interests of the Gentry in the Parliament of 1841–1847.* European Social Class, Stability and Change. (Ed) E. Barber & E. G. Barber. Macmillan, New York, 1965.

Blanco, Richard L, *Attempts to Abolish Branding and Flogging in the Army of Victorian England Before 1881*. The Journal of Army Historical Research. Autumn 1968.

Bond, Brian, M A Thesis, London 1962. *The Introduction and Operation of Short Service and Localisation in the British Army, 1868–1892.*.

Dietz, P J, and Stone, J F, *The British All Volunteer Army*. Armed Forces and Society, Published Chicago University, 1975.

Green, Miriam, *Journal*. In The Gibraltar Garrison Library, reproduced from an early but unidentified RE Journal.

HMG *Statement on Defence Estimates. 1987 and 1988.*

HMG *National Audit Office Report. Ministry of Defence. Costs and Financial Control of British Forces, Germany*. No. 236. Published 11 January 1988.

Kirke, Major C M St G, *Social Structures in the Peninsular Army*. RUSI Journal, Summer, 1988.

Otley, CB, PhD Thesis. *The Origins and Recruitment of the British Army Elite*. Copy at the Ministry of Defence Library, Whitehall; and II, *The Social Origins of British Army Officers*. Sociological Review N.S. Vol 18, 1970.

Razzell, P, *Social Origins of Officers in the Indian and British Home Army; 1758–1962*. Journal of Sociology, Vol 14, 1963.

Reresby, Sir John, *Diary* At York City Library.

Schon, Donald, *Loss of the Stable State*. BBC Reith Lectures 1970, reproduced in *The Listener*.

Shils, Edward and Janowitz, Morris, *Cohesion and Disintegration in the Wehrmacht in World War II*, Public Opinion Quarterly, 1948.

Tylden, Major G, *The Accoutrements of the British Infantryman, 1640–1940*. Journal of Army Historical Research, Vol 47, No. 189, Spring 1969.

Thomas, Jean-Pierre, *The French Armed Forces Since the Second World War*. Prepared for *Defence, The Services and Public Opinion in Britain and Germany*. A University, Services Scotland, Study Group Report 1971/2 (Ed) P Dietz. Subsequently held over. Published Army HQ, Scotland.

War Office Files Consulted at the Public Record Office

Abolition of Purchase, 1870s	PRO/WO/33/26
Aiding Civil Power in Ireland	
Issue of Booklet, 1870	PRO/WO33/21/417
Apprehension of Deserters, 1878	PRO/WO/33/32/669
Army Lists, 1877	PRO/WO/33/31/881
Army Reform, 1840s	PRO/WO/112
Bureaucracy at the WO. 1877	PRO/WO/33/30/635
Branding of Soldiers, 1871	PRO/WO/33/22/462
Comparative Costs	
Indian/British Soldiers, 1860s	PRO/WO/32/750 and 33/32/691
Courts Martial, Officers, Overseas, 1870s	PRO/WO/71/309
Diplomacy in the Field, 1878	PRO/WO/33/32/682
Enlistment of Boys, 1878	PRO/WO/33/29/632
Newspaper Correspondents, 1878	PRO/WO/33/32/490
Officers on Full Pay	
as MPs, 1878	PRO/WO/33/32/687
'Out Book' of Deputy	
A/G Ireland, 1849	PRO/WO/35/28
Recruiting Reports, 1871	PRO/WO/33/22/480
Recruiting, Future, 1871	PRO/WO/33/32/465
Short Service and Localisation, 1868/92	PRO/WO/33/46 and 33/41
Wellington and Chartism, 1848	PRO/WO/32/111
Wellington and the Limited Service Bill of, 1846	PRO/WO/30/118

Index